A WAR OF INTERVENTION

THE RUSSO-GEORGIAN WAR 2008

A WAR OF INTERVENTION

THE RUSSO-GEORGIAN WAR 2008

Col Harjeet Singh (Retd)

PENTAGON PRESS

A WAR OF INTERVENTION: THE RUSSO-GEORGIAN WAR 2008
Col Harjeet Singh (Retd)

First Published in 2016
Reprinted July 2016, April 2017

ISBN 978-81-8274-867-5

Published by
PENTAGON PRESS
206, Peacock Lane, Shahpur Jat,
New Delhi-110049
Phones: 011-64706243, 26491568
Telefax: 011-26490600
email: rajan@pentagonpress.in
website: www.pentagonpress.in

Printed at Aegean offset Printers Greater Noida (U.P.)

Contents

MAPS AND ILLUSTRATIONS

MAPS

ILLUSTRATIONS

ABBREVIATIONS

ASSR	Autonomous Soviet Socialist Republic
APC	Armoured Personnel Carrier
BMO	Border Monitoring Operation
BTC	Baku-Tbilisi-Ceyhan Pipeline
CERD	International Convention on the Elimination of All Forms of Racial Discrimination
CERT	Computer Emergency Response Team
CFE	Treaty on Conventional Armed Forces in Europe
CFSP	Common Foreign and Security Policy
CIS	Commonwealth of Independent States
CIS PKF	CIS Peacekeeping Force
CSCE	Conference on Security and Cooperation in Europe
CSTO	Collective Security Treaty Organisation
DDoS	distributed denial of service
EAPC	Euro-Atlantic Partnership Council
EC	European Commission
ECHO	European Community Humanitarian Office
ECHR	European Court for Human Rights
EConvHR	European Convention for the Protection of Human Rights and Fundamental Freedoms
ECRML	European Charter of Regional Minority Languages
ENP	European Neighbourhood Policy
ERA	Explosive Reactive Armour
ESDP	European Security and Defence Policy
EUMM	European Union Monitoring Mission
EU	European Union
EUSR	European Union Special Representative

GAF	Georgian Armed Forces
GLONASS	Global Navigation Satellite System
GPS	Global Positioning System
GRENA	Georgian Research and Educational Networking Association
GSSR	Georgian Soviet Socialist Republic
GTEP	Georgia Train and Equip Programme
GUAM	Organisation for Democracy and Economic Development, including Georgia, Ukraine, Azerbaijan, Moldova
HRAM	Human Rights Assessment Mission
HRL	Human Rights Law
HROAG	Human Rights Office in Abkhazia, Georgia
HRW	Human Rights Watch
ICC	International Criminal Court
ICCPR	International Covenant on Civil and Political Rights
ICJ	International Court of Justice
ICRC	International Committee of the Red Cross
ICTY	International Criminal Tribunal for the former Yugoslavia
IDP	Internally Displaced Person
IED	Improvised Explosive Device
IHL	International Humanitarian Law
IIFFMCG	Independent International Fact-Finding Mission on the Conflict in Georgia
IGO	International Governmental Organisation
ILC	International Law Commission
INGO	International Non-Governmental Organisation
IP	Internet protocol
IPAP	Individual Partnership Action Plan
JCC	Joint Control Commission
JPKF	Joint Peacekeeping Forces
KGB	Komitet gosudarstvennoi bezopasnosti
km	kilometres
MANPADS	man-portable air defence systems
MAP	Membership Action Plan
mm	millimetres
MR	Motorized Rifle
MRLS	Multiple Rocket Launching System
NAC	North Atlantic Council
NAM	Needs Assessment Mission

NATO	North Atlantic Treaty Organisation
NGO	Non-Governmental Organisation
NRC	NATO-Russia Council
NSC	National Security Council (Georgia)
ODIHR	Office for Democratic Institutions and Human Rights
OHCHR	Office of the High Commissioner for Human Rights
OSCE	Organisation for Security and Cooperation in Europe
PACE	Parliamentary Assembly of the Council of Europe
PCA	Partnership and Cooperation Agreement
PFP	Partnership for Peace
PGM	Precision-Guided Munitions
RBN	Russian Business Network
SAM	Security Assessment Mission
SF	Special Forces
SSOP	Sustainment and Stability Operation Programme
SSR	Soviet Socialist Republic
TACIS	Technical Assistance for the CIS
TSFSR	Trans-caucasian Soviet Federative Socialist Republic
UAV	Unmanned Aerial Vehicle
UN	United Nations
UNDHA	UN Department of Humanitarian Affairs
UNDP	UN Development Programme
UNHCR	UN High-Commissioner for Refugees
UNOMIG	UN Observer Mission in Georgia
UNSC	UN Security Council
UNSG	UN Secretary-General
US	United States of America
USSR	Union of Soviet Socialist Republics
VCLT	Vienna Convention on the Law of Treaties
WTO	World Trade Organisation

RUSSIAN FEDERATION
GEORGIA
ABKHAZIA
NORTH OSSETIA
SOUTH OSSETIA
AJARA (AJARIA)
BLACK SEA
TURKEY
ARMENIA
AZERBAIJAN
El'brus 5642 m
Kodori Gorge
Roki Tunnel
Karachayevsk
Prokhladnyy
Mozdok
Nal'chik
Vladikavkaz
Gagra
Pitsunda
Pskhu
Gudauta
Novyy Afon
Sukhumi
Gulripsh
Lata
Otap
Omarishara
Tqvarcheli
Ochamchira
Gali
Pichori
Anaklia
Mestia
Khaishi
Lentekhi
Jvari
Tsalenjhikha
Zugdidi
Khobi
Senaki
Poti
Tskhaltubo
Samtredia
Kutaisi
Khvanchkara
Ambrolauri
Tqibuli
Chiatura
Zestaponi
Lanchkhuti
Chokhatauri
Ozurgeti
Kobuleti
Batumi
Bakhmaro
Baghdati
Khashuri
Abastumani
Borjomi
Bakuriani
Atskuri
Akhaltsikhe
Vale
Keda
Khulo
Kvaisi
Kurta
Tskhinvali
Akhalgori
Mleta
Pasanauri
Dusheti
Gori
Mtskheta
T'bilisi
Archilo
Akhmeta
Telavi
Qvareli
Lagodekhi
Gurjaani
Tsnori
Rustavi
Marneuli
Bolnisi
Kazreti
Akhalkalaki
Ninotsminda
Dedoplis Tsqaro
Balakän
Zaqatala
Agstafa
Gäncä
Vanadzor
Gyumri
Hrazdan
Sevan
Zod
Lake Ritsa
Lake Tabatskuri
Lake Paravani
Lake Sevan
Mingachevir Reservoir
Kuban
Terek
Inguri
Rioni
Supsa
Qvirila
Aragvi
Alazani
Iori
Mtkvari (Kura)
Kür (Kura)
National capital
Autonomous republic capital
Town, village
Major airport
International boundary
Autonomous republic boundary
Main road
Secondary road
Railroad
0 25 50 75 km
0 25 50 mi
40°
41°
42°
43°
44°
45°
46°

1

INTRODUCTION

Georgia was a constituent republic of the former Union of Soviet Socialist Republics (USSR). In 1991, the dissolution of the Soviet Union led to the independence of Georgia. In turn, the autonomous regions of Georgia, namely South Ossetia and Abkhazia, attempted to break away from Georgia, resulting in civil strife in the early 1990s. These conflicts were settled with Russian involvement with the United Nations (UN) Mission in Georgia deploying in a peacekeeping role in Abkhazia and a Russian peacekeeping force deploying under a Joint Control Commission in South Ossetia. This is the background to the conflict that suddenly broke out in the Caucasus while the Olympics were in progress in Beijing.

The political context of the conflict was the ascendance of Mr. Saakashvili in Georgia. He had risen to the presidency in the aftermath of the Rose Revolution of late 2003. He followed a policy of reassertion of Georgian control over areas that had attempted to break away. He had earlier managed to regain control of Ajaria in the south west and had sent troops into the Kodori gorge in Abkhazia. Georgia was eager to join the North Atlantic Treaty Organization (NATO) and perhaps the ploy of a threat from Russia, heightened by the war, was to serve to hasten the process. In the event, the strategy backfired badly, with NATO expansion to include Georgia being seen by the world as an avoidable risk.

However, the international context is the more important aspect leading to the outbreak of hostilities. Russia had seen an eclipse in power after the break-up of the Soviet Union, under Boris Yeltsin. In the Putin era, it has managed to regain some vitality with additional oil and gas revenues coming its way due to discoveries, operation of pipelines and the rise in prices. It has, therefore, wanted to reassert itself in face of the steady expansion of NATO in its vicinity to include states of the erstwhile Warsaw Pact and even former Soviet republics. The immediate perceived affront was the recognition by the US and its allies of Kosovo, a breakaway autonomous province of Serbia, as an independent state. Russia saw a chance of returning the compliment received in the Balkans in the Caucasus. Two other causal factors are the oil and pipeline politics in the region and US interests in the region.

The conflict began with an artillery and rocket bombardment of South Ossetia by Georgia on 7 August 2008. Georgia captured Tshinkvali, the capital of South Ossetia by the next day. In this about 1,500 people were reportedly killed including ten Russian peacekeepers. This led to the Russian military response. Within five days Russian troops were in control of both Abkhazia and South Ossetia and were on the doorsteps of Tbilisi, the capital of Georgia. A ceasefire was negotiated on 15 August 2008 and Russian troops had withdrawn by 22 August 2008. Russia recognised both Abkhazia and South Ossetia as independent states on 26 August 2008.

Georgia has a military strength of about 27,000 and has Soviet-era equipment interspersed with fresh purchases from the United States of America (US). These troops are US-trained with a training team of about 127 trainers deployed for the purpose in Georgia. A joint exercise had just been completed with US troops of its European Command in July so as to prepare a Georgian brigade for deployment in Iraq to replace its brigade of 2,000 troops already there. In the event, those deployed in Iraq were speedily flown back in US transport aircraft during the conflict. However, the brigade that was readying to deploy to Iraq and was ostensibly being trained by the US for the purpose was instead employed to capture South Ossetia with another brigade in reserve. A third brigade was employed to gain Abkhazia. Clearly, there appears to have been some prior preparation for this attack with US awareness of the same.

Russian aims were to secure both regions while weakening Georgia at the same time, and through this to send a wider message of the re-emergence of Russia. Russian muscle flexing also served the purpose of sensitising the US of the vulnerability of its Baku-Tbilisi-Ceyhan (BTC) oil pipeline that had been built for the express purpose of bypassing Russia. Towards this end, it also appears to have made prior preparation, having conducted Exercise Caucasian Frontier in July and having trained troops readily at hand for immediate response. Russia had issued passports to people in South Ossetia and when Georgia tried on 7 August to reassert its control by use of force, Russia responded with military means for protecting Russian citizens.

The two-pronged Russian onslaught was through both regions. It involved about 18,000 troops of 58th Army and supported by 4th Air Army. Air operations were conducted against Tbilisi airport and elements of the Russian Black Sea Fleet, based at Sevastopol in the Crimea (on lease from Ukraine) conducted operations for the capture of Poti port. However, despite the victorious showing, Russian military actions have come in for some critical scrutiny in terms of preparedness. Interestingly, the use of cyber war was witnessed for perhaps the first time with Russia-based computer networks targeting Georgian servers in 'botnets' and 'distributed denial of service (DDOS)' attacks. Apparently, the website of the Georgian president under attack had to be shifted to a Polish server. Eventually, the Russians retreated into a security zone around South Ossetia ending the conflict that resulted in 2,000 dead, 30,000 refugees and 160,000 displaced people.

The US response was to condemn Russian actions. It sent humanitarian aid by air and through ships of its Sixth Fleet in the Mediterranean and is reported to have helped Georgia with military advisers from the training team in location. It may have helped precipitate matters by giving Mr. Saakashvili signals that he could go ahead with his adventurist enterprise of a military takeover in the hope of testing newly-elected Russian President Medvedev. In this context the visit of US Secretary of State Rice to Georgia in July is notable. It has cut off the US-Russian nuclear deal that was under discussion and it has signed a missile shield deal with Poland.

The international response was swift in trying to bring the conflict to a close. The United Nations Security Council (UNSC) was not very effective since Russia is a member of the P5. However, the European Union (EU) under the French presidency drew up a ceasefire agreement that came to fruition after a few problem areas were sorted out. Divisions in Europe came to the fore on the approach to be adopted towards Russia. The EU suspended talks on EU-Russian partnership. NATO was divided over supporting Georgia since its major members are dependent on Russia for oil and gas. However, it held in abeyance planned joint exercises. While Georgia pulled out of the Commonwealth of Independent States (CIS), there was no avid support witnessed for Russia from among countries of it's 'near abroad' that comprise this grouping. Most states with Russian ethnic population, such as Ukraine and Kazakhstan, are worried by the Russian reason of support to its citizens as *casus belli.*

The war itself was a minor one and on that account may vanish into military history. However, there are a few issues, that it has helped flag, that should receive attention. First is the problem of overlapping ethnicities. South Ossetia has a population of about 100,000 people of Persian origin, who differ from their Georgian neighbours but have affiliation with the North Ossetians who belong to Russia. This is indicative of the intricate and overlapping nature of problems in areas such as the Balkans and Caucasus and indeed elsewhere, not excluding South Asia. These are subject to being manipulated by external motivated forces. Recognition to 'statelets' as independent states such as has occurred with respect to Kosovo in February 2004 and with South Ossetia and Abkhazia would make the world order unstable. Second is the well-noted point that Russia has unmistakably arrived back on the strategic scene. Lastly, there are grave implications of the increasing resort to military means by states for UN Charter norms regulating the use of force in the international system.

2

THE CAUCASUS

The large region known as the Caucasus is not really part of Eastern Europe, Central Asia, or the Middle East. It is at the crossroads of Asia and Europe, wedged between Russia to the north, Turkey and Iran to the south, and between the Black Sea to the West and the Caspian Sea to the east. During the Soviet years, the entire Caucasus area was part of the Soviet Union, with Chechnya and Dagestan as semi-autonomous regions of the Russian Republic and Georgia, Armenia, and Azerbaijan as separate Soviet republics.

Physical Geography

The Caucasus range is about 1,100 kilometres long, extending in a west-northwest to east-southeast direction. Its total area is about 145,000 square kilometres, and it is 180 kilometres wide in the region of Mount Elbrus. A dozen or so peaks have an elevation exceeding 5,000 metres. On its north side the range rises gradually in a series of parallel chains. On the south side it towers over the basins of the Transcaucasia and the Caspian Sea. In addition to this dissymmetry between the northern and southern faces, the range is divided by Mounts Elbrus and Kazbek into three distinct regions on its southern side: the western, central, and eastern Caucasus.

The northern side of the range consists of a series of ridges, with escarpments facing toward the main chain and the more gradual back slopes fanning out into plateaus of varying sizes, all inclining toward the

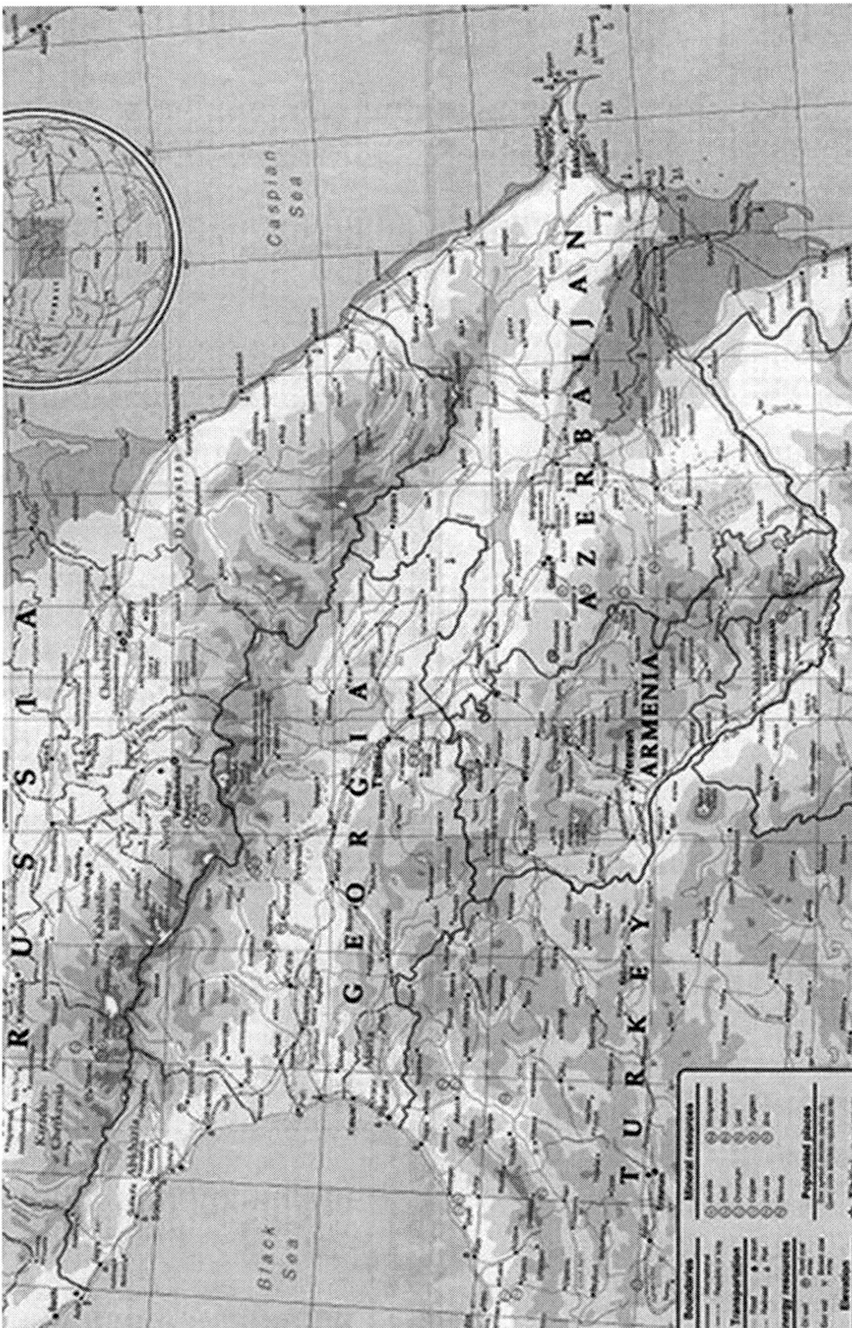

Map 1: The Caucasus

north at angles of from 5 to 15 degrees. Each ridge is steeply cut by the deep gorges of rivers (e.g., the Kuban, Baksan, and Terek). In the eastern Caucasus, particularly in Dagestan, the flat lands are much more extensive and part of a more complex structure that dominates the Koysu gorges.

The principal chain is in the central part of the Caucasian watershed. It consists of ridges which rise above 4,000 metres. The highest peaks include the volcanic cones of Mount Elbrus (5,642 metres) and Mount Kazbek (5,033 metres). In this axial zone of the central Caucasus the most beautiful high-mountain topography is found and glaciation is most extensive.

In the western Caucasus the elevations gradually diminish. Several peaks in the eastern Caucasus rise above 4,000 metres (Mount Tebulos Mta 4,493 metres, Bazar Dyuzi 4,466 metres, Shakh Dag 4,260 metres). The steep, narrow southern face of the range measures barely 20 kilometres from the crest of the principal chain to the Alazani valley.

Georgia is a small country of approximately 69,875 square kilometres. To the north and northeast, Georgia borders the Russian republics of Chechnya, Ingushetia, and North Ossetia (all of which began to seek autonomy from Russia in 1992). Neighbours to the south are Armenia, Azerbaijan, and Turkey. The shoreline of the Black Sea constitutes Georgia's entire western border.

Despite its small area, Georgia has one of the most varied topographies of the former Soviet republics. Georgia lies mostly in the Caucasus Mountains, and its northern boundary is partly defined by the Greater Caucasus range. The Lesser Caucasus range, which runs parallel to the Turkish and Armenian borders, and the Surami and Imereti ranges, which connect the Greater Caucasus and the Lesser Caucasus, create natural barriers that are partly responsible for cultural and linguistic differences among regions. Because of their elevation and a poorly developed transportation infrastructure, many mountain villages are virtually isolated from the outside world during the winter. Earthquakes and landslides in mountainous areas present a significant threat to life and property. Among the most recent natural disasters were massive rock and mudslides in Ajaria in 1989 that displaced thousands of people in south-western Georgia, and two earthquakes in 1991 that destroyed several villages in north-central Georgia and South Ossetia.

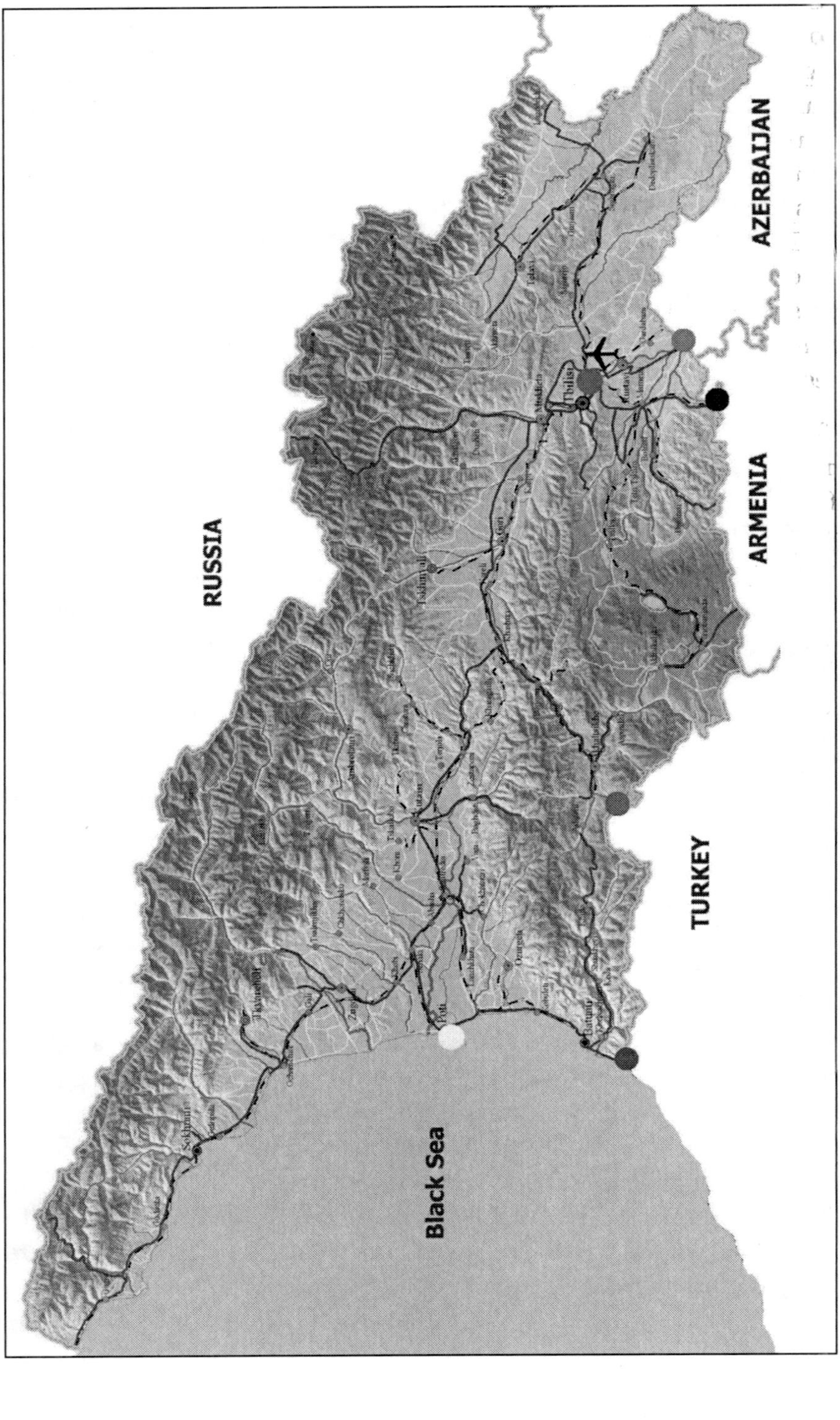

Map 2: Geography of the Caucasus Region

Georgia has about 25,000 rivers, many of which power small hydroelectric stations. Drainage is into the Black Sea to the west and through Azerbaijan to the Caspian Sea to the east. The largest river is the Mtkvari (formerly known by its Azerbaijani name, Kura, which is still used in Azerbaijan), which flows 1,364 kilometres (km) from northeast Turkey across the plains of eastern Georgia, through the capital, Tbilisi, and into the Caspian Sea. The Rioni River, the largest river in western Georgia, rises in the Greater Caucasus and empties into the Black Sea at the port of Poti. Soviet engineers turned the river lowlands along the Black Sea coast into prime subtropical agricultural land, embanked and straightened many stretches of river, and built an extensive system of canals. Deep mountain gorges form topographical belts within the Greater Caucasus.

The Caucasus is situated on the boundary between the temperate and subtropical climatic zones, and the orientation and height of the range reinforce the contrasts between the two. At sea level the average annual temperatures are approximately 10°C in Northern Caucasia and 16° C in Transcaucasia. The differences are more pronounced in winter, when Northern Caucasia is subject to thermal anticyclones from Russia, bringing average January temperatures of -5°C on the Kuban plains and an absolute minimum of -35°C, whereas in the more sheltered Transcaucasia the January average is 3°C in the west and 6°C in the east, with an absolute minimum close to -20°C on the plains. In summer the temperatures are very similar in all parts of the Caucasus, though slightly higher in the east at noon, owing to more continental location (23-24°C in the west, 25-29°C in the east). Winters are not much more severe in the mountains.

In addition, the Caucasus is also the region of translation between humid Atlantic and Mediterranean winds, on one hand, and dry continental air currents, on the other. On the plains the transition occurs on the Stavropol and Surami sills and in the mountains between Mounts Elbrus and Kazbek. Precipitation comes from the west, in storm systems that are replenished over the waters of the Black Sea, which explains the contrasts between the eastern and western ends of the Caucasus range and also between the well-watered Colchian face and the dryer northern slopes. In the western Caucasus maximum rainfall occurs in winter, in the central and eastern Caucasus in summer. Furthermore, the depth and duration of the snow cover also vary between the western and eastern sections of the range. At an elevation of 1,900 metres the western Caucasus receives an average of 1,200 millimetres (mm) of solid precipitation between November and March, compared to only 395 mm at the same elevation in the eastern Caucasus. These figures can vary considerably, however. The permanent snow line rises from 2,900-3,100 metres in the western Caucasus to 3,200-3,500 metres in the central Caucasus and 3,600-3,900 metres in the eastern Caucasus.

There are 2,047 glaciers in the Caucasus range, covering a total of 1,424 square kilometres. More than half (1,110) are situated in the central Caucasus; they cover an area of 1,033 square kilometres, that is, 72.5 percent of the total glaciated surface in the entire range. There are 565 glaciers in the western Caucasus and 372 in the eastern Caucasus, with surface areas of 278 square kilometres and 113 square kilometres respectively. The total volume of ice in the 1980s was estimated at 118.6 square kilometres.

The large rivers—the Kuban, Baksan, Terek, Sulak, and Samur on the northern slope and the Inguri, Rioni, Aragvi, and Iori on the southern slope—are fed by the glaciers, and the period of high water thus begins in March, when the snow melts, and lasts into July and August. The greatest volume occurs in summer, when the silt content of the streams is considerable. It is even greater in the east, where there is less vegetation cover.

Climate

Georgia's climate is affected by subtropical influences from the west and Mediterranean influences from the east. The Greater Caucasus range moderates local climate by serving as a barrier against cold air from the north. Warm, moist air from the Black Sea moves easily into the coastal lowlands from the west. Climatic zones are determined by distance from the Black Sea and by altitude. Along the Black Sea coast, from Abkhazia to the Turkish border, and in the region known as the Kolkhida Lowlands inland from the coast, the dominant subtropical climate features high humidity and heavy precipitation (1,000 to 2,000 mm per year; the Black Sea port of Batumi receives 2,500 millimetres per year). Several varieties of palm trees grow in these regions, where the midwinter average temperature is 5°C and the midsummer average is 22°C.

The plains of eastern Georgia are shielded from the influence of the Black Sea by mountains that provide a more continental climate. Summer temperatures average 20°C to 24°C, winter temperatures 2°C to 4°C. Humidity is lower, and rainfall averages 500 to 800 millimetres per year.

Alpine and highland regions in the east and west, as well as a semi-arid region on the Iori Plateau to the southeast, have distinct microclimates. At higher elevations, precipitation is sometimes twice as heavy as in the eastern plains. In the west, the climate is subtropical to about 650 metres; above that altitude (and to the north and east) is a band of moist and moderately warm weather, then a band of cool and wet conditions. Alpine conditions begin at about 2,100 metres, and above 3,600 metres snow and ice are present year-round.

Vegetation

The geographical position of the Caucasus provides favourable conditions for a great range of flora. More than 6,000 species have been enumerated in the region. The distribution of flora, which is determined by the terrain and climate, permits identification of several distinct regions, each with its own sequence of zones of elevation.

In the western and central Caucasus the lower forest zone consists of deciduous trees on gray or brown forest soils; oaks predominate, along with hornbeams. The zone of transition to piedmont vegetation distinguishes the Kuban regions on the north from the Colchian slopes in the south. In the former these oak and birch forests yield to a wooded steppe, which gradually gives way to the steppe proper.

Above 900-1,100 metres in the western Caucasus there are wide expanses of beech trees on brown soils, the most common formation in the mountains. On the moist southern slopes they are succeeded above 1,500-1,600 metres by a mixed forest of conifers and beeches, often succeeded in the upper mountain zone by a forest of dark conifers up to 2,000-2,200 metres. In the more arid valleys on the northern slopes beeches and spruces do not appear; instead above the oak trees there is a zone of pine trees. Conversely, on the southern face of the central Caucasus, beeches cover the entire slope up to the limit of the forest zone, though the upper part of this zone, between 1,800 and 2,500 metres, generally consists of a mixture of small deciduous trees (birches, maples, and even beeches).

The lower reaches of the alpine zone (2,000-2,500 metres) in the western Caucasus are characterized by tall grasses, which stand taller than a man, mingled with flowering shrubs. In these high meadows from 2,500 metres up to the snow line (3,200 metres in the western Caucasus, 3,600 in the central Caucasus) the ground is covered with alpine grasses and wild grains.

In the eastern Caucasus the vegetation is different because of the greater aridity. On the interior southern slopes the characteristics are comparable to those of the northern slopes, but the forests are more abundant and the steppes do not constitute a separate zone.

Owing to its natural features, the Caucasus exhibits a degree of bio-geographical continuity with the north-western regions of Iran, but its mountainous terrain has served as an important obstacle to population movements between the two areas.

Population

The population within the boundaries of the Caucasus range has been estimated at 1.25 million in an area of 103,000 square kilometres, an average density of more than twelve per square kilometres. In fact, a large part of the western Caucasus is almost uninhabited, as are several valleys in the central Caucasus, whereas in the eastern Caucasus the population density is often extremely high and greater in the mountains than on the plains. These differences partly reflect natural conditions like the broad expanses of the Dagestan plateaus but even more the history of the 19th and 20th centuries.

The population has experienced and is still experiencing the effects of the Russian conquest of the northern piedmont. For example, after their defeat in 1864 the Circassians were driven from the mountains; this displaced population has been estimated at about half a million. The western Caucasus remains almost entirely uninhabited because no group has come to replace the Circassians. In the central and eastern Caucasus colonization of the piedmont by the Cossacks drove the Caucasians into the mountains. Then, when the Cossacks went to war in 1914, their departure was followed by massive migrations of mountain dwellers into the abandoned Cossack villages.

After the establishment of Soviet power there was an administrative reorganization, based primarily on national and linguistic criteria. The Caucasus today is thus partitioned among three federated republics (Russian Soviet Federated Socialist Republic, Azerbaijan Soviet Socialist Republic, Georgian Soviet Socialist Republic), five autonomous republics

(Kabardino-Balkarian Autonomous Soviet Socialist Republic, North Ossetian Autonomous Soviet Socialist Republic, Checheno-Ingush Autonomous Soviet Socialist Republic, Dagestan Autonomous Soviet Socialist Republic, Abkhazian Autonomous Soviet Socialist Republic), and three autonomous oblasts(Adygei Autonomous Oblast, Karachayevo-Cherkess Autonomous Oblast, and South Ossetian Autonomous Oblast). All these entities also include territory outside the mountains. Their capitals are located on the piedmont and, except for Tbilisi in Georgia and Baku in Azerbaijan, have long been inhabited mainly by Russians, a circumstance that for a considerable time slowed the exodus of the mountain people, who were hesitant to leave their villages and settle in a milieu unfamiliar to them. Subsequently, however, new villages were founded on the plain and large-scale migrations organized. In the 1920s the populations of twenty-two Karachai villages were transplanted to the plain, 30,000 mountain dwellers from North Ossetia came to settle in fifteen new villages, and 12,000 Chechen families were also involved in these mass migrations. The situation was different in Georgia, where Georgians are the main component of the population, both in the urban centres of the piedmont and in the mountains. The latter was rapidly depopulated to the benefit of the piedmont, where living conditions are much less difficult. Between 1942 and 1945 many inhabitants of the Caucasus were evacuated or deported; Balkars, Chechens, Ingush, and Karachai even lost their national rights for a time. Although a number of them returned to their lands after 1956, the population density has never reached its pre-war level.

Today the population of the mountains remains almost exclusively rural. The upper limit of permanent habitation is at an elevation of 2,400 metres. Forms of settlement vary with the region. In the damp climate of the western Caucasus no trace of the old wooden villages of the Circassians survives. The fields of the very large agricultural villages on the piedmont, each with several thousand residents, are laid out along the streams in almost continuous strips. At higher elevations they yield to occasional pastoral and forest villages; the higher the elevation the more widely spaced these villages are and the smaller the number of inhabitants. There are no permanent settlements above 1,300 metres in this part of the Caucasus. The houses are built of stone and set in gardens, so that they are separated from one another.

There are also a few larger towns scattered in the mountains. Most often they are characterized by single economic activities (e.g., extractive industries at Tyrny Auz, Sadon, and Chiatura; tourism at Teberda; hot springs at Tskhaltubo). Small urban centres located in proximity to the mountains, like Karachayevsk, Kuba, Shemakha, Ambrolauri, Tsageri, and Oni, have more diversified functions, notably commercial, administrative, and service.

Economy

For reasons of geography (e.g. peripheral location within the Russian Federation and constraints of the physical environment), history (e.g., relatively late conquest by the Russians), and ethnic composition (e.g., the presence of many national minorities), the Caucasus, especially its eastern regions, remained poorly integrated into the Soviet economy and has been only slightly affected by the changes that have transformed the latter. Income in the mountains is lower than on the plains; in Georgia individual productivity in the mountains is two or three times lower than the average for the republic as a whole. Economic and social structures have been modified on the same pattern as in the rest of the country. Nevertheless, the systems of production have changed little in the mountains, and the Caucasus is still primarily characterized by an agricultural and pastoral mountain economy. More than half the working population is employed in the agricultural sector.

Production is organized within a tripartite framework, consisting of *kolkhozes* (collective farms), *sovkhozes* (state farms), and the auxiliary domestic sector. Each collective farm encompasses several villages. In the central and eastern Caucasus, there are cultivated lands near the *auls*, high summer pastures on the axial chain of the mountain range, and winter pastures and irrigated cultivation on the piedmont. The private sector has for a long time been limited to parcels of land for personal use and flocks of twenty to fifty sheep.

The specific nature of agricultural activities is determined by the zone of elevation, and there are also differences between the western Caucasus, where cattle raising predominates, and the rest of the range, where sheep and goats are the main livestock. Cattle breeding plays an essential economic role, accounting for 40-90% of the income of the mountain people. Cattle-raising in the more humid west requires seasonal shifts between villages and summer farms.

In the high mountains a much smaller proportion of the land is cultivated. In the high valleys crops, mainly potatoes are grown only on the private plots. At medium elevations they are more important, and the total area devoted to them is increasing as specialized crops are introduced or expanded, at least in the eastern Caucasus. In addition to cereals (rye and corn), which are grown on the plateaus, on slopes divided into strips and terraces, such forage crops as beets have been developed; in the valleys of the eastern Caucasus legumes, fruit trees (e.g., apricots and pears), and grapes are grown on irrigated plots.

There is a rich handicraft tradition in the eastern Caucasus. The goldsmiths and silversmiths of Kubachi and the weavers of Khuchni and Akhty have been celebrated for centuries, and their work is well known outside the Caucasus. In the Soviet period, masters and journeymen have formed craft cooperatives, and this sector, which has been able to maintain a high level of production owing to the Soviet market, has remained vital to the present day. Few industries have been established in the mountains; the primary exceptions are mining (wolfram and molybdenum, manganese, and polymetallic minerals) and quarrying.

Industrialization is hampered, however, by inadequate infrastructure, though all the permanently inhabited villages are electrified. At first small hydroelectric plants or groups of generators were used, but gradually the distribution grid has been extended. The piedmonts are supplied by large dams and powerful hydroelectric plants, which power several large factories in the valley. In the high mountains, on the other hand, where power plants must occupy arable land, the necessary equipment was installed only rather late, for technical reasons arising particularly from the frequency of earthquakes. There are no good roads in the Caucasus. The main axial roads bypass it, and it can be crossed only by the Georgian military road through the Krestov pass or by the Mamison pass. The transverse valleys in the north (e.g., those of the Kuban and Baksan rivers) are accessible, but many villages can be reached only by stony roads. A Transcaucasian railway exists between Tbilisi and Ordzhonikidze via the Aragvi and Terek valleys.

The difficulties of travel have also slowed the development of tourism, for which the Caucasus is otherwise well suited. Certain regions (like Svanetia and the interior of Dagestan) are blessed with architectural riches and many picturesque villages, virtual open-air museums. Although springs are abundant, they are still only partially exploited as thermal spas.

The largest resorts are outside the mountains or on their periphery. Excursions into the mountains are organized from these and other large resorts on the Black Sea coast (Sochi, Gagra). Since the 1970s winter-sports resorts have been established at Teberda-Dombay, Tse-, and Gudauri. Because of growing urbanization on the piedmonts an increasing number of people have second homes in the mountains, often original family homes that have been preserved after migration to the lowlands.

Language, Religion, and Culture

For centuries, Georgia's geographic position has opened it to religious and cultural influences from the West, Persia, Turkey, and Russia. The resultant diversity continues to characterize the cultural and religious life of modern Georgia. However, the Georgian language displays unique qualities that cannot be attributed to any outside influence.

To sum up, the general features of the Caucasus are:

(a) **The Caucasus is mountainous.** In this part of the world geography is destiny. The Greater Caucasus Range, with its highest peak being Mt. Elbrus, divides the region into the North Caucasus and the South Caucasus; other mountains split the area further. The North Caucasus includes several small republics that are part of the Russian Federation. The South Caucasus comprises the independent states of Armenia, Georgia, and Azerbaijan among the 15 national republics.

(b) **The Caucasus is culturally diverse.** A glance at a political map of the region suggests that simple borders separate the political entities in the Caucasus, but in fact crossing from, say, Georgia to Chechnya involves traversing high mountain passes that are open only part of the year or using one of a few strategic tunnels. Such natural barriers mean that many groups in the region have existed in isolation for millennia. In fact, this compact region with its population of around 20 million includes upwards of 50 ethnic groups, and a great linguistic variety. A few languages like Azerbaijani are members of the Turkic language family, and others like Armenian and Ossetian are part of the Indo-European language family (which includes Russian and English). Most are part of three distinct language families found nowhere else in the world. This linguistic diversity is accompanied by religious and political variation. The focus on Islam in current discussions of the Caucasus might leave the impression that the entire region is Muslim, and to be sure there are many Muslims there. But many in nominally Muslim regions such as Azerbaijan are quite secular, and Armenia and Georgia have been Christian since the fourth century.

(c) **There are deep historical roots for just about everything in the Caucasus.** Historical roots in the region are indeed impressive: Petroglyphs from 10,000 years ago can be found in Azerbaijan and Georgia is the site of the world's first cultivation of grapes for wine, some 8,000 years ago. In medieval times the Caucasus was overrun by Arabs, Mongols, Persians, and Turks as they tried to control this strategically important area. And for the past two centuries Russia has been the major player in the region. The peoples of the Caucasus have a reputation of being fiercely independent, and some highland groups were never conquered—or even discovered—by invading powers. The result is a set of competing national narratives that extend much further back in time than what we are accustomed to. In Georgia, for example, twelfth century king "David the Builder" retains a living presence in politics.

(d) **The Caucasus is in a "dangerous neighbourhood."** Throughout their long history, Caucasian clans and nations have engaged in warfare, and this continues today. In some cases the hostilities are between local groups. Just three decades ago, for example, more than 30,000 people died in a conflict between Armenia and Azerbaijan over the territory of Nagorno-Karabakh. But most major hostilities since 1800 have grown out of Russian efforts to subjugate the region, especially the North Caucasus. In the 1990s a brutal war in Chechnya between militants and Russian forces left well over 70,000 dead. This sort of violence stems from the time of Tsars' efforts to expand the Russian empire into the region and subdue the local populations. Authors like Lev Tolstoy and Alexandre Dumas described both the romantic and brutal sides of the Caucasus War, which dragged on from 1817 to 1864. In many respects, it is a war that continues to this day.

(e) **Russian suppression of national resistance in the Caucasus has encouraged fundamentalist movements.** Russian efforts to suppress local groups have often led to radicalization. Numerous conflicts in the North Caucasus started out as ethnic or national resistance, but when brutally suppressed by Russia, morphed

> into extreme reactions, often with Islamist overtones. Time and again Russia's heavy-handed efforts have had this result, and as violent resistance emerged the unfortunate Russian response has been to double down on the use of brutal force. Today discussions of autonomy or non-violent acts of resistance in the Caucasus are often labelled as terrorist and ruthlessly stamped out by Russians or their proxies. In an age of instant global communication, one ominous result is that the fundamentalist identities that have emerged locally are tied to worldwide networks. In addition to fighting against Russia, for example, radicalized Chechens can now be found fighting with Islamists in Afghanistan and Syria.

The North Caucasus is a place of spectacular beauty with most people wanting nothing more than to live in peace and see their children prosper. The cycles of violence continue to be very hard to break, however, and occasionally the targets of revenge go beyond Russians to anyone taken to be an enemy of Islam.

3

HISTORY OF GEORGIA

Georgia's location at a major commercial crossroads and among several powerful neighbours has provided both advantages and disadvantages through some 25 centuries of history. Georgia comprises regions having distinctive traits. The ethnic, religious, and linguistic characteristics of the country as a unit coalesced to a greater degree than before under Russian rule in the 19th century. Then, beneath a veneer of centralized economic and political control imposed during 70 years of Soviet rule, Georgian cultural and social institutions survived, thanks in part to Georgia's relative distance from Moscow. As the republic entered the post-Soviet period in the 1990s, however, the prospects of establishing true national autonomy based on a common heritage remained unclear.

Historical Background

Although Saint George is the country's patron saint, the name Georgia derives from the Arabic and Persian words, Kurj and Gurj, for the country. In 1991 Georgia—called Sakartvelo in Georgian and Gruziia in Russian—had been part of a Russian or Soviet empire almost continuously since the beginning of the 19th century, when most of the regions that constitute modern Georgia accepted Russian annexation in order to gain protection from Persia. Prior to that time, some combination of the territories that make up modern Georgia had been ruled by the Bagratid Dynasty for about 1,000 years, including periods of foreign domination and fragmentation. Throughout history the territory comprising the Georgian state varied considerably in size as foreign forces occupied some regions and as centrally ruled federations controlled others.

Christianity and the Georgian Empire

In the last centuries of the pre-Christian era, Georgia, in the form of the kingdom of Kartli-Iberia, was strongly influenced by Greece to the west and Persia to the east. After the Roman Empire completed its conquest of the Caucasus region in 66 B.C., the kingdom was a Roman client state and ally for some 400 years. In A.D. 330, King Marian Ill's acceptance of Christianity ultimately tied Georgia to the neighbouring Byzantine Empire, which exerted a strong cultural influence for several centuries. Although Arabs captured the capital city of Tbilisi in A.D. 645, Kartli-Iberia retained considerable independence under local Arab rulers. In A.D. 813, the Armenian prince Ashot I became the first of the Bagrationi family to rule Georgia. Ashot's reign began a period of nearly 1,000 years during which the Bagratids, as the house was known, ruled at least part of what is now Georgia.

Western and eastern Georgia were united under Bagrat V (r. 1027-72). In the next century, David IV (r. 1099-1125) initiated the Georgian golden age by driving the Turks from the country and expanding Georgian cultural and political influence southward into Armenia and eastward to the Caspian Sea. That era of unparalleled power and prestige for the Georgian monarchy concluded with the great literary flowering of Queen Tamar's reign (1184-1212). At the end of that period, Georgia was well known in the Christian West (and relied upon as an ally by the Crusaders). Outside the national boundaries, several provinces were dependent to some degree on Georgian power: the Trabzon Empire on the southern shore of the Black Sea, regions in the Caucasus to the north and east, and southern Azerbaijan.

Occupation and Inclusion in the Russian Empire

The Mongol invasion in 1236 marked the beginning of a century of fragmentation and decline. A brief resurgence of Georgian power in the 14th century ended when the Turkic conqueror Timur (Tamerlane) destroyed Tbilisi in 1386. The capture of Constantinople by the Ottoman Turks in 1453 began three centuries of domination by the militant Ottoman and Persian empires, which divided Georgia into spheres of influence in

1553 and subsequently redistributed Georgian territory between them. By the 18th century, however, the Bagratid line again had achieved substantial independence under nominal Persian rule. In this period, Georgia was threatened more by rebellious Georgian and Persian nobles from within than by the major powers surrounding the country. In 1762 Herekle II was able to unite the east Georgian regions of Kartli and Kakhetia under his independent but tenuous rule. In this period of renewed unity, trade increased and feudal institutions lost influence in Georgia. In 1773 Herekle began efforts to gain Russian protection from the Turks, who were threatening to retake his kingdom. In this period, Russian troops intermittently occupied parts of Georgia, making the country a pawn in the Russian-Turkish rivalry of the last three decades of the 18th century. After the Persians sacked Tbilisi in 1795, Herekle again sought the protection of Orthodox Russia.

Within the Russian Empire

Annexation by the Russian Empire began a new stage of Georgian history, in which security was achieved by linking Georgia more closely than ever with Russia. This subordinate relationship would last nearly two centuries.

Because of its weak position, Georgia could not set the terms of protection by the Russian Empire. In 1801 Tsar Alexander I summarily abolished the kingdom of Kartli-Kakhetia, and the heir to the Bagratid throne was forced to abdicate. In the next decade, the Russian Empire gradually annexed Georgia's entire territory. Eastern Georgia (the regions of Kartli and Kakhetia) became part of the Russian Empire in 1801, and western Georgia (Imeretia) was incorporated in 1804. After annexation Russian governors tried to rearrange Georgian feudal society and government according to the Russian model. Russian education and ranks of nobility were introduced, and the Georgian Orthodox Church lost its autocephalous status in 1811. In the second half of the 19th century, Russification intensified, as did Georgian rebellions against the process.

By 1850 the social and political position of the Georgian nobility, for centuries the foundation of Georgian society, had deteriorated. A new worker class began to exert social pressure in Georgian population centres. Because the nobility still represented Georgian national interests, its decline meant that the Armenian merchant class, which had been a constructive part of urban life since the Middle Ages, gained greater economic power within Georgia. At the same time, Russian political hegemony over the Caucasus now went unopposed by Georgians.

By the end of the 19th century, Russia, fearing increased Armenian power in Georgia, asserted direct control over Armenian religious and political institutions. In the first decade of the 20th century, a full-fledged Georgian national liberation movement was established by Marxist followers of the Russian Social Democrat Party. By 1900 migration from rural areas and the growth of manufacturing had generated a fairly cohesive working class led by a new generation of Georgian intellectuals, who called for elimination of both the Armenian bourgeoisie and the Russian government bureaucracy. The main foe, however, was tsarist autocracy.

In 1905 a large-scale peasant revolt in western Georgia and general strikes in industrial centres throughout the Caucasus caused Russia to declare martial law. As elsewhere in the Russian Empire, the political reforms of 1905 temporarily eased tensions between the Georgian population and the Russian government. For the next decade, the Georgian revolutionaries of the Social Democrat Party were split between the gradualist Menshevik and the radical Bolshevik factions, and the incidences of strikes and mass demonstrations declined sharply between 1906 and 1917. Mensheviks, however, occupied all the Georgian seats in the first two seatings of the Duma, the Russian parliamentary institution established in 1905. In this period, Joseph V. Stalin (a Georgian who changed his name from Ioseb Jugashvili around 1910) became a leader of Bolshevik conspiracies against the Russian government in Georgia.

World War I and Independence

Because Turkey was a member of the Central Powers in World War I, the Caucasus region became a major battleground in that conflict. In 1915 and 1916, Russian forces pushed southwest into eastern Turkey from bases in the Caucasus, with limited success. As part of the Russian Empire, Georgia officially backed the Allies, although it stood to gain little from victory by either side. By 1916 economic conditions and mass immigration of war refugees had raised social discontent throughout the Caucasus, and the Russian Empire's decade-old experiment with constitutional monarchy was judged a failure. The revolution of 1917 in Russia intensified the struggle between the Mensheviks and the Bolsheviks in Georgia. In May

1918, Georgia declared its independence under the protection of Germany. Georgia turned toward Germany to prevent opportunistic invasion by the Turks; the move also resulted from Georgians' perception of Germany as the centre of European culture. The major European powers recognized Georgia's independence, and in May 1920, Russian leader Vladimir I. Lenin officially followed suit. The few years of post-war independence were economically disastrous, however, because Georgia did not establish commercial relations with the West, Russia, or its smaller neighbours.

In seven decades as part of the Soviet Union, Georgia maintained some cultural independence, and Georgian nationalism remained a significant—though at times muted—issue in relations with the Russians. In economic and political terms, however, Georgia was thoroughly integrated into the Soviet system.

After independence was declared in 1918, the Georgian Bolsheviks campaigned to undermine the Menshevik leader Zhordania, and in 1921 the Red Army invaded Georgia and forced him to flee. From 1922 until 1936, Georgia was part of a united Transcaucasian Soviet Federated Socialist Republic (TSFSR) within the Soviet Union. In 1936 the federated republic was split up into Armenia, Azerbaijan, and Georgia, which remained separate Soviet socialist republics of the Soviet Union until the end of 1991.

Although Stalin and Lavrenti Beria, his chief of secret police from 1938 to 1953, were both Georgians, Stalin's regime oppressed Georgians as severely as it oppressed citizens of other Soviet republics. The most notable manifestations of this policy were the execution of 5,000 nobles in 1924 as punishment for a Menshevik revolt and the purge of Georgian intellectuals and artists in 1936-37. Another Georgian Bolshevik, Sergo Ordzhonikidze, played an important role in the early 1920s in bringing Georgia and other Soviet republics into a centralized, Moscow-directed state. Ordzhonikidze later became Stalin's top economic official.

World War II and After

Georgia was not invaded in World War II. It contributed more than 500,000 fighters to the Red Army, however, and was a vital source of textiles and munitions. Stalin's successful appeal for patriotic unity eclipsed Georgian nationalism during the war and diffused it in the years following.

Restoration of autonomy to the Georgian Orthodox Church in 1943 facilitated this process.

The last two decades of Stalin's rule saw rapid, forced urbanization and industrialization, as well as drastic reductions in illiteracy and the preferential treatment of Georgians at the expense of ethnic minorities in the republic. The full Soviet centralized economic planning structure was in place in Georgia by 1934. Between 1940 and 1958, the republic's industrial output grew by 240 percent. In that time, the influence of traditional village life decreased significantly for a large part of the Georgian population.

Upon Stalin's death in 1953, Georgian nationalism revived and resumed its struggle against dictates from the central government in Moscow. In the 1950s, reforms under Soviet leader Nikita S. Khrushchev included the shifting of economic authority from Moscow to republic-level officials, but Khrushchev's repudiation of Stalin set off a backlash in Georgia. In 1956 hundreds of Georgians were killed when they demonstrated against Khrushchev's policy of de-Stalinization. Long afterward many Stalin monuments and place-names—as well as the museum constructed at Stalin's birthplace in the town of Gori, northwest of Tbilisi—were maintained. Only with Mikhail S. Gorbachev's policy of *glasnost* in the late 1980s did criticism of Stalin become acceptable and a full account of Stalin's crimes against his fellow Georgians become known in Georgia.

Between 1955 and 1972, Georgian communists used decentralization to become entrenched in political posts and to reduce further the influence of other ethnic groups in Georgia. In addition, enterprising Georgians created factories whose entire output was "off the books". In 1972 the long-standing corruption and economic inefficiency of Georgia's leaders led Moscow to sponsor Eduard Shevardnadze as first secretary of the Georgian Communist Party. Shevardnadze had risen through the ranks of the Communist Youth League (*Komsomol*) to become a party first secretary at the district level in 1961. From 1964 until 1972, Shevardnadze oversaw the Georgian police from the Ministry of Internal Affairs, where he made a reputation as a competent and incorruptible official.

The First Shevardnadze Period

As party first secretary, Shevardnadze used purges to attack the corruption and chauvinism for which Georgia's elite had become infamous even among the corrupt and chauvinistic republics of the Soviet Union. Meanwhile, a small group of dissident nationalists coalesced around academician Zviad Gamsakhurdia, who stressed the threat that Russification presented to the Georgian national identity. This theme would remain at the centre of Georgian-Russian relations into the new era of Georgian independence in the 1990s. Soviet power and Georgian nationalism clashed in 1978 when Moscow ordered revision of the constitutional status of the Georgian language as Georgia's official state language. Bowing to pressure from street demonstrations, Moscow approved Shevardnadze's reinstatement of the constitutional guarantee the same year.

In the 1970s and early 1980s, Shevardnadze successfully walked a narrow line between the demands of Moscow and the Georgians' growing desire for national autonomy. He maintained political and economic control while listening carefully to popular demands and making strategic concessions. Shevardnadze dealt with nationalism and dissent by explaining his policies to hostile audiences and seeking compromise solutions. The most serious ethnic dispute of Shevardnadze's tenure arose in 1978, when leaders of the Abkhazian Autonomous Republic threatened to secede from Georgia, alleging unfair cultural, linguistic, political, and economic restrictions imposed by Tbilisi. Shevardnadze took a series of steps to diffuse the crisis, including an affirmative action programme that increased the role of Abkhazian elites in running their region, despite the minority status of their group in Abkhazia.

Shevardnadze initiated experiments that foreshadowed the economic and political reforms that Gorbachev later introduced into the central Soviet system. The *Abasha* economic experiment in agriculture created new incentives for farmers similar to those used in the Hungarian agricultural reform of the time. Reorganization in the seaport of Poti expanded the role of local authorities at the expense of republic and all-union ministries. By 1980 Shevardnadze had raised Georgia's industrial and agricultural production significantly and had dismissed about 300 members of the party's corrupt hierarchy.

When Shevardnadze left office in 1985, considerable government corruption remained, however, and Georgia's official economy was still weakened by an extensive illegal "second economy." But his reputation for honesty and political courage earned Shevardnadze great popularity among Georgians, the awarding of the Order of Lenin by the Communist Party of the Soviet Union in 1978, and appointment as minister of foreign affairs of the Soviet Union in 1985.

Patiashvili

Jumber Patiashvili, a nondescript party loyalist, succeeded Shevardnadze as head of the Georgian Communist Party. Under Patiashvili, most of Shevardnadze's initiatives atrophied, and no new policy innovations were undertaken. Patiashvili removed some of Shevardnadze's key appointees, although he could not dismiss his predecessor's many middle-echelon appointees without seriously damaging the party apparatus. In dealing with dissent, Patiashvili, who distrusted radical and unofficial groups, returned to the usual confrontational strategy of Soviet regional party officials. The party head met major resistance when he backed a plan for a new Transcaucasian railroad that would cut a swath parallel to the Georgian Military Highway in a historic, scenic, and environmentally significant region. In a televised speech, Patiashvili called opponents of the project "enemies of the people"—a phrase used in the 1930s to justify liquidation of Stalin's real and imagined opponents. By isolating opposition groups, Patiashvili forced reformist leaders into underground organizations and confrontational behaviour.

Gorbachev's simultaneous policies of glasnost and continued control energized the forces of nationalism in Georgia, which pushed the republic out of the central state before the Soviet Union fell apart. The first years of independence were marked by struggle among Georgians for control of the government and by conflict with ethnic minorities seeking to escape the control of Tbilisi.

Nationalism Rises

In April 1989, Soviet troops broke up a peaceful demonstration at the government building in Tbilisi. Under unclear circumstances, twenty Georgians, mostly women and children, were killed. The military authorities and the official media blamed the demonstrators, and opposition leaders were arrested. The Georgian public was outraged. What was afterward referred to as the April Tragedy fundamentally radicalized political life in the republic. Shevardnadze was sent to Georgia to restore calm. He arranged for the replacement of Patiashvili by Givi Gumbaridze, head of the Georgian branch of the Committee for State Security (*Komitet gosudarstvennoi bezopasnosti*—KGB)

In an atmosphere of renewed nationalist fervour, public opinion surveys indicated that the vast majority of the population was committed to immediate independence from Moscow. Although the communist party was discredited, it continued to control the formal instruments of power. In the months following the April Tragedy, the opposition used strikes and other forms of pressure to undermine communist power and set the stage for de facto separation from the Soviet Union.

The Rise of Gamsakhurdia

Partly as a result of the conspiratorial nature of anti-government activity prior to 1989, opposition groups tended to be small, tightly knit units organized around prominent individuals. The personal ambitions of opposition leaders prevented the emergence of a united front, but Zviad Gamsakhurdia, the most widely honoured and recognized of the nationalist dissidents, moved naturally to a position of leadership. The son of Georgia's foremost contemporary novelist, Gamsakhurdia had gained many enemies during the communist years in acrimonious disputes and irreconcilable factional splits.

Opposition pressure resulted in a multi-party election in October 1990. Despite guarantees written into the new law on elections, many prominent opposition parties boycotted the vote, arguing that their groups could not compete fairly and that their participation under existing conditions would only legitimize continuation of Georgia's "colonial status" within the Soviet system.

As an alternative, the opposition parties had held their own election, without government approval, in September 1990. Although the minimum turnout for a valid election was not achieved, the new "legislative" body, called the Georgian National Congress, met and became a centre of opposition to the government chosen in the official October election. In the officially sanctioned voting, Gamsakhurdia's Round Table/Free Georgia coalition won a solid majority in the Supreme Soviet, Georgia's official parliamentary body.

Arguably the most virulently anti-communist politician ever elected in a Soviet republic, Gamsakhurdia was intolerant of all political opposition. He often accused his opposition of treason or involvement with the KGB. The quality of political debate in Georgia was lowered by the exchange of such charges between Gamsakhurdia and opposition leaders of the National Democratic Party.

After his election, Gamsakhurdia's greatest concern was the armed opposition. Both Gamsakhurdia's Round Table/Free Georgia coalition and some opposition factions in the Georgian National Congress had informal military units, which the previous, communist Supreme Soviet had legalized under pressure from informal groups. The most formidable of these groups were the Mkhedrioni (horsemen), said to number 5,000 men, and the so-called National Guard. The new parliament, dominated by Gamsakhurdia, outlawed such groups and ordered them to surrender their weapons, but the order had no effect. After the elections, independent military groups raided local police stations and Soviet military installations, sometimes adding formidable weaponry to their arsenals. In February 1991, a Soviet army counterattack against Mkhedrioni headquarters had led to the imprisonment of the Mkhedrioni leader.

Gamsakhurdia moved quickly to assert Georgia's independence from Moscow. He took steps to bring the Georgian KGB and Ministry of Internal Affairs (both overseen until then from Moscow) under his control. Gamsakhurdia refused to attend meetings called by Gorbachev to preserve a working union among the rapidly separating Soviet republics. Gamsakhurdia's communications with the Soviet leader usually took the form of angry telegrams and telephone calls. In May 1991, Gamsakhurdia ended the collection in Georgia of Gorbachev's national sales tax on the grounds that it damaged the Georgian economy.

Soon Georgia ceased all payments to Soviet government took steps to isolate the republic economically. Rather than consent to participate in Gorbachev's March 1991 referendum on preserving a federation of Soviet republics, Gamsakhurdia organized a separate referendum on Georgian independence. The measure was approved by 98.9 percent of Georgian voters. On 9 April 1991, the second anniversary of the April Tragedy, the Georgian parliament passed a declaration of independence from the Soviet Union. Once the Soviet Union collapsed at the end of 1991, Georgia refused to participate in the formation or subsequent activities of the

Commonwealth of Independent States (CIS), the loose confederation of independent republics that succeeded the Soviet Union.

The Struggle for Control

In May 1991, Gamsakhurdia was elected president of Georgia (receiving over 86 percent of the vote) in the first popular presidential election in a Soviet republic. Apparently perceiving the election as a mandate to run Georgia personally, Gamsakhurdia made increasingly erratic policy and personnel decisions in the months that followed, while his attitude toward the opposition became more strident. After intense conflict with Gamsakhurdia, Prime Minister Tengiz Sigua resigned in August 1991.

The August 1991 coup attempt against Gorbachev in Moscow marked a turning point in Georgian as well as in Soviet politics. Gamsakhurdia made it clear that he believed the coup, headed by the Soviet minister of defence and the head of the KGB, was both inevitable and likely to succeed. Accordingly, he ordered Russian president Boris N. Yeltsin's proclamations against the coup removed from the streets of Tbilisi. Gamsakhurdia also ordered the National Guard to turn in its weapons, disband, and integrate itself into the forces of the Ministry of Internal Affairs. Opposition leaders immediately denounced this action as capitulation to the coup. In defiance of Gamsakhurdia, National Guard commander Tengiz Kitovani led most of his troops out of Tbilisi.

The opposition to Gamsakhurdia, now joined in an uneasy coalition behind Sigua and Kitovani, demanded that Gamsakhurdia resign and call new parliamentary elections. Gamsakhurdia refused to compromise, and his troops forcibly dispersed a large opposition rally in Tbilisi in September 1991. Chanturia, whose National Democratic Party was one of the most active opposition groups at that time, was arrested and imprisoned on charges of seeking help from Moscow to overthrow the government.

In the ensuing period, both the government and extra-parliamentary opposition intensified the purchase and "liberation" of large quantities of weapons—mostly from Soviet military units stationed in Georgia—including heavy artillery, tanks, helicopter gunships, and armoured personnel carriers. On 22 December, intense fighting broke out in central Tbilisi after government troops again used force to disperse demonstrators. At this point, the National Guard and the Mkhedrioni besieged Gamsakhurdia and his supporters in the heavily fortified parliament building. Gunfire and artillery severely damaged central Tbilisi, and Gamsakhurdia fled the city in early January 1992 to seek refuge outside Georgia.

The Military Council

A Military Council made up of Sigua, Kitovani, and Mkhedrioni leader Jaba Ioseliani took control after Gamsakhurdia's departure. Shortly thereafter, a Political Consultative Council and a larger State Council were formed to provide more decisive leadership. In March 1992, Eduard Shevardnadze returned to Georgia at the invitation of the Military Council. Shortly thereafter, Shevardnadze joined Ioseliani, Sigua, and Kitovani to form the State Council Presidium. All four were given the right of veto over State Council decisions.

Gamsakhurdia, despite his absence, continued to enjoy substantial support within Georgia, especially in rural areas and in his home region of Mingrelia in western Georgia. Gamsakhurdia supporters now constituted another extra-parliamentary opposition, viewing themselves as victims of an illegal and unconstitutional *putsch* and refusing to participate in future elections. Based in the neighbouring Chechen Autonomous Republic of Russia, Gamsakhurdia continued to play a direct role in Georgian politics, characterizing Shevardnadze as an agent of Moscow in a neo-communist conspiracy against Georgia. In March 1992, Gamsakhurdia convened a parliament in exile in the Chechen city of Groznyy. In 1992 and 1993, his armed supporters prevented the Georgian government from gaining control of parts of western Georgia.

The autonomous areas of South Ossetia and Abkhazia added to the problems of Georgia's post-Soviet governments. By 1993 separatist movements in those regions threatened to tear the republic into several sections. Intimations of Russian interference in the ethnic crises also complicated Georgia's relations with its giant neighbour.

South Ossetia

The first major crisis faced by the Gamsakhurdia regime was in the South Ossetian Autonomous Region, which is largely populated by Ossetians, a separate ethnic group speaking a language based on Persian. In December 1990, Gamsakhurdia summarily abolished the region's autonomous status

The breakaway republics of Abkhazia, South Ossetia and Nagorno-Karabakh within the Caucasus region (after August 2008)

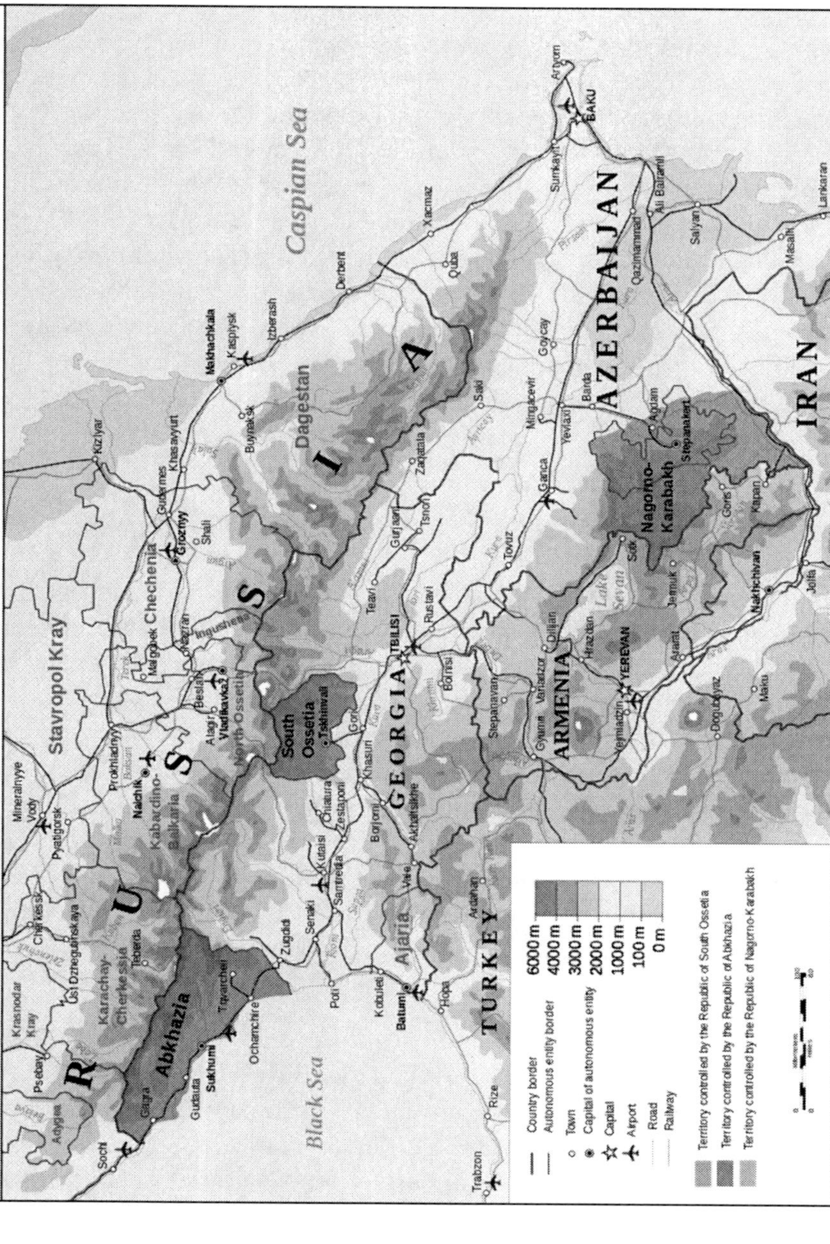

Map 3: Caucasus—Breakaway Regions

within Georgia in response to its long-time efforts to gain independence. When the South Ossetian regional legislature took its first steps toward secession and union with the North Ossetian Autonomous Republic of Russia, Georgian forces invaded. The resulting conflict lasted throughout 1991, causing thousands of casualties and creating tens of thousands of refugees on both sides of the Georgian-Russian border. Russian President Boris Yeltsin mediated a ceasefire in July 1992. A year later, the ceasefire was still in place, enforced by Ossetian and Georgian troops together with six Russian battalions. Representatives of the Conference on Security and Cooperation in Europe (CSCE) attempted mediation, but the two sides remained intractable. In July 1993, the South Ossetian government declared negotiations over and threatened to renew large-scale combat, but the cease-fire held through early 1994.

Abkhazia

In the Abkhazian Autonomous Republic of Georgia, the Abkhazian population, like the Ossetians a distinct ethnic group, feared that the Georgians would eliminate their political autonomy and destroy the Abkhaz as a cultural entity. On one hand, a long history of ill will between the Abkhaz and the Georgians was complicated by the minority status of the Abkhaz within the autonomous republic and by periodic Georgianization campaigns, first by the Soviet and later by the Georgian government. On the other hand, the Georgian majority in Abkhazia resented disproportionate distribution of political and administrative positions to the Abkhaz. Beginning in 1978, Moscow had sought to head off Abkhazian demands for independence by allocating as much as 67 percent of party and government positions to the Abkhaz, although, according to the 1989 census, 2.5 times as many Georgians as Abkhaz lived in Abkhazia.

Tensions in Abkhazia led to open warfare on a much larger scale than in South Ossetia. In July 1992, the Abkhazian Supreme Soviet voted to return to the 1925 constitution, under which Abkhazia was separate from Georgia. In August 1992, a force of the Georgian National Guard was sent to the Abkhazian capital of Sukhumi with orders to protect Georgian rail and road supply lines and to secure the border with Russia. When Abkhazian authorities reacted to this transgression of their self-proclaimed sovereignty hundreds were killed in fighting between Abkhazian and Georgian forces, and large numbers of refugees fled across the border into

Russia or into other parts of Georgia. The Abkhazian government was forced to flee Sukhumi.

For two centuries, the Abkhaz had viewed Russia as a protector of their interests against the Georgians: accordingly, the Georgian incursion of 1992 brought an Abkhazian plea for Russia to intervene and settle the issue. An unknown number of Russian military personnel and volunteers also fought on the side of the Abkhaz, and Shevardnadze accused Yeltsin of intentionally weakening Georgia's national security by supporting separatists. After the failure of three ceasefires, in September 1993 Abkhazian forces besieged and captured Sukhumi and drove the remaining Georgian forces out of Abkhazia. In the fall of 1993, mediation efforts by the UN and Russia were slowed by Georgia's struggle against Gamsakhurdia's forces in Mingrelia, south of Abkhazia. In early 1994, a de facto ceasefire remained in place, with the Inguri River in northwest Georgia serving as the dividing line. Separatist forces made occasional forays into Georgian territory, however.

In September 1993, Gamsakhurdia took advantage of the struggle in Abkhazia to return to Georgia and rally enthusiastic but disorganized Mingrelians against the demoralized Georgian army. Although Gamsakhurdia initially represented his return as a rescue of Georgian forces, he actually included Abkhazian troops in his new advance. Gamsakhurdia's forces took several towns in western Georgia, adding urgency to an appeal by Shevardnadze for Russian military assistance. In mid-October the addition of Russian weapons, supply-line security, and technical assistance turned the tide against Gamsakhurdia and brought a quick end to hostilities on the Mingrelian front. His cause apparently lost, Gamsakhurdia committed suicide in January 1994.

Rose Revolution and Re-establishing Power over South Ossetia

The President of Georgia, Eduard Shevardnadze, was first elected into office in 1995. Shevardnadze was re-elected in 2000, but the results were revealed to be fraudulent three years later during the parliamentary elections in 2003. Mikheil Saakashvili had claimed he had won the 2000 elections and political unrest soon rose. The political protests of 2003 are now known as the Rose Revolution. As a result of the Rose Revolution, Saakashvili won the 2004 presidential election in a landslide. On a regional scale, the politics in Georgia inspired the Ukrainian Orange Revolution and November 2004 Ukrainian presidential election.

President Saakashvili made Georgian nationalism his top priority, particularly by strengthening Georgia's military. Saakashvili's efforts were successful in the south-western Ajaria when the Georgian army deposed the authoritarian Adjarian leader, Aslan Abashidze. After redefining terms of Ajaria's autonomy, Saakashvili decided to re-establish Georgian power over other autonomous areas within the country's borders.

Saakashvili first attempted to restore Georgian power in South Ossetia by starting an anti-smuggling campaign in the region. According to Georgian authorities, Russia was smuggling goods into Georgia without passing through customs. Roadblocks were set up in Gori by the Georgian government in 2004 in order to restrict traffic from South Ossetia. Once again, hostilities increased between Georgia and the Russian-supported South Ossetia. After several small skirmishes, Georgia changed tactics and began supporting a pro-Tbilisi Ossetian platform headed by Dmitry Sanakoev. This ultimately ended with the secessionist de facto government headed by South Ossetia's current president, Eduard Kokoity. Sanakoev maintains authority over the scattered ethnic Georgian cities in South Ossetia, while Kokoity oversees the rest of South Ossetia from the capital of Tskhinvali.

Georgia continued to speak against the Russian presence in the Georgian republics and openly expressed the desire for international intervention. In particular, Georgia was officially interested in joining the European Union in 2004 and NATO in 2005. Still concerned over border security, Georgia used drones in Abkhazia and South Ossetia. The South Ossetian elections in 2006 resulted in a declaration of independence, which Georgia did not recognize. In April of 2008, a Russian airplane shot down a Georgian drone.

Since the Rose Revolution of 2003 that swept Mikhail Saakashvili to power in Georgia, Russia's relationship with its Caucasian neighbour has evolved through four clearly delineated, increasingly unhappy stages. The first, more hopeful stage came during Saakashvili's first months in office, when elites of both nations seemed genuinely interested in cooperating to raise relations above their hitherto post-Soviet nadir towards the end of the Eduard Shevardnadze era. Persistent disagreements, including Russia's reluctance to reduce its military presence in Georgia, Georgia's increasingly

Western leanings and apparent ingratitude for Russian assistance in solving the Ajara crisis, and ultimately Georgian bellicosity towards South Ossestia, found the relationship moving away from cooperation to an atmosphere of "passive containment" by Russia. Persistent tensions combined with the spy scandal of 2007 moved the environment into the third stage of "active containment," wherein Russia recalled its ambassador and cut off almost all links between the countries. Finally, in August 2008, the small-scale post-Soviet cold war escalated into a military confrontation that lasted for five days and may be repeated in a future.

Ethnic Minorities

Regional ethnic distribution is a major cause of the problems Georgia faces along its borders and within its territory. In the census of 2002, the distribution of ethnic groups, in a total population of 4,371,535 was as under:

	Total	*Percentage*
Georgians	3,661,173	83.8
Azerbaijanis	284,761	6.5
Armenians	248,929	5.7
Russians	67,671	1.5
Ossetians	38,028	0.9
Yazidis	18,329	0.4
Greeks	15,166	0.3
Kists (Chechens)	7,110	0.2
Ukrainians	7,039	0.2
Abkhazians	3,527	0.1
Assyrians	3,299	0.1
Kurds	2,514	0.1
Jews	2,333	0.1
Others	11,656	0.2

Russians, who make up the fourth largest ethnic group in the country, do not constitute a majority in any district. The highest concentration of Russians is in Abkhazia, but the overall dispersion of the Russian population restricts political representation of the Russians' interests.

Azerbaijanis are a majority of the population in the districts of

Marneuli and Bolnisi, south of Tbilisi on the Azerbaijan border, while Armenians are a majority in the Akhalkalaki, Ninotsminda, and Dmanisi districts immediately to the west of the Azerbaijani-dominated regions and just north of the Armenian border. Despite the proximity and intermingling of Armenian and Azerbaijani populations in Georgia, in the early 1990s few conflicts in Georgia reflected the hostility of the Armenian and Azerbaijani nations over the territory of Nagorno-Karabakh. Organizations in Georgia representing the interests of the Armenian and Azerbaijani populations had relatively few conflicts with authorities in Tbilisi in the first post-communist years.

Under Soviet rule, a large part of Georgian territory was divided into autonomous areas that included concentrations of non-Georgian peoples. The largest such region was the Abkhazian Autonomous Soviet Socialist Republic (Abkhazian ASSR); after Georgian independence, it was re-designated the Abkhazian Autonomous Republic. The distribution of territory and the past policies of tsarist and Soviet rule meant that in 1989 the Abkhaz made up only 17.8 percent of the population of the autonomous republic named for them (compared with 44 percent Georgians and 16 percent Russians). The Abkhaz constituted less than 2 percent of the total population of Georgia. Although Georgian was the prevailing language of the region as early as the eighth century A.D., Abkhazia was an autonomous republic of Russia from 1921 until 1930, when it was incorporated into Georgia as an autonomous republic.

In the thirteenth century, Ossetians arrived on the south side of the Caucasus Mountains, in Georgian territory, when the Mongols drove them from what is now the North Ossetian Autonomous Republic of Russia. In 1922 the South Ossetian Autonomous Region was formed within the new Transcaucasian republic of the Soviet Union. The autonomous region was abolished officially by the Georgian government in 1990, then reinstated in 1992. South Ossetia includes many all-Georgian villages, and the Ossetian population is concentrated in the cities of Tskhinvali andJava. Overall, in the 1980s the population in South Ossetia was 66 percent Ossetian and 29 percent Georgian. In 1989 more than 60 percent of the Ossetian population of Georgia lived outside South Ossetia.

The Ajarian Autonomous Soviet Socialist Republic (Ajarian ASSR) in southwest Georgia was re-designated the Ajarian Autonomous Republic in 1992. The existence of that republic reflects the religious and cultural differences that developed when the Ottoman Empire occupied part of Georgia in the sixteenth century and converted the local population to Islam. The Ajarian region was not included in Georgia until the Treaty of Berlin separated it from the Ottoman Empire in 1878. An autonomous republic within Georgia was declared in 1921. Because the Ajarian population is indistinguishable from the Georgian population in language and belongs to the same ethnic group, it generally considers itself Georgian. Eventually, the term "Ajarian" was dropped from the ethnic categories in the Soviet national census. In the 1979 census the ethnic breakdown of the region showed about 80 percent Georgians (including Ajars) and 10 percent Russians. Nevertheless, the autonomous republic remains an administrative subdivision of the Republic of Georgia, local elites having fought hard to preserve the special status that this distinction affords them.

The Meskhetian Turks are another potential source of ethnic discord. Forcibly exiled from southern Georgia to Uzbekistan by Stalin during World War II, many of the estimated 200,000 Meskhetian Turks outside Georgia sought to return to their homes in Georgia after 1990. Many Georgians argued that the Meskhetian Turks had lost their links to Georgia and hence had no rights that would justify the large-scale upheaval that resettlement would cause. However, Shevardnadze argued that Georgians had a moral obligation to allow this group to return.

Within the leading ethnic groups, the fastest growth occurred in the Azerbaijani population and among the Kurds, whose numbers increased by 20 percent and 30 percent, respectively. This trend worried Georgians, even though both groups combined made up less than 7 percent of the republic's population. Over the same period, the dominant Georgians' share of the population increased from 68.8 percent to 70.1 percent. Ethnic shifts after 1989—particularly the emigration of Russians, Ukrainians, and Ossetians—were largely responsible for the Georgians' increased share of the population.

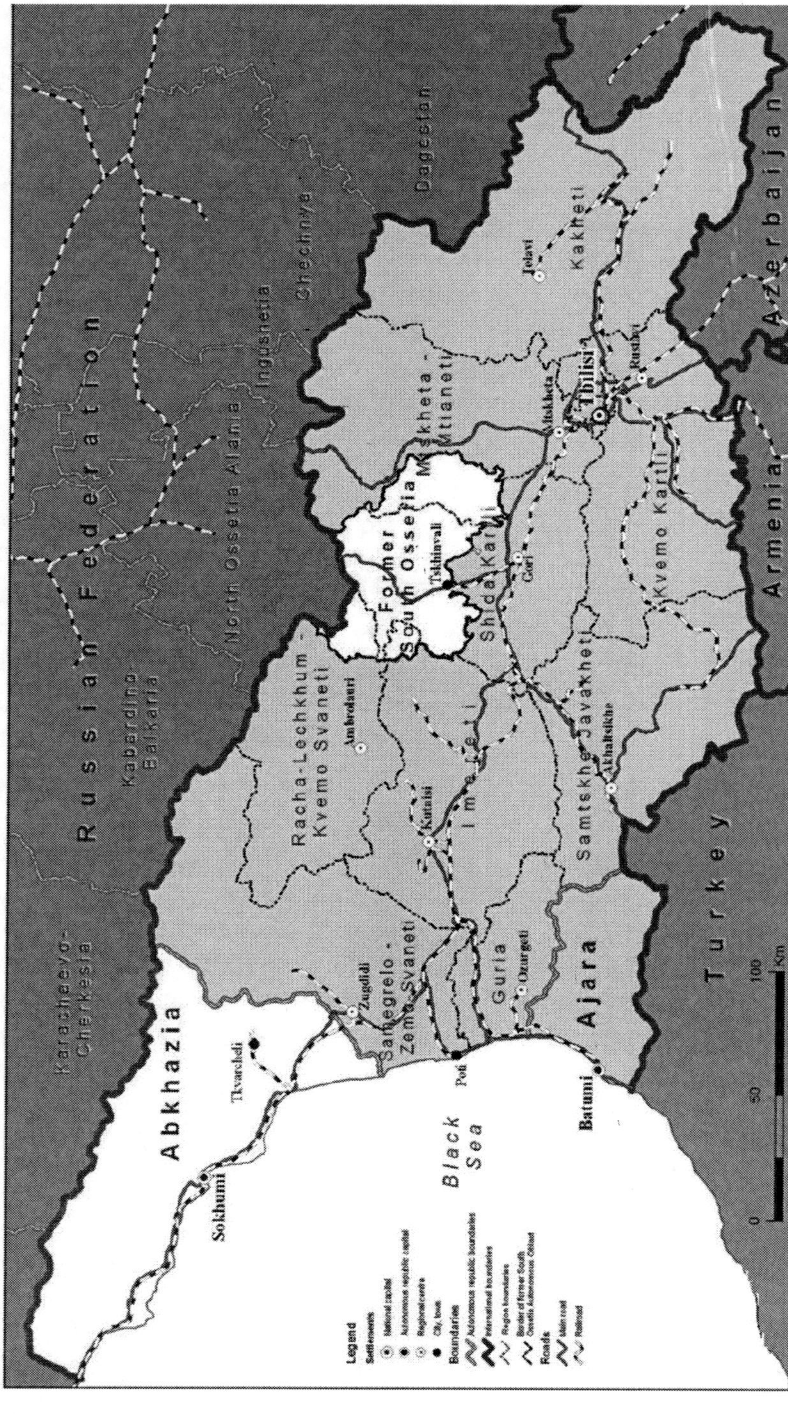

Map 4: Administrative Map of Georgia

1. Mikheil Saakashvili and Vladimir Putin

2. Mikheil Saakashvili with the Georgian Army on training

3. Russian army troops entering Georgia

4. Russian mechanised forces entering Georgia

5. The terrain of Central Georgia

6. Russian convoys in Georgia

7. Russian military convoy in Tskhinvali

8. Russian tanks advancing

9. Destroyed Russian tank

10. Russian special forces

11. Georgian snipers in action

12. Russian forces advancing

13. Georgian forces in retreat from South Ossetia

14. Georgian forces in Gori

15. Russian forces advancing

16. Destroyed Russian tank in Gori

4

RELATIONS BETWEEN GEORGIA AND RUSSIA

The historical and political circumstances of the armed conflict between Russia and Georgia in August 2008 reveal two sets of historically complex relations which overlap—bilateral relations between Georgia and Russia on the one hand, and internal conflictual relations between Georgia and the breakaway territories of South Ossetia and Abkhazia on the other. This context is furthermore entrenched in a broader geopolitical environment in which the Caucasus has been a theatre of competing influence between external powers.

History of an Ambivalent Relationship

Georgian national identity claims historical origins dating as far back as the establishment of an autocephalous Georgian church in the 4th century and the emergence of the Georgian language with its own alphabet in the 5th century. Nevertheless, for centuries Georgia was divided into diverse local sub-ethnic entities, each with its own characteristic traditions, manners, dialects, and with separate languages similar to Georgian. However, ethnic consolidation and nation-making had not been completed. Earlier Georgian history culminated in the united Georgian Kingdom of the 11th to 13th centuries, when Georgia was a regional power in the Caucasus. In ensuing periods it split up into several political entities and weakened after repeated attacks by foreign powers like the Mongols and

Timurids. From the 16th century onward, Ottoman Turkey and Safavid Iran began to subjugate western and eastern regions of Georgia respectively.

Seeking greater political influence in the Black Sea region, the Russian empire extended into the South Caucasus beginning in the second half of the 18th century. The situation in Georgia was dramatic at that time. Turkish and Persian armed invasions destroyed the country. King Erekle II, who had succeeded in unifying two Georgian kingdoms in the eastern part of the country, solicited the Russian Empress Catherine II for protection. A treaty to this effect was signed on 24 July 1783 and eastern Georgia became a Russian protectorate. Yet Georgia fought alone against the next Persian invasion in 1795 and suffered the destruction of its capital. Erekle's son and successor, George XII, again asked Russia for protection while simultaneously trying to reach a separate bilateral agreement with Persia. In response, Russia proclaimed the annexation of his kingdom: on 8 January 1801 Tsar Paul I signed a decree incorporating Georgia into the Russian Empire.

Tsarist rule over Georgia can be divided into three periods:

1) From 1801-1844 Georgia was under Russian military administration.
2) From 1844-81 it was known as the Viceroyalty of the Caucasus, and
3) From 1881-1917 it was fully integrated into the Russian Empire and experienced intensified russification. Tbilisi became the informal capital of the Caucasus and Georgian nobility was raised to equal status with its Russian counterpart. A Georgian intelligentsia, which emerged as of the 1870s, gave rise to a national awakening.

Historically, Russia and Georgia view this annexation differently. Russia describes it in terms of helping an ancient Christian nation threatened by Islamic neighbours. It emphasises the unification of Georgian territories and stabilisation of the country under the Tsar. Georgian historiography underlines the negative consequences of the annexation: the abolition of the autocephaly of the Georgian Church in 1811 and its subordination to the Russian Orthodox Church, denationalisation and russification were among the disadvantages. The advantages included Russian protection against external (Muslim) powers, the unification of all Georgian lands within one state organism and social progress such as the reform of the educational system. To some extent, Georgians were a privileged nation within the Empire. Nevertheless, Russia is treated by the Georgian historical narrative mainly as a threat to the very existence of the Georgian nation.

Georgia's independence as the *Democratic Republic of Georgia* (1918-1921) was due more to the collapse of the Russian Empire than to its own efforts of national liberation. Georgia considers this "first independence" as its first important experience of modern democratic statehood. At the time, Georgian politicians were not determined to break ties with Russia. In 1918-1920 Bolshevik groups organised uprisings in the province of Shida Kartli, inhabited mainly by the Ossetian minority. The uprisings were brutally suppressed in 1920 by the Georgian army. The Ossetians believe their nation was the target of Georgian repression but the Georgians claim they were struggling against the Bolsheviks, not the Ossetians.

The Bolsheviks established a Georgian Soviet Socialist Republic on 25 February 1921, which a year later became part of a Transcaucasian Soviet Federative Socialist Republic (TSFSR, also including the Soviet Republics of Armenia and Azerbaijan). When this Transcaucasian entity was dissolved in December 1936, all three Republics were incorporated into the USSR. Soviet Georgia had a complicated territorial structure: the Autonomous Republics of Abkhazia and Ajara and the Autonomous District (*Oblast*) of South Ossetia were included within its borders, covering about 22 percent of its territory. The Georgian elite were convinced that these entities had been created by the Soviets to limit Georgian jurisdiction over its own territory.

A Georgian national revival emerged in post-Stalinist decades. In April 1978, for example, thousands of people protested in Tbilisi against changes in the Georgian constitution which would give the Russian and Georgian languages equal status. Soviet authorities yielded to the demand to maintain the previous exclusive status of the Georgian language.

The Soviet period in Georgia ended tragically, on 9 April 1989, when Soviet troops broke up a peaceful demonstration in the centre of Tbilisi killing at least 19 people and wounding hundreds. The trauma resulted in a radicalisation of the Georgian national movement in the *perestroika* era, prompting even many Georgian communists to consider independence as the only viable perspective for the country.

Two years later, symbolically on 9 April 1991, the Georgian Parliament proclaimed independence. The most challenging heritage of the Soviet period – also in terms of Georgian-Russian relations – remained the country's territorial structure with its three autonomous entities (Abkhazia, South Ossetia, Ajara). During the transition period to post-Soviet sovereignty under the leadership of Zviad Gamsakhurdia, the national movement did much to alienate these regions and national minorities from the Georgian independence project, branding ethno-centrist slogans such as "Georgia for Georgians".

Following the dissolution of the USSR, Russia declared former Soviet territory as its sphere of vital interest. Expecting international recognition of its position as a guarantor of peace and stability in this area, Russia defined the post-Soviet newly independent states as it's "near abroad", stressing their proximity and close ties with Russia. It was probably important for Russia to have influence in the South Caucasus to maintain control over a region neighbouring Iran and Turkey and its own North Caucasus, in which centrifugal tendencies were on the rise.

Relations between Moscow and Tbilisi were tense in 1990-1993, during the mandate of first Georgian President, Zviad Gamsakhurdia, and the initial period of Eduard Shevardnadze's rule. They then improved significantly until the late 1990s following Georgian accession to the CIS in 1993 but deteriorated once again in the early 2000s. Zviad Gamsakhurdia's authoritarian rule represented strong anti-Russian sentiments that were widely shared by the Georgian elite.

In October 1993, after Georgia's unsuccessful military engagement in South Ossetia and Abkhazia, Eduard Shevardnadze asked Moscow for assistance to suppress an insurrection instigated by supporters of Zviad Gamsakhurdia in the western province of Samegrelo. Russian troops provided this assistance but at the price of a reorientation of Georgia's foreign policy. Eduard Shevardnadze signed the decree on Georgia's accession to the CIS in October 1993. In 1994 Georgia also joined the Russian-controlled Collective Security Treaty. Four Russian military bases, present since Soviet times, were to be maintained on Georgian territory, and Russian border troops deployed along the Georgian border with Turkey and at the sea border. The Russian military presence in Georgia also included peacekeeping forces in Abkhazia and South Ossetia.

With the location of foreign military bases on its territory, Georgia not only lost its territorial integrity *de facto*, but partially also its sovereignty. Georgian disenchantment with Russia coincided with the West's growing interest in the South Caucasus since the mid-1990s and the rising significance of the Caucasian-Caspian region for the independent supply of oil and gas to the global market. Georgia supported important projects promoted by Washington as well as EU-fostered transport projects. Russia perceived such projects as an attempt to undermine its own geo-economic position in the wider Caspian region. In the late 1990s, Georgia began to increase its relations with the West. In 1999 it joined the Council of Europe, intensified its relations with NATO and left the Russian-dominated Collective Security Treaty. Relations between Moscow and Tbilisi continued to deteriorate, worsening with Russia's second war in Chechnya beginning in late 1999 and the Georgian refusal to allow Russian troops access along the Chechen segment of the Russian-Georgian border.

From the late 1990s, the Georgian authorities made new efforts to reduce the Russian military presence in the country. In 1993, Georgia and Russia signed an agreement on the withdrawal of Russian troops from Georgia by 1995, but the agreement did not come into force. In ensuing years, bilateral agreements on the deployment of Russian military bases were signed, the most important one on 15 September 1995. Under this agreement, four Russian bases were deployed in Georgia: in Batumi (Ajara), in Gudauta (Abkhazia), in Akhalkalaki (region of Samtskhe-Javakheti, inhabited by Armenians), and in Vaziani (near Tbilisi). An agreement on the withdrawal of Russian border troops was signed in November 1998 and all Russian border troops left Georgia in 1999.

During the Istanbul OSCE Summit in 1999, Russia had committed to dismantling its military bases in Georgia. In 2001 the base in Vaziani was withdrawn and the infrastructure of the base in Gudauta was transferred to the CIS (in fact Russian) Peacekeeping Force in Abkhazia. The dismantling of the two other bases was the subject of difficult negotiations but was eventually implemented in 2007. Russia, or at least certain forces proceeding from the territory of the Russian Federation, had intervened in Georgia's conflicts with Abkhazia and South Ossetia from the beginning of the 1990s. The military victory of pro-Abkhaz fighters in their armed conflict with Georgian troops would not have been possible without this interference. But in the early 1990s this Russian involvement had an inconsistent character. The political situation in Russia itself influenced its policy in the region. Local Russian commanders stationed in Abkhazia actively supported the Abkhaz side.

The ensuing peace processes in Abkhazia and South Ossetia were largely in the hands of Russia. For around 15 years it was possible to preserve a minimum of stability in the region, i.e. to keep large military operations suspended. The conflicts were in effect frozen. At the turn of the millennium it became increasingly apparent that the resolution of the conflicts in Abkhazia and South Ossetia was not in the offing. Major geopolitical changes occurred in the first years of the new millennium in connection with the reorientation of America's foreign policy after 9/11 (2001) and EU enlargement, leading to a new policy towards its new neighbours. These changes further included NATO's eastward enlargement.

Under the presidency of Vladimir Putin, Russia became wealthier, more stable and more assertive of its claims to influence in its "near abroad". Increasingly, Russia saw the West as a rival in the South Caucasus and elsewhere. This new international environment did not prove to be favourable to the resolution of the conflicts in Abkhazia and South Ossetia. However, both Russia and Georgia developed an "enemy image" and negative stereotypes of each other.

Growing Confrontation 2004–2008

Under the leadership of Vladimir Putin and Mikheil Saakashvili, bilateral relations became the most precarious ever between the Russian Federation and a neighbouring state formerly belonging to the USSR. Problems poisoning bilateral relations included:

(a) The Georgian demand for a Russian troop withdrawal and the dismantling of military bases on Georgian territory in accordance with commitments made by Russia at the Istanbul OSCE Summit in 1999;
(b) Georgian participation in the construction of the Baku-Tbilisi-Ceyhan oil pipeline (BTC);
(c) Russian demands for military access to Georgian territory to fight armed Chechen rebels in uncontrolled areas like the Pankisi Gorge; and
(d) increased US military support for the modernisation of the Georgian army.

In this context, Georgia's unresolved conflicts with Abkhazia and South Ossetia were a crucial matter. For the Georgians, the territorial integrity of their country and the reintegration of Abkhazia and South Ossetia were a matter of unquestionable national consensus. On the Russian side, there was a similar consensus that the majority of non-Georgian residents of both territories—with their anti-Georgian and pro-Russian leaning and with Russian passports distributed to them by the Kremlin on a massive scale—were to be protected as Russian citizens against possible Georgian aggressions.

President Saakashvili declared the restoration of Georgia's territorial integrity to be his political priority. He practised a policy of accelerated, enhanced reintegration whereas Russia increased its support to Abkhazia and South Ossetia. Russia was engaged in these conflicts as the main peacekeeper, as facilitator and as a member of the Group of Friends of the UN Secretary-General, but it was demonstrating a clear bias in favour of the "separatist" parties to the conflict. Besides its main peacekeeping role in Georgia's unresolved conflicts, Russia had at its disposal strong economic resources permitting a coercive Georgia policy. Georgia had no equivalent means for an adequate response with the exception, perhaps, of its veto power on Russia's admission to the World Trade Organisation.

In trying to normalise Russian-Georgian relations, in the Russian point of view, the main pre-conditions for normalization of relations with Georgia were:

(a) Renunciation of a unilateral orientation toward the US and NATO;
(b) Acknowledgement of Russia's special interest in Abkhazia and South Ossetia, home to tens of thousands of people who had recently obtained Russian passports;
(c) Permission for Russian security forces to fight Chechen rebels from Georgian territory, mainly in the Pankisi Gorge.

The main argument for persuading the new Georgian authorities to accept these conditions was economic. Georgia owed Russia more than $300 million, mainly for electricity. Other forms of leverage at that time were the high number of Georgian migrant workers in Russia, and Georgia's dependency on Russia for trade and energy supply. Hence, bilateral relations between Moscow and Tbilisi were already burdened and relations further deteriorated in ensuing years.

Most analysts assessed the Russian economic influence in Georgia to be one stable factor in the relationship. For a while, the rhetoric on both sides changed and a Russian-Georgian political dialogue gained fresh momentum. At the same time President Saakashvili presented Georgia as Washington's main geopolitical partner and pressed his western partners for help in restoring Georgia's territorial integrity. Although Russia allegedly had supported the peaceful outcome of the power change in Tbilisi, the Rose Revolution was perceived as a challenge to Russia's new assertiveness in CIS space. It was the first of subsequent "colour revolutions", which were described in Russian commentaries as a "geopolitical aggression" steered by Western powers against Russia's strategic position in the post-Soviet space. The political affinity between Presidents Putin and Saakashvili changed into the most problem-ridden personal relationship between state leaders in the CIS.

The Ajara Crisis in Spring 2004

In this period, the disputed question of military bases merged with a political conflict around Ajara. The new Georgian leadership wanted to re-establish control over this territory. It counted on the support of the local population but was concerned about the risk of Russian intervention in this conflict. Russia's potential leverage into this crisis was amplified by the fact that nearly 70 percent of the residents of the Russian military base in Batumi were locals, but all of them had Russian citizenship. Aslan Abashidze, the leader of Ajara, looked to Moscow for support in his political confrontation with the new power elite in Tbilisi.

At the height of the Ajara crisis in April/May 2004, when President Saakashvili gave Aslan Abashidze a 10-day ultimatum calling for his resignation and the disbanding of his militia forces, the Kremlin helped to resolve the conflict peacefully. This crisis resulted in the reintegration of Ajara into the Georgian jurisdiction. Georgia considered the outcome of this crisis as a precursor for a near-term reintegration of other breakaway territories.

The Ajara crisis had never been a secessionist or ethno-territorial conflict and was, indeed, incomparable to the Abkhazia or South Ossetia scenarios. The conflict between Tbilisi and Batumi lacked deeper historical and ethnic roots. There is no ethno-linguistic difference between Ajarians and Georgians. There is a religious difference with many Ajarians being

Muslim, but this was never a factor in the conflict. There had never been an Ajarian declaration of secession from Georgia. And above all, Georgians and Ajarians had never known the wider armed clashes and the experience of mutual violence and brutality that constitute the crucial psychological element in Georgian-Abkhaz and Georgian-Ossetian relation.

The South Ossetia Crisis in Summer 2004

At the beginning of his presidency, Mikheil Saakashvili promised that he would restore Georgia's territorial integrity by the end of his tenure. Shortly after the reintegration of Ajara, the new government in Tbilisi began an anti-smuggling offensive in South Ossetia where the marketplace of Ergneti had become a centre of illegal trade in the Caucasus. Special forces from the Georgian Ministry of Internal Affairs were sent to some villages in South Ossetia, mainly under Georgian control. In Russia, this security reinforcement was seen as an attempt to re-establish control over the whole of South Ossetia, and the beginning of a new conflict between Moscow and Tbilisi.

Georgia announced that Tbilisi intended to resort to arms if Russian peacekeepers tried to shut down a police post that was blocking attempts to smuggle contraband from Russia to Georgia via South Ossetia. The flow of contraband, indeed, decreased after police posts were opened in Georgian villages around Tskhinvali and not far from the Ergneti market. At the same time, Tbilisi offered that South Ossetian autonomy would be re-established. Saakashvili promised to pay Georgian pensions to residents of South Ossetia even if they had already received pensions from Moscow as bearers of Russian passports. Georgia was prepared to grant South Ossetia the same degree of autonomy that North Ossetia had as one of the republics within the Russian Federation.

A verbal skirmish between Moscow and Tbilisi ensued. Georgian authorities intended to use a strategy similar to the one that was successful in the Ajara crisis. They tried to drive a wedge between the separatist authorities and the local population of South Ossetia. But the Georgian approach to regain control over the region and the Russian support for the challenged regime of *de facto* President Eduard Kokoity of South Ossetia led to a confrontation that escalated into armed clashes in the villages surrounding Tskhinvali. On 10 July 2004 the Georgian President called on his military to be ready to mount protracted, full-scale operations to defend the country's territory. All available resources would be used for defence. On the other side volunteers from the Russian North Caucasus and from the separatist Transnistria region in Moldova reportedly came to South Ossetia to help the Ossetians counter a Georgian aggression.

The conflict over South Ossetia took on international dimensions. Georgia pushed for internationalisation of the peacekeeping forces in South Ossetia and Abkhazia, seeking to end the Russian dominance of the existing format. In early August, President Saakashvili warned that vessels attempting to dock in Abkhazia without Georgian authorisation would be targeted, including tourist ships from Russia. The Georgian coast guard had already fired at a freighter reportedly registered in Turkey. Russian commentators linked the Georgian demands with US military support and Georgian NATO ambitions.

In August 2004 the crisis reached its high point with shelling of Tskhinvali and nearby villages and escalating armed clashes. Georgia was on the verge of a large-scale armed conflict with its former autonomous region. But the Georgian Government knew that an armed conflict would derail its plans to rebuild the Georgian state and economy, and most of President Saakashvili's main campaign promises. Russia was threatening to impose a total transportation blockade on Georgia. Abkhazia announced its withdrawal from all talks with Tbilisi as a result of the freighter incident.

Georgian security forces stopped their offensive in the conflict zone. But the Georgian side now had a fundamental commitment problem when addressing new peace initiatives and autonomy offers to the South Ossetian and the Abkhaz conflict sides. The Georgian military initiative reactivated the memory of wars in South Ossetia and Abkhazia in 1991-1992 and 1992-1994 respectively, raising the already high psychological barrier to confidence-building even higher. Furthermore, the crisis marked an important step in the further deterioration of bilateral relations between Georgia and Russia.

In the years thereafter, the Georgian Government continued to focus on South Ossetia as its primary object for its declared policy of reintegration and restoration of territorial integrity. In July 2005, President Saakashvili announced a new peace plan for South Ossetia that offered substantial autonomy and a three-stage settlement, consisting of demilitarization, economic rehabilitation, and a political settlement. South Ossetia's *de facto* President Kokoity rejected the plan, asserting in October 2005 "we are citizens of Russia". In November 2006, a popular referendum was held in South Ossetia to reaffirm its "independence" from Georgia. Many South Ossetians voted in the 2007 Russian Duma election and the 2008 Russian presidential election.

For the purpose of reintegration, the Georgian strategy changed from using security forces in South Ossetia to building a political bridgehead in the breakaway region. "Presidential" elections in South Ossetia in November 2006 re-elected *de facto* President Kokoity. An alternative election held in parallel at the same time among the ethnic Georgian population (and those displaced from South Ossetia) elected Dimitri Sanakoyev, an Ossetian politician committed to political dialogue with Tbilisi and opposed to the power elite around Eduard Kokoity. In 2007 Tbilisi appointed Dimitri Sanakoyev head of a "provisional administration in South Ossetia" with official residence in the village of Kurta. A dual power structure had thus emerged in this tiny region with its 70,000 residents (of whom more than 20,000 ethnic Georgians).

The Dispute over Russian Peacekeeping Role in Georgia's Conflict Zones

Russia's peacekeeping role in Abkhazia and South Ossetia was a fundamental bone of contention in Georgian-Russian bilateral relations, and a focus of Georgia's diplomatic efforts. Georgia increasingly demanded a revision of the existing negotiation formats and the internationalisation of peacekeeping forces in the conflict zones. The existing formats were based on ceasefire agreements ending the 1991-1994 armed conflicts between Georgia and both regions.

A paradox of the Russian peacekeeping role in Georgia was that Russia behaved with self-interest, but at the local level, the Russian presence seemed to be indispensable and was presented as part of the former superpower's burden. Consequently, there was no substantial international pressure for a revision of the Russian peacekeeping format. In the Georgian perception, however, the Russian peacekeepers had become border guards defending the administrative borders of Georgia's breakaway territories. In October 1997, Georgia together with Ukraine, Azerbaijan and Moldova established a consultative forum known as GUAM. In the framework of GUAM, Georgia's demand for an internationalisation and revision of the existing peacekeeping formats was supported by Ukraine. Together with Tbilisi, Kiev preferred to see other players such as the European Union and NATO as mediators and providers of peacekeeping troops in post-Soviet secessionist conflicts.

Georgian criticism of Russian peacekeeping in Abkhazia's security zone flared up again in October 2007 when a Russian unit allegedly attempted to take control of a Georgian "patriotic youth camp", situated within Georgian-controlled territory near the Georgian-Abkhaz demarcation line in Ganmukhuri.

Georgia's demand to internationalise the peacekeeping formats in Abkhazia and South Ossetia met with restraint in the West. International organisations and Georgia's Western partners conceded the peacekeeping and mediator role to Russia reasoning that Russia recognised Georgian sovereignty at least formally. It was only since March 2008 with the escalation of Russian-Georgian relations over the unresolved conflicts that they began to perceive Russia's role as being much closer to that of a party to the conflict. It became more and more untenable to argue that Russia was an impartial arbiter.

The European Union's engagement in unresolved conflicts with Russia was characterised as "working around the conflict", i.e. not working on the conflict. It was a soft policy confining itself to measures confidence-building between the parties to the conflict, the support of the mediation efforts made by other actors, economic rehabilitation of war damaged conflict zones and support for economic projects uniting the parties to the conflict. The EU was not involved in "hard" security issues, as the Russian Federation was not supportive of its more active engagement such as providing peacekeeping troops.

Creeping Annexation

Georgia's objection to the dominant Russian role in the peacekeeping operation in its conflict zones was motivated mainly by the perception that Russia was seen as the protagonist responsible for keeping the conflicts in the region frozen, in order to maintain a "controllable instability" for the purposes of its own power projection in the South Caucasus. Moreover, Russia was promoting progressive annexation of Abkhazia and South Ossetia by integrating these territories into its economic, legal and security space. The open annexation of these territories was blocked by several obstacles, ranging from Russia's military conflict in Chechnya to its interest in avoiding a massive confrontation with the West.

The clearest demonstration of this Russian policy of integrating separatist entities of neighbouring states into its own legal jurisdiction was "passportisation", i.e. the awarding of Russian passports and citizenship of the Russian Federation to residents of Abkhazia and South Ossetia.

In 2007 Russia paid residents of Abkhazia a total of 590 million roubles in the form of pensions and allocated 100 million roubles to South Ossetia, where the overwhelming majority of the non-Georgian population were already holders of Russian passports. Russia was thus using economic means to try to caution Georgia against attempts to take back the unrecognised republics by force.

Another aspect of "creeping annexation" was the fact that the separatist governments and security forces were manned by Russian officials. Russia appointed its former civilian and military leaders to serve in key posts in Abkhazia and especially in South Ossetia, including the *de facto* Defence Ministers of Abkhazia (Sultan Sosnaliev) and South Ossetia (Anatoly Barankevich) and the *de facto* Chief of the Abkhaz General Staff (Lt Gen Gennadi Zaytsev).

The Spy Scandal in Autumn 2006

Another incident provided an example of the depth of the Russian-Georgian crisis and its emotional dimension. On 27 September 2006 Georgian authorities arrested four Russian military officers, accusing them of being members of an espionage network whose main goal was to prevent Georgia's integration into NATO. This marked a new low point in bilateral relations and triggered an exchange of mutual accusations. On the Russian side the incident strongly reinforced the intention to punish Georgia. Moscow imposed heavy trade and financial sanctions against Georgia and recalled its diplomats from Tbilisi. The Georgian authorities handled the "spy affair" in a manner considered provocative not only in Russia. Georgia overplayed the incident: it did not expel the arrested officers discreetly – acceptable and standard *modus operandi* in such cases—but the men were released and transferred to OSCE officials in theatrical circumstances.

On 28 September, Russia asked the UN Security Council to condemn

Georgia for taking dangerous and unacceptable step that could destabilise the region. There was no such condemnation but members requested more information about the situation. The dispute intensified on 29 September 2006 with a statement from the Georgian Interior Ministry to the effect that Russian military movements had begun in territory bordering Georgia with the mobilisation of Russia's 58th Army, deployed in North Ossetia.

Russia continued to seek support for punitive measures against Georgia. However, this provoked negative reactions from Armenia and Azerbaijan. By imposing a blockade on Georgia, which serves as Armenia's main land route to Russia, the Kremlin strengthened the effects of the blockade imposed by Turkey and Azerbaijan on Armenia. Russia's blockade measures towards Georgia also adversely affected its own North Caucasian republics by closing the main border crossing between North Ossetia and Georgia. But above all, this crisis had an impact on Russian domestic affairs and affected the behaviour of Russian authorities toward the Georgian diaspora living in Russia in a way that damaged Russia's image in the world. Some ethnic Georgians, including children, were loaded in cargo planes and expelled from Russia. Prominent Georgian intellectuals living in Russia were harassed by the tax police, Georgian businesses in Moscow were singled out by law enforcement authorities. Georgians were portrayed as the most criminal of all ethnic minorities in Russia. The campaign took an especially ugly turn when some Moscow schools were ordered to submit to the police lists of children with Georgian names.

On 3 October 2006 in connection with the spy scandal, Russia cut air, land, sea, postal, and banking communications with Georgia. Earlier in 2006 it had slapped a ban on Georgian wine, fruit, vegetables, and mineral water, citing health concerns. Georgian officials downplayed the consequences of the sanctions. Russia was Georgia's main trade partner in 2006 despite restrictions on import of Georgian agricultural products. In the previous year, imports from Russia included 53% of electricity and 95% of natural gas consumed in Georgia.

As a result of Russia's economic sanctions Georgian exports to Russia in 2007 amounted only to USD 53 million, a 30 percent decline from the previous year. The sanctions spurred Georgia to restructure and reorient its export policies. Eventually, they did not lead to a dramatic decline of Georgian economic growth rates. They remained high, at reportedly 12 percent of GDP.

Incidents of Violation of Georgian Airspace

There had been five incidents of violation of Georgian airspace by Russian airplanes in 2001–2002 and Russia had denied them all. In October 2001, nine unidentified jets bombed areas of the Kodori Valley under Georgian control. In August 2002, Georgia accused Russia of bombing its northern Pankisi Gorge. In March 2007, Mi-24 helicopters bombed the Kodori and Chkhalta Valleys, and the Chuberi Pass. In August 2007 there was an air strike on the village of Tsitebulani near South Ossetia. And in April 2008, a MiG-29 fighter was videotaped downing an unarmed Georgian reconnaissance drone over the Gali region.

Additionally Georgia claimed that Russia periodically moved military equipment into Abkhazia and South Ossetia in violation of the ceasefire agreements of 1994 and 1992 respectively. In reply to Georgian accusations of military violations by the Russian side the Russian Foreign Ministry reported that in 2007 alone peacekeepers in Abkhazia claimed 158 instances in which Georgian warplanes allegedly flew over the security zone. The first time that Russia acknowledged the violation of Georgian airspace was shortly before the armed conflict of August 2008. At the time, Russian routine references to Georgia's territorial integrity had already disappeared from official statements. On 10 July, Russia's Ministry of Foreign Affairs confirmed that Russian air force planes had flown a mission over South Ossetia the preceding day. The flight was allegedly meant to prevent a Georgian military attack in this conflict zone.

Countdown to the Armed Conflict: the Geopolitical Context

Developments in the context of Georgia's unresolved regional conflicts and the bilateral Russian-Georgian relationship was overshadowed by two supra-regional international issues in 2008. The first was Kosovo's declaration of independence and its official recognition by around fifty states. The second was the NATO procedure for a decision on a Membership Action Plan (MAP) for Georgia and Ukraine. Both issues may have challenged Russia's *Weltanschauung* of a post-bipolar world. For many years Russia had felt deeply irritated by NATO enlargement. In terms of emotional impact, the dispute on Kosovo's independence brought Russia back to the year 1999 when it perceived the NATO war in Yugoslavia as a fundamental challenge to its own position in the international arena.

Georgia's Aspiration to Join NATO

Among all external variables the greatest impact of the Russian-Georgian conflict has been on NATO enlargement policy, in particular with regard to the possible integration of Georgia and Ukraine. Moscow's coercive Georgia policy was initially meant to prevent NATO expansion into CIS space. This policy gained momentum with the discussion on the MAPs for Georgia and Ukraine. Russian moves against both countries were intended to show that Moscow could stop them from joining NATO.

Admission to NATO had become a national project in Georgia. Around 80 percent of the public supported NATO-membership – the highest popular vote among applicant countries in the past decades. The Georgian Government repeatedly tried to set dates for admission to full membership. Within NATO this drive was met partly with strong support, partly with scepticism. Strong support came from Washington. Within Europe it came from a nucleus of eight countries, supporting an active policy by NATO and the EU in Europe's East. Initiated in 2005 in Tbilisi by the three Baltic states, Poland, Ukraine, Romania and Bulgaria joined by Sweden and the Czech Republic supported Georgia's goal to advance to a MAP at NATO's summit in Bucharest in the spring of 2008.

Russia's Kosovo Precedent Formula

Kosovo's declaration of independence refuelled debates about the linkage between the fundamental international legal principles of self-determination, sovereignty and territorial integrity. Western governments and regional organisations that recognised Kosovo's declaration of independence argued a case of *sui generis*. However, even within the EU this argument was not accepted by all member states and there was no common position among them. Some of them feared the case of Kosovo would set a precedent for secessionist conflicts on their own territories. Russia in particular rejected the *sui generis* argument and hinted at the Kosovo issue as a precedent for unresolved ("frozen") secessionist conflicts in the CIS space where Moldova, Georgia and Azerbaijan were involved in conflicts over breakaway regions such as Transnistria, Abkhazia, South Ossetia and Nagorno-Karabakh.

But Russia made use of this Kosovo precedent formula selectively, mainly as an instrument to pressure Georgia and less in the case of the Karabakh conflict between Azerbaijan and Armenia. Its involvement in this conflict differed from that in Georgia's conflicts with Abkhazia and South Ossetia and from its political position in Moldova's conflict with Transnistria. In the Karabakh conflict Russia was less directly involved and did not hold a dominant position as peacekeeper as it did in Abkhazia and South Ossetia (and Transnistria). Though Russia has a close security relationship to Armenia, in the Karabakh conflict it was less supportive of the Armenian-bound *de facto* state of Nagorno-Karabakh in comparison to its clear support for Abkhazia and South Ossetia.

In the Transnistrian conflict Russia also stood at the side of the separatist party to the conflict extending financial and political support to the Transnistrian authorities and keeping its 14th army (around 1,200 troops) stationed in the breakaway region. But with the Moldovan Government's commitment to neutrality, Russia supported a peaceful settlement of this conflict.

Thus the Kosovo precedent had its deepest impact on the unresolved secessionist conflicts of Georgia and on the bilateral relations between Georgia and Russia. In January 2006, President Vladimir Putin had called for universal principles to settle the "frozen conflicts" in the CIS. He insisted: "We need common principles to these problems for the benefit of all people living in conflict-stricken territories... If people believe that Kosovo can be granted full independence, why then should we deny it to Abkhazia and South Ossetia?" This line of reasoning became official Russian policy. In June 2006 the Russian Foreign Ministry reacted to Montenegro's referendum on whether it should end its union with Serbia and to Kosovo's accelerated movement toward independence. "Moscow respects the principle of territorial integrity, but it points out that South Ossetia's right to self-determination is an equally respected principle in the world community".

Moscow and its protégés in Sukhumi and Tskhinvali now had to find a way to apply the main arguments that the West was citing in favour of Kosovo's independence also to Abkhazia and South Ossetia. The first of these was that the claim to independence was supported by a majority of the local population living in those territories. The second argument was that alleged genocide had been committed there by forces of the metropolitan state. In support of the second argument, Parliaments in Russia and in North and South Ossetia held Georgia responsible for "genocide" committed against Ossetians in 1920 and again in the conflict of 1989-1992. This position was strongly expressed in the first Russian statements on the August 2008 Georgian artillery offensive on Tskhinvali, which was described by the Russian and the South Ossetian sides as a Georgian "genocide" of Ossetians, having cost the life of 2,000 people. In the weeks that followed, the number of victims was revised significantly downward.

With Kosovo's unilateral declaration of independence in February 2008 and its subsequent official recognition by several states, the precedent formula had gained strength. Early in March, the *de facto* Parliaments of Abkhazia, South Ossetia and Transnistria addressed appeals to the Russian Parliament, the UN and other international organisations for recognition of their independence. On 6 March 2008, the Russian Foreign Ministry announced that it was lifting all restrictions against Abkhazia stipulated in a CIS agreement of 1996. International commentaries deemed these measures to be Russian diplomacy's final departure from recognition of Georgia's territorial integrity. President Putin justified them as "exclusively socio-economic goals which distinguishes them in principle from a number of countries' politicised and unlawful decisions to recognise the unilaterally proclaimed independence of Kosovo, decisions which, as has repeatedly been stressed, are precedent-setting in nature". The *de facto* Presidents of Abkhazia and South Ossetia underpinned this formula with statements like, "We have more political and legal grounds for recognition than Kosovo does".

Russia kept the promise it had made immediately after Kosovo declared independence to reassess its relations with the unrecognised entities. But it made use of this precedent formula selectively: it was used in the case of Georgia, constituted the key feature of Russia's coercive policy against Georgia and was closely connected to Georgia's NATO ambitions. But even with this enhanced use of Russia's Kosovo precedent formula Russian, Georgian and Western experts did not expect an imminent diplomatic recognition of Abkhazia and South Ossetia by the Kremlin.

This restraint finally disappeared with the armed conflict of August 2008. Already before its official recognition of Abkhazia's and South Ossetia's independence on 26 August 2008, Russia had significantly increased cooperation with the unrecognised entities. One day after President Putin's decree on 16 April 2008 on the close cooperation of

Russian authorities with their counterparts in Sukhumi and Tskhinvali a Russian newspaper quoted Abkhaz *de facto* Foreign Minister Shamba with the following triumphant remarks: "We can see the ribbon at the finish line on the road to our recognition. And we'll cut that ribbon. We're not afraid of any backlash from Tbilisi. We're prepared for the fact that the situation in the conflict zone will heat up; Georgia may instigate that". President Saakashvili did instigate that with the offensive against Tskhinvali and provided Russia with arguments to pursue its policy toward the Georgian secessionist conflicts.

The Escalation in 2008

The year 2008 began with Mikheil Saakashvili's re-election to his second presidential term with 53.4% of the vote. As four years before, both Georgian and Russian officials expressed a desire to improve their bilateral relations. In his inaugural address on 20 January 2008, re-elected

President Saakashvili offered to "extend the hand of partnership and cooperation to Russia." In his first news conference he invited President Putin to visit Georgia and added that "one of my main regrets is that during my first presidential term relations with Russia were spoiled".

The Russian Government reacted by sending Foreign Minister Sergei Lavrov to President Saakashvili's inauguration, contrary to expectations that Moscow would boycott this ceremony in Tbilisi or send a low-level delegation. Foreign Minister Lavrov was the highest-ranking Russian Government official to visit Georgia since the spy scandal in 2006. On 21 February, Presidents Putin and Saakashvili met in the Russian presidential residence Novo-Ogaryovo. President Saakashvili expressed his interest in achieving at least a limited reconciliation. At the summit, the two sides agreed to re-establish direct civilian air links. Reportedly there were talks of a joint control of borders on the Psou river and at the Roki tunnel, which provoked protests from the leaders of Abkhazia and South Ossetia.

However, the fundamental variable affecting Russian-Georgian relations did not change with President Saakashvili's second term. The re-elected President strongly reaffirmed his intention to pursue Georgia's "Euro-Atlantic orientation" and to deepen its ties with NATO. During the election campaign all of his main opponents also professed to support this orientation in Georgian foreign and security policies.

War rhetoric repeatedly flared up on all conflict sides from March-April 2008. This bellicose rhetoric around the unresolved regional conflicts in the South Caucasus was accompanied by a process of armament and a sharp rise in defence budgets in the region between 2004 and 2008. Growth in military spending in the three South Caucasian states in 2008 exceeded GDP growth dramatically. Georgia increased its military spending during this period from below 1 percent of its GDP to more than 8 percent. Likewise, the separatist entities became more militarised. Georgia made a standard accusation of Russia that it used the rotation of its peacekeeping contingents to deploy additional military forces into the conflict zones.

At first global attention with regard to the escalation was focused on Abkhazia. In May Russia moved to increase the troop levels of its peacekeeping force in Abkhazia to 2,500 and sent railway troops on a "humanitarian mission" into the region. The Abkhaz leadership claimed that territorial defence forces had shot down five Georgian reconnaissance drones in recent weeks. NATO Secretary-General Jaap de Hoop Scheffer demanded that Moscow withdraw its railway troops and urged both sides to "engage quickly in a high-level and open dialogue to de-escalate tensions". In July 2008 Germany initiated a three-stage plan for a settlement of the Georgian-Abkhaz conflict. The first stage involved measures to rebuild trust between the conflict sides to lead to their signing of an agreement on the non-use of force, and the initiation of a process to bring Georgian IDPs/refugees back to Abkhazia.

The second stage provided for reconstruction work financed by donor states. Not until the third stage was it planned to tackle Abkhazia's political status. Abkhaz *de facto* President Sergei Bagapsh turned down the plan and put forward his own conditions for beginning talks with the Georgian side. First, Georgia has to pull its troops out of the upper Kodori Valley in Abkhazia. Second, it must sign an agreement on not resuming military operations.

Meanwhile the conflict escalation on the ground shifted from Abkhazia to South Ossetia. Both the Georgians and Ossetians launched artillery attacks on each other's villages and checkpoints. But even in July many experts did not expect that one of the parties to the conflict could be rationally intending to open hostilities.

Conclusion

Russian-Georgian relations are paradoxical. On the one hand there are many traditional ties, primarily socio-cultural. For over 200 years Georgia had been part of the Russian and Soviet Empire. Its political class was incorporated into the Tsarist establishment. Georgia was Russia's bridgehead in its Caucasus wars of the 19th century, the imperial outpost for the establishment of Russian military and administrative power in the whole of the region. Later on, Georgia was a Soviet Republic with its very specific experience of Stalinist terror, but a comparatively high standard of cultural autonomy in the decades after Stalin's death. The Georgian historical narrative emphasises the two annexations by Russia in 1801 and 1921 as national traumas. A burden of mutual claims and contradictions was inherited from the Soviet and post-Soviet periods.

The April 1989 events, when Soviet forces brutally broke up a demonstration in Tbilisi, marked a turning point in Georgia's tough independence course. In the period under Zviad Gamsakhurdia this course translated into a Georgian ethnocentric attitude with nationalistic slogans and enforced anti-Russian sentiments deterring non-Georgian minorities and autonomous regions from Georgia's independence projects. Georgia's drive for its emancipation from Russian power projection gained renewed strength after the peaceful power change from Shevardnadze to Saakashvili. The idea of "fleeing the Russian Empire" which made virtually no distinction between the contexts of pre-1917 Russia, the Soviet Empire and the post-Soviet Russian Federation had become the keynote of its foreign policy.

Thus the question of who was responsible for the 2008 August armed conflict cannot be focused solely on the night from 7 to 8 August and the Georgian offensive against Tskhinvali. It has to include a broader run-up to the conflict, a longer process comprising mutual accusations, military threats, violent incidents in conflict zones, acts of a great power's coercive policy toward an insubordinate neighbour, this neighbour's unrealistically accelerated policy of reintegration and presenting its Western-oriented foreign and security policies as fleeing the Russian Empire.

In this growing confrontation, challenges and opportunities for security and economic cooperation between Russia and Georgia were ignored or missed. Both sides should have realised that they had a shared interest in the stability of their common neighbourhood. The South and the North Caucasus constitute a single organism. A region like Pankisi was a symbol for such mutual security challenges to both Georgia and Russia. The whole border between Georgia and Russia runs along critical zones of intersection between North and South Caucasian security challenges. Both sides shared economic interests. Russia remained Georgia's most important export market and the largest labour market for the Georgian diaspora. For Russia, Georgia was important to its political, military and economic actions in the whole of the South Caucasus. More than once, Russia's punitive acts against Georgia affected Armenia. With its policy of partitioning Georgia and recognising Abkhazia and South Ossetia as independent states after the 2008 August conflict, Russia did not gain any support even from its closest allies. On the other hand, Georgia had done much to alienate its breakaway regions and push them away from its own independence project. On all sides negative stereotypes and emotions prevailed over shared interests.

5

ARMED FORCES OF GEORGIA

Throughout history, Georgia was involved in many conflicts, constantly defending itself from larger powers such as the Persian, Ottoman, Byzantine and Russian Empires, as well as Mongols, Arabs and Seljuk Turks. There always has been great interest of large countries in Georgia because of the country's important geopolitical location.

Compared to the other countries in the Caucasus region, Georgia has the smallest military force. In case of intervention by other countries, the Georgian military has to counter forces many times larger and better equipped. Considering the small size of Georgia in terms of territory as well as limitations of other resources such as demographic, natural, economic and industrial, as well as military equipment, it is difficult for Georgia to maintain a large professional military force to counter any possible aggression.

Almost from its inception in late 1990, after the breakup of the Soviet Union, the National Guard became directly involved in Georgian politics. By 1992 repeated human rights offences against Gamsakhurdia supporters brought calls to change this role. At the same time, the political rivalry between Ioseliani and Kitovani, the leaders of the Mkhedrioni (horsemen) and the National Guard, respectively, became one of the key conflicts in the Georgian government hierarchy, and many political parties continued to retain private armies in the guise of armed bodyguards or security teams. Discipline problems in the ranks of both the National Guard and the Mkhedrioni and their ineffectiveness as fighting forces led the Georgian government to plan for a professional army. In April 1992, the State Council adopted a resolution to form a unified armed force of up to 20,000 soldiers.

At the time the government announced its plans for a professional army, however, neither existing military group had sufficient internal discipline to carry out major restructuring. Efforts to disband the National Guard and Mkhedrioni were delayed by continued violence in western Georgia, by an attempted coup in Tbilisi by Gamsakhurdia supporters, and by the political ambitions of Kitovani and Ioseliani. In May 1992, Kitovani was designated minister of defence in an effort to bring the National Guard under central control. Instead, during the following year Kitovani turned his position into a power centre rivalling Shevardnadze's. In May 1993, Shevardnadze induced Kitovani and Ioseliani to resign from their powerful positions on the Council for National Security and Defence, depriving both men of influence over national security policy and enhancing the stature of the head of state.

From lessons learned from the past, it is very important for Georgia to be able to defend its interests with Georgia's organic forces as long as required in order to preserve its sovereignty. To achieve these goals requires conducting a number of very complex measures and preparations mainly on the political and strategic level. However, whatever political ways or methods the Georgian government chooses to stop such an intervention, it is still paramount for Georgia to have capable military forces to oppose such acts. Generally, the role of the Georgian Armed Forces (GAF) in case of external military aggression can be to defend the country's sovereignty through military force to give the government enough time and freedom of action to employ effective measures to stop the aggression.

Military intervention by larger countries may be aimed at the full or partial occupation of Georgian territories; overthrow of the government or change of the political system in Georgia. Neither result will be acceptable for the Georgian people. If such an intervention from a larger country occurs in Georgia, it is not certain that other organizations, such as NATO or the UN will be able to intervene in a timely and effective manner (diplomatically, economically, or militarily) to stop the aggression. It may take several weeks or even months before the international community, political or military organizations can make a decision to intervene and find ways to influence the aggressor to cease military actions against Georgia.

In 1992, Georgia joined the North Atlantic Cooperation Council and in 1994 joined the Partnership for Peace (PFP) programme. On 21-22 November 2002, at the NATO Summit in Prague, Georgia made a declaration of its aspiration to NATO membership and expressed its desire to participate in the Individual Partnership Action Plan (IPAP) programme. On 29 October 2004, NATO approved this and in 2005, two agreements were signed. In 2010, during the NATO Defence Ministerial and North Atlantic Council meeting in Lisbon and 2012, NATO Chicago Summit, NATO member countries reaffirmed the 2008 Bucharest Summit decision that "Georgia will become a member of NATO," and reiterated continued support to the sovereignty and territorial integrity of Georgia. Possible reason for an intervention into Georgian internal affairs by any country may be geopolitical, economic, strategic security interests or conflicts of interest's between the countries.

The National Military Strategy of Georgia describes the criteria for determination of the effectiveness of the Armed Forces. These are the training level of the forces, modern technical equipment, and an effective management system. Currently, the GAF is still experiencing significant shortfalls in all three areas.

Land Forces

This is the largest component of the GAF. It also incorporates aviation and air defence units. The land forces consist of:

(a) HQ Land Forces Command
(b) Five infantry brigades
(c) Two artillery brigades
(d) One engineer brigade
(e) One air defence brigade
(f) One aviation brigade
(g) Two separate light infantry battalions
(h) One technical reconnaissance battalion
(i) One signal battalion, one medical battalion, and one military police battalion.

The Special Forces (SF) are directly subordinated to the Joint Staff as an MOD Main Special Operations Division and are responsible for conducting reconnaissance, unconventional warfare, and counter-terrorism operations. SF command consists of one SF Brigade and Special Operations

Main Division. The Special Forces Brigade consists of Special Operations Battalion, Naval Special Operations Squadron, Support Battalion, and Special Forces Training Centre; The Department of the National Guard of Georgia organizes and trains reservists in peacetime and mobilizes them during a crisis or wartime. The National Guard is organized into a light infantry brigade (1,578 active reservists).

A Reserve of the Military Forces has been created to support the military during emergency or/and combat situations, and other situations. There are three categories of the reserve forces in Georgia:

(a) **Active Reserve**, staffed with the persons who are discharged from the compulsory military or professional military service.
(b) **Reserve of the National Guards**, which aims to participate in logistic operations of the military forces during the combat activities. It is staffed with citizens according to their place of residence and administrative-territorial divisions.
(c) **Individual Reserve**, which aims to fill and rotate active subunits of the Armed Forces.

Paramilitary Forces. Their strength is about 11,700, consisting of:

(a) Ministry of Interior Troops - 6,300
(b) Border Guard - 5,400

Coast Guard. The Georgian Navy was abolished 2009, and was incorporated in to the Coast Guard under the Border Guard of Georgia which is subordinated to the Ministry of Internal Affairs with HQ in Poti.

Training

In early stages of development, the GAF experienced a lack of the expertise and professionalism in its officers and Non-commissioned Officers. Many officers did not even have any professional military education. Improvements in the Georgian military began when the Georgian government, in the early 2000s, took decisive steps to create a professional military and make Georgia part of western collective defence organizations such as NATO. Georgia joined NATO's Partnership for Peace Programme in 1994. Since 2002, several training programmes were conducted with the support of different western allies, mainly with the US military.

The Georgian Army is using the US Army Training Management System to train its units. Live, virtual, and constructive simulation training systems are actively used for training GAF units on different levels from individual to brigade level. These simulation systems help both, to minimize the training costs and increase the efficiency of the training by adding realism to the training.

Major training organizations in the GAF are the National Training Centre, Sachkhere Mountain School, NCO School, and Armour Training Centre, which organize different courses to support the GAF needs of professional development of its servicemen.

The expertise and professionalism gained with participation in stability operations in Iraq and Afghanistan, and introduction of the advance training systems i.e. simulation training systems and training management system, help the GAF to raise their performance level and become more interoperable with its western allied countries which is a significant factor in the matter of Georgian aspiration for joining NATO. However, the GAF has lack of the resources and expertise for conduct of major combat operations, which are critical for defence of the Nation.

The Georgian terrain allows the deployment of maximum two division-size mechanized formations at a time in each area of operation or direction. Even deployment of these division-size formations will be highly restricted by terrain in many areas. Mechanized units will be forced to operate along the existing roads and have to canalize in order to negotiate choke points, thus becoming vulnerable to the anti-tank weapons systems and artillery fire.

The GAF does not possess enough capabilities to defend itself from cyber-attacks.

Inventory

Main Battle Tanks	**93** (T-72)
Armoured Infantry Fighting Vehicles	**63** (17 BMP-1; 45 BMP-2; 1 BRM-1K);
Armoured Personnel Carriers	**137** APC (T) 45 (MT-LB); APC (W) 92: (25 BTR-70; 17 BTR-80; 50 *Ejder).*
Artillery Systems	**185** SP: 35 (152mm 32 DANA; 13 2S3; 1 2S19; 203mm 1 2S7); Towed: 68 (122mm: 55 D-30; 152mm 13: 3 2A36; 10 2A65); MRL: 37 (122mm: 13 BM-21; 6 GRADLAR; 18 RM-70); Mortar: 43

	(120mm: 13 2S12; 21 M-75; 9 M-120); AT: å50 (MSL å10; GUNS å40) AD: SAM, SP (9K35 *Strela*-10 (SA-13 *Gopher*)).
Aviation and Air Defence Assets	**ATK: 12** (3 Su-25 *Frogfoot*; 7 Su-25K *Frogfoot* A; 2 Su-25UB *Frogfoot* B) TPT, Light: 9 (6 An-2 *Colt*; 1 Tu-134A *Crusty* (VIP); 2 Yak-40 *Codling)* TRG 9 L-29 *Delfin;* **Helicopters**: TPT 29 Medium 17 Mi-8T *Hip;* Light 12 Bell 205 (UH-1H) SAM: 1AMBBN 9K37 *Buk*-M1 (SA-11 *Gadfly*), 8(two batteries)—9K33 *Osa*-AK (SA-8B *Gecko*), 6-10 9K33 *Osa*-AKM (updated SAM systems).
Naval Assets	**Patrol and Coastal Combatants**: 17 PBF 1 *Kaan 33* PB 16: 7 *Zhuk* (3 ex-UKR); 2 *Point*; 2 *Dauntless*; 2 *Dilos*(ex-GRC); 1 *Akhmeta* **Amphibious Landing Craft** LCU:1-*Vydra* (ex-BUL) **Logistic and Support** YTL: 1

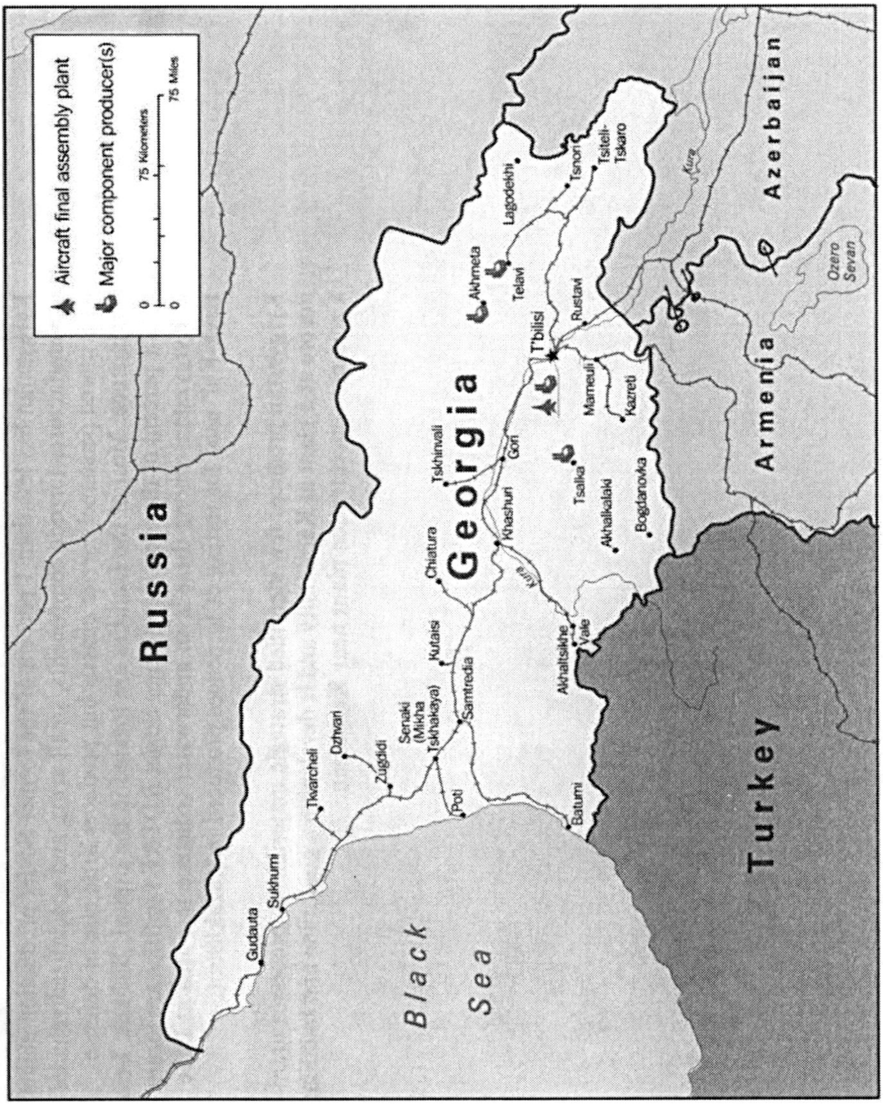

Map 5: Defence Industries in Georgia

6

TERRAIN ANALYSIS

The Republic of Georgia has a land area of 69,700 square kilometres, with territorial boundaries of 1,461 kilometres (Armenia 164 kilometres, Azerbaijan 322 kilometres, Russia 723 kilometres, and Turkey 252 kilometres). It has a coastline of 310 kilometres bordering the Black Sea.

Georgia is divided into nine regions, 65 districts, one city, and two Autonomous Republics. Its horizontal width is 336 kilometres from North-West to Southeast. Its vertical length is 112 kilometres from South to North (in its widest section). The highest elevation is Mt. Shkhara 5,201 metres.

Georgia is a mountainous country. 85 percent of its territory is covered by high mountains. Its territorial boundaries mainly run along the high mountain ridges. Mountainous terrain limits the trafficability of vehicles to the existing road network. Deployment of the large mechanized formations is greatly restricted by mountain ridges, narrow valleys, and deep river ravines.

In the North the country is bordered by the Great Caucasus Mountain Ridge, where some of the great peaks exceed 5,000 metres. In the South, Georgia's territorial borders also mainly run along the high mountain ridges of the Lesser Caucasus Mountains. (The Lesser Caucasus Mountain Ridge mainly runs parallel to the Greater Caucasus Ridge). The highest mountains of this ridge rise more than 3,000 metres above sea level.

On the West, Georgia is bordered by the Black Sea. The coastline constitutes 310 kilometres of the territorial borders of Georgia, approximately 180 kilometres of which is part of Abkhazian Autonomous Republic, currently occupied by Russia. The coastline in the Northern and Southern parts is mostly mountainous with narrow strips of flat ground between the sea and mountains. In the centre, the coastline is more flat and lowland stretches for several kilometres deep in to the hinterland (Kolkhida Lowland).

The Kolkhida lowland has a rough triangle shape and stretches from the town of Poti on the Black sea coast for approximately 100 kilometres deep eastwards to the town of Grigoleti. The west side of the triangle is also approximately 80 kilometres wide and runs along the Black Sea coast from town of Kobulety to the North, up to Gali and Ochamchira districts of Abkhazia. This lowland provides good mobility for mechanized and armoured units. Even though many rivers cross the area, mainly from North to South they do not represent major obstacles. Multiple bridges that cross these rivers can support movement of medium tanks. There are many fords as well, which can be used to cross those rivers, in case the bridges are destroyed.

The Likhi ridge runs from north to south, connecting the Greater and Lesser Caucasus ridges and divides Georgia approximately in two halves. This area can also greatly degrade the mobility of mechanized formations.

In the easternmost part of Georgia, the terrain is relatively open and less mountainous. Small mountain ridges without forests run generally from East to West. Here too Georgian territorial boundaries are defined by natural terrain. The boundaries run along the Alazani and Iori rivers, which generally do not constitute any obstacle, but in some places, in combination with the mountain ridges, they can limit the number of the mobility corridors.

The central parts of Eastern Georgia are more open and flat and provide good mobility for battalion and brigade size mechanized formations. Most of the major towns of Georgia are located in these lowland areas along the East-West highway, and can constitute an obstacle for the attacking mechanized formations.

The two largest rivers in Georgia are Kura and Rioni. The Rioni River flows from the North to South in Western Georgia from the Greater Caucasus Mountains and then turns to the West. In some places, the river's steep banks provide good natural obstacles. The Kura River flows from

Northeast Turkey to the north in Georgia, then turns to the East, crossing the southern part of Georgia, and flows to Azerbaijan. The river mainly flows in restricted terrain and its steep banks are an obstacle for mechanized formations.

Mobility Corridors/Avenues of Approach

Because of its strategic location on the east side of the Black Sea and to the south of the Greater Caucasus Mountains, Georgia controls most of the mountain passes through them. Due to the very restricted terrain all along the Georgia's international borders, the mobility of mechanized formations into Georgia is restricted and limited to the existing roads. There are limited numbers of mobility corridors that hypothetically may be used as avenues of approach. To the north, due to the limited number of passes through the Greater Caucasus Ridge, there are only four mobility corridors which can support movement or deployment of mechanized units. Similar to the Northern Mountains, the terrain along the Southern border of Georgia provides limited amount of mobility corridors for mechanized formations.

Operationally the mobility corridors can be divided into Western and Eastern theatres by the Likhi range in the centre of Georgia.

In the Western Theatre, there are two mobility corridors for mechanized formations, one to the north and one to the south.

(a) **The north-western corridor.** This runs along the Black Sea coast from Russia, through the occupied Georgian region of Abkhazia into the Samegrelo region of Georgia. At the border of Abkhazia this corridor is approximately 20 kilometres wide, contains several roads, and is able to support deployment of a division-sized formation.

(b) **The south-western corridor:** This corridor starts at the Georgian-Turkish border and runs along the Black Sea coast to the north, toward the Kolkhida lowland. It runs through restricted terrain, with several narrow passes and chokepoints. It is limited from the East by the high mountain ridges and from the West by the Black Sea. This corridor can only support deployment of a battalion and in some places brigade-sized mechanized formations.

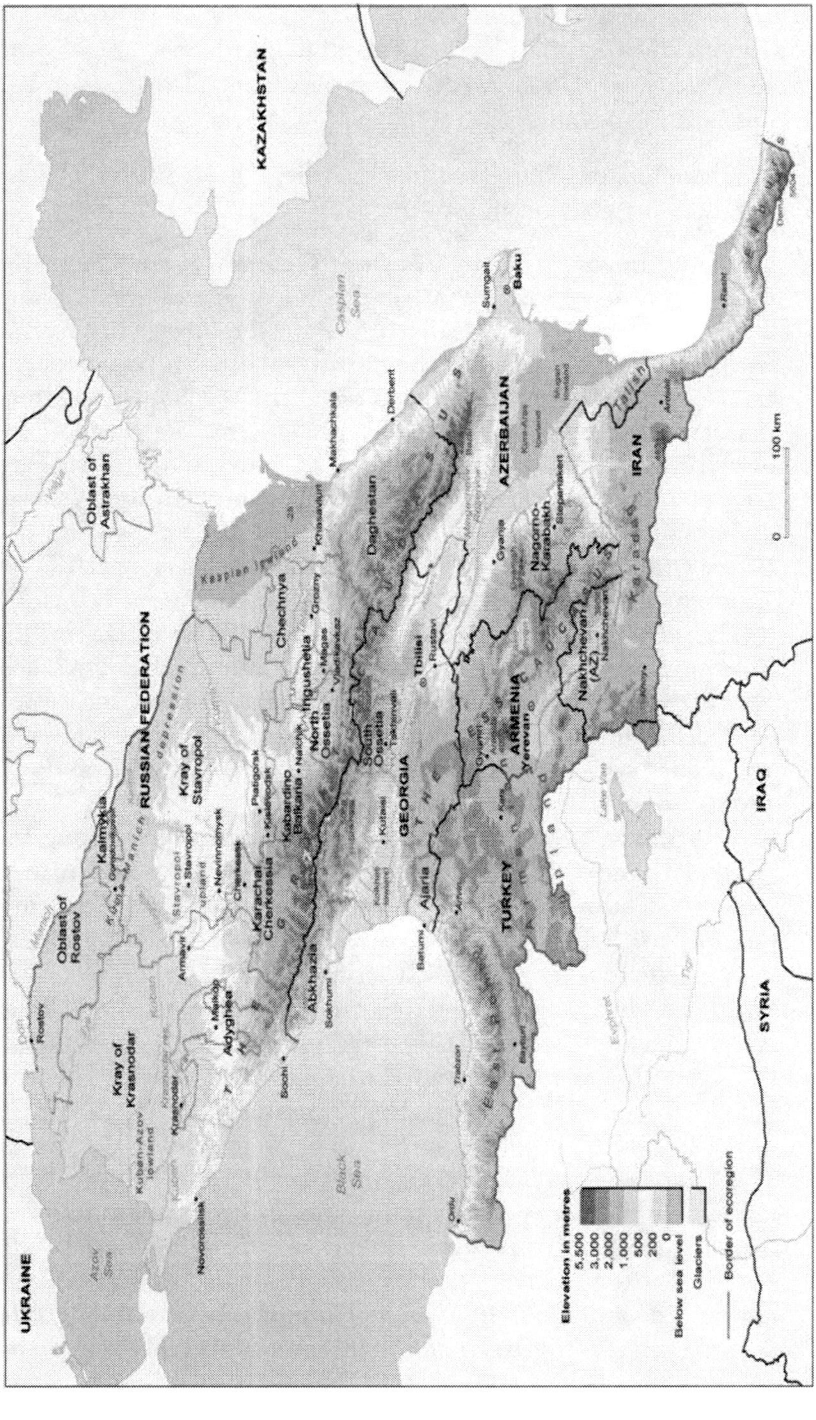

Map 6: Topography of Georgia

Both these mobility corridors in the west open on to the Kolkhida Lowland where terrain becomes more open and flat, with an average width about 30 kilometres. It can support the deployment of a mechanized division-plus size force elements.

In the Eastern theatre, there are three mobility corridors on the north and two mobility corridors on the south:

(a) **From the northern part of Eastern Georgia**. It runs from the Russian border through the occupied Georgian region of South Ossetia. It starts at the Rocky tunnel, at the border of Georgia with Russia, runs through the narrow mountain passes of the Caucasus Mountains and opens on to the flat terrain south of Tskhinvali. At the beginning of this mobility corridor, mechanized units can only move along the limited roads, but the southern part of this corridor can support deployment of one or two division-size formations.

(b) **From the Russian border southwards.** This corridor is approximately 70 kilometres east of the afore-mentioned corridor. It has only one road, from the town of Stepantsminda, on the Russian-Georgian border, through narrow mountain valleys, and ends approximately 10 kilometres northeast of Tbilisi, the capital of Georgia. In this corridor, there is extremely restricted terrain, and it does not allow deployment of any mechanized formations and can be used by infantry columns only.

(c) **The northeast corridor**. This runs from East to West, along the Southern edge of the Greater Caucasus ridge from Azerbaijan to Georgia. From the south, several mountain ridges limit movement. It is approximately 20 kilometres wide and can support deployment of one division size formations.

(d) **South of Tbilisi.** This corridor contains two main roads from Azerbaijan and Armenia. This corridor mainly constitutes open terrain with a width of approximately 30 kilometres and can support deployment of a division-plus size mechanized formation.

(e) **The Samtskhe-Javakxeti corridor.** It has two main roads from Armenia and Turkey. These roads join at the southern town of Akhaltsikhe approximately 15 kilometres from the border with Turkey. The terrain in this corridor is severely restricted and does not provide good mobility for mechanized formations. Roads in the area run through deep mountain ravines and there are many

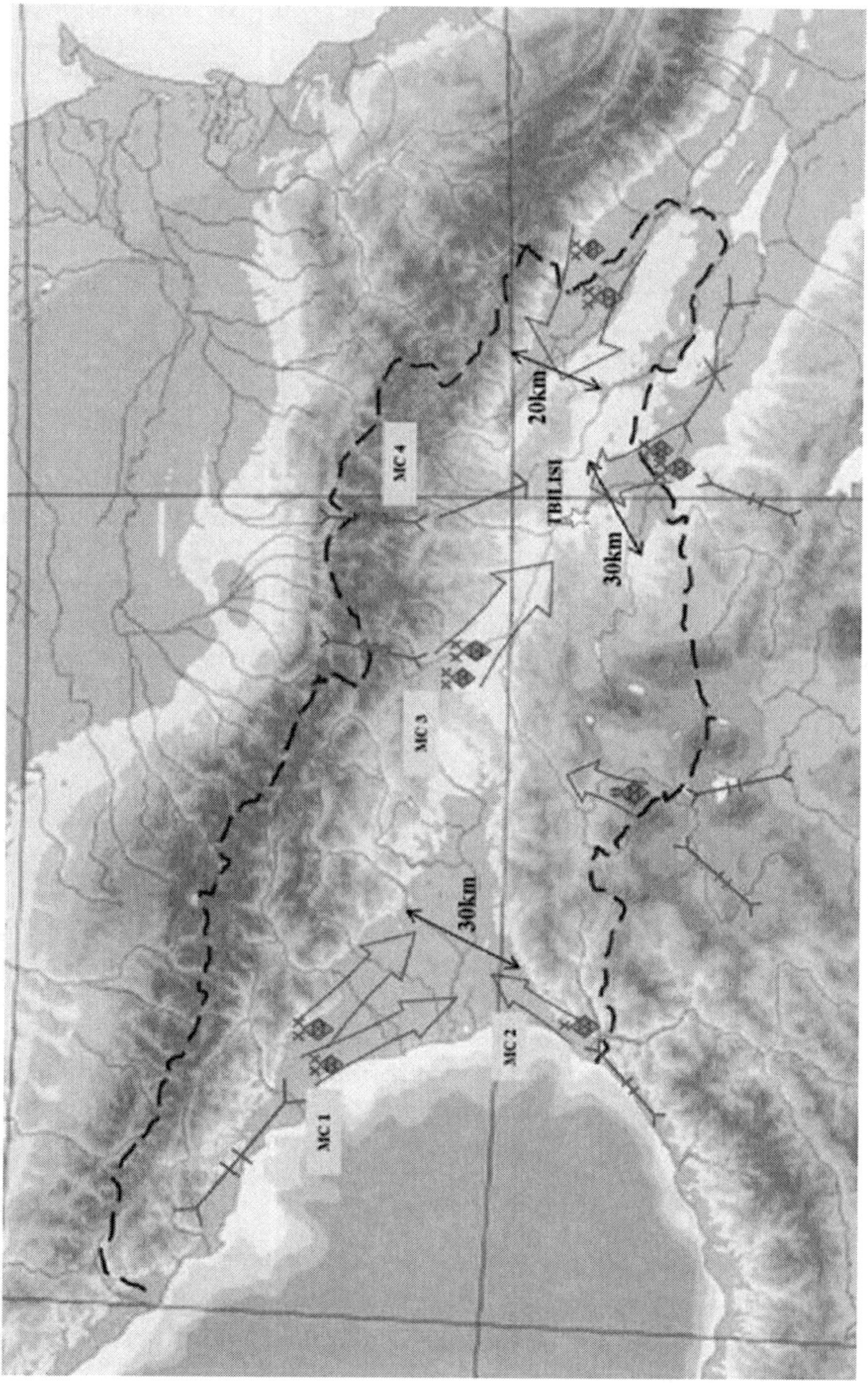

Map 7: Avenues of Approach into Georgia

chokepoints along the roads. Some sectors of the corridor can support deployment of one or two-battalion size mechanized formations simultaneously.

Beside these mechanized mobility corridors, there are several mountain passes that can be used by small light formations mainly for shaping operations, such as diversion, deep operations, and disruption of the lines of communications.

In addition, the territories of the breakaway regions of the Abkhazia and the South Ossetia, which are outside of the control of the Georgian Government, can serve as a bridgehead and may be used for staging areas of large military forces.

Key Terrain

There are many areas in each corridor that can be identified as key terrain, according to the specific operational plans. These chokepoints can be exploited by a defending side to produce maximum effect with fewer resources. The dominating mountains may serve as good locations for observation posts. They can also be used for coordination of indirect fire and intelligence gathering.

Observation/Fields of Fire

Forests and brush cover more than one third of Georgia's territory. The mountain ridges of west Georgia as well as the flat area of the Kolkhida Lowland are almost entirely covered by forests. In conjunction with mountainous terrain, it greatly limits observation and ability to conduct effective fire from tanks and anti-tank weapon systems at the maximum ranges. On the other hand, observation is better conducted from the high grounds. The area gives more opportunities to the defending side to exploit the advantages of the terrain. By appropriate selection of the areas of engagements, ambush sites, and counterattack routes, a smaller defending force may achieve parity or even superiority over numerically superior attacking forces.

Absence of forests on the hills of the East and Southeast parts of Georgia provides better observation, but here too it is limited by restricted terrain. In some places of eastern Georgia, such as the Kartli Plain, the valleys of the Alazani and Iori rivers, the terrain is more open with very less vegetation and provides good observation over long ranges. Larger mechanized and tank forces will have advantage over smaller forces in this terrain.

Cover and Concealment

Restricted terrain and overhead cover provided by thick forests provide good cover and concealment to both sides in the mountains. In the open areas of west and east Georgia, terrain does not offer good cover and concealment to either side.

Air

Because of its small size in terms of territory, the airspace of Georgia is limited. This gives a likely aggressor an advantage to establish air superiority over Georgian airspace. On the other hand, defence of the airspace by air defence systems is relatively easy.

Maritime

Georgia does not possess large naval assets. A strong navy can easily overwhelm the small Georgian coast guard. Georgia faces the threat of intervention by military forces from the sea, and may be left without sea lines of communications. In case of control of those lines of communication, Georgia can be denied external support, in terms of humanitarian and military assistance, food, and medical supplies.

The domination of the sea also gives advantage to the opponent in terms of inserting forces into Georgia from the sea by conducting amphibious operations. There are the some locations along the Black Sea coast of Georgia that support the conduct of amphibious operations.

7

FORCE LEVELS

RUSSIAN ARMED FORCES IN GEORGIA
(by 12 August 2008)

The Russian order of battle involved a significant portion of the Russian 58th Army, one of Russia's premier combat formations, having more than twice the number of troops, five times the number of tanks, ten times the number of armoured personnel carriers and twelve times the number of combat aircraft as the Georgian Armed Forces.

In South Ossetia

58th Army

19th Motorized Rifle Division

135th Motorized Rifle Regiment (two battalions, one for peacekeeping)

429th Motorized Rifle Regiment (two battalions, two tank companies)

503rd Motorized Rifle Regiment (two battalions, one tank company)

693rd Motorized Rifle Regiment (3 battalions, one tank battalion)

481st Air-Defence Missile Regiment

292nd Self-propelled Artillery Regiment

141st Independent Tank Battalion

239th Independent Reconnaissance Battalion

1493rd Independent Engineer Battalion

344th Independent Maintenance Battalion

42nd Motorized Rifle Division

70th Motorized Rifle Regiment (two battalions, one tank company)
71st Motorized Rifle Regiment (three battalions, one tank battalion)
50th Self-propelled Artillery Regiment
417th Independent Reconnaissance Battalion
"Vostok" Battalion (one company) (from Chechnya)
"Zapad" Battalion (one company) (from Chechnya)

76th Guards Air Assault Division

104th Air Assault Regiment (one battalion)
234th Air Assault Regiment (one battalion)

98th Airborne Division

217th Airborne Regiment (two battalions)

10th Independent Spetsnaz Brigade (four companies)

22nd Independent Spetsnaz Brigade (one company)

45th Independent Reconnaissance Spetsnaz Regiment (one company)

(Total: 16,000 soldiers, 130 MBT, 105 SP-Guns, 40 MRL, 400 IFV, 400 APC, 60 AIFV)

2,500 South Ossetian troops were initially present.

Russian peacekeeping forces

496 from Russian battalion
488 from North Ossetia

In Abkhazia region

15th Independent Motorized Rifle Brigade (for peacekeeping—without heavy equipment)

43rd Independent Motorized Rifle Battalion

131st Independent Motorized Rifle Brigade (for peacekeeping, without heavy equipment)

526th Independent Motorized Rifle Battalion
558th Independent Motorized Rifle Battalion

7th Air Assault Division

108th Air Assault Regiment (two battalions)
247th Air Assault Regiment (two battalions)

1141st Artillery Regiment

31st Independent Air Assault Brigade (two battalions)

45th Independent Reconnaissance Spetsnaz Regiment (one company)
(Total: 6,500 soldiers, 20 SP-Guns, 100 APC, 100 AIFV)
Two battalions of Black Sea Fleet Marines

4th Air Army

GEORGIAN ARMED FORCES
(August 2008)

1st Infantry Brigade (Gori)
- 11th Light Infantry Battalion
- 12th Light Infantry Battalion
- 13th Light Infantry Battalion
- 14th Armoured Battalion
- Artillery Battalion
- Logistics Battalion

2nd Infantry Brigade (Senaki and Batumi)
- 21st Light Infantry Battalion
- 22nd Light Infantry Battalion
- 23rd Light Infantry Battalion
- 24th Armoured Battalion
- Artillery Battalion
- Logistics Battalion

3rd Infantry Brigade (Kutaisi and Ahaltsihe)
- 31st Light Infantry Battalion
- 32nd Light Infantry Battalion
- 33rd Light Infantry Battalion
- 34th Armoured Battalion
- Artillery Battalion
- Logistics Battalion

4th Infantry Brigade (Tbilisi and Muhrovani)
- 41st Light Infantry Battalion
- 42nd Light Infantry Battalion
- 43rd Light Infantry Battalion
- 44th Armoured Battalion
- Artillery Battalion
- Logistics Battalion

5th Infantry Brigade (Batumi and Poti)

51st Light Infantry Battalion
52nd Light Infantry Battalion
53rd Light Infantry Battalion
54th Armoured Battalion

1st Artillery Brigade

Self-propelled Artillery Battalion
MRL Battalion
Independent Armoured Battalion
Independent Light Infantry Battalion
Independent Air-Defence Battalion
Independent Engineer Battalion
Independent Signals Battalion

(Total: 18,000 soldiers, 120 MBT, 30 SP-Guns, 40 MRL, 80 Guns, 120 AIF and APCs)

Initial Deployments

Deployment of the opposing sides prior to the conflict was as follows:

The Georgian military, before the conflict, numbered approximately 20,000 combat troops, with another 10,000 logistical and administrative personnel and a further 7,000 of Interior Ministry troops (with armoured vehicles). Equipment was generally of Soviet make, with official pre-war strength at 82 T-72 and 110 T-55 tanks of all marks with first-generation ERA (Explosive Reactive Armour); about 150 BMP armoured fighting vehicles, another 80-100 medium and heavy APCs and at least 100 light wheeled APCs; roughly 40-50 self-propelled (all 152mm) and 130 towed (about 100 122mm, the rest 152mm) artillery pieces, plus 35-45 multiple rocket launch systems; 15-20 combat aircraft plus another 15 light jet trainers and roughly 80 helicopters of all types.

Unofficially, the numbers vary somewhat; for example, Russian data as of 20 July 2008 suggested that the Georgians had 165 T-72s (75 T-72M, the rest T-72 B1 and AV; the AV model has first-generation ERA, the T-72M is the export version with downgraded weapon systems, and the B1 has improved armour and fire control systems plus ERA but without the ATGM capability) and 40 T-55-AM tanks (the modernized version but with a weaker engine than the upgraded version of T-55s), rather than 82 and 110, respectively; 373 artillery pieces of all types excluding multiple rocket launchers rather than the 170-180 implied above; just over 20 combat aircraft (mostly Su-25s) plus 33 light attack aircraft (L-159 ALCA) and 25-26 rather than 80 combat helicopters; and a number of missile boats and patrol ships.

The numbers above should also be viewed in light of the following disclosures about arms shipments to Georgia between 2004 and 2008:

(a) 10 UH-1-H helicopters and 230 wheeled vehicles (including 15 *Hummers*) from the US, with 15 UH-60 *Blackhawk* helicopters;
(b) 7 152mm self-propelled guns, 16 ZSU-23 AD guns, and 300 RPG-7s, 500 *Igla* MANPADS (man-portable air defence systems) and 150 *Kornet* and *Konkurs* ATGMs, 4 Su-25 attack aircraft, two light troop ships, 10 thousand crates of AK-47 assault rifles and RPG 22s plus ammunition, and 650 tons of ammunition from Bulgaria;
(c) 66 APCs, 1,186 AMD-65 assault rifles, 44 PKM machine-guns, 600 82mm mortar rounds and an unspecified amount of 7.62mm ammunition from Hungary;
(d) 1 missile boat and 2 patrol ships plus 60 mortars from Greece;
(e) 14,000 AK assault rifles from Lithuania;
(f) 60 RN-94 APCs, 2 UH-1 helicopters, one patrol ship, 2,500 MP5A1 SMGs, 1,500 G3 A3 assault rifles, 4,000 122mm rockets and 20,000 155mm artillery shells, plus a large amount of 7.62mm ammunition and hand grenades from Turkey;
(g) 1 multiple rocket launcher with 4 *Mirage* fighter aircraft, 2 missile boats and upwards of 60-65 *Mistrale* and *Mistrale*-2 MANPADS from France;
(h) 120 T-54 or T-55 and 55 T-72 tanks, plus 24 *Dana* 152mm self-propelled artillery vehicles, 25 M-75 120mm mortars, 200 *Strela* MANPADs and more than 40 tons of ammunition of all types from the Czech Republic;
(i) 8 *Hermes*-450 and *Skylark* unmanned reconnaissance aircraft from Israel;
(j) 45 120mm and 25 82mm mortars plus 500 262mm rockets from Bosnia & Herzegovina;
(k) 20 million 7.62mm bullets, plus 1,000 HEAT and 1,690 APFSDS tank shells and other ammunition from Serbia;
(l) 31 T-72s, 20 BTR-80s, 40 BMP-2s, 12 152mm *Akatsia* self-propelled artillery vehicles, 9 Mi-24, 2 Mi-8MT and 2 Mi-4 helicopters, 40 tons of ammunition, multiple other specialist vehicles and at least three *Buk*-M1-2 medium-range mobile SAM systems (basically a next-generation version of the SA-11) from the Ukraine.

The US had 95 advisors and 130 "civilian contractors" in Georgia when war broke out.

Georgia had a small air force, almost all of it ground-attack oriented. During the Soviet days, Tbilisi was the home of the USSR's main Su-25 manufacturing plant, which explains why such a small country had 20 of them still operational (at least 5 upgraded by the Israelis with new avionics and targeting systems). [The Su-25 is the Soviet version of the US A-10 *Warthog* ground attack aircraft, except it looks more like a conventional fighter-bomber, and has had considerably more combat experience. Specifically, flying 60,000 sorties for 21 combat losses during the Afghanistan war in the 1980s, then thousands more during the many wars that followed the USSR's collapse, e.g. the two Chechen conflicts, as well as 900 sorties during the Iran-Iraq War. Basically it is very effective at acting against ground troops and armour]

Abkhazia had between 5,000 and 10,000 regular troops (the number varied year-to-year) plus 28,000 reservists; roughly 60 tanks, about 40 of them T-72s and the remainder T-55s; 116 APCs and BMP IFVs; 85 artillery pieces and mortars (total); 5 Su-25 aircraft, about a half-dozen other fixed-wing and 2 rotary aircraft, and 21 patrol boats, i.e. a brigade, maybe two, with modest armour and artillery support.

Finally, in South Ossetia—a region with a total population significantly lower than 120,000 (just how much lower depends on whether one counts ethnic Georgians, most of whom fled; 70,000 to 80,000 is likely the real number)—had 3,000 regular troops and 15,000 reservists, plus 200 militarized SWAT and 900 police; nominally 75 T-72s and 12 T-55s, 80 BMP-1 and BMP-2 IFVs and 85 BTR-70 and BTR-80 APCs; 42 122mm and 152mm *Gvozdika* and *Akatsia* self-propelled artillery vehicles plus another 80 towed artillery and mortar pieces; a few ZSU-23 *Schilka* and towed 100mm AAA, plus *Igla* MANPADS, an unspecified amount of RPG-7 and RPG-22 weapons, and 4 Mi-8 helicopters. There may have been a few more combat helicopters, including at least 3 American UH-1s. Basically, one brigade minus.

The Russians had designated the entire area as the "Caucasus Military District", with the bulk of the military forces provided by the 58th Army, with air support provided by the 4th Air and Air Defence Army. The 58th Army's order of battle included the 19th Motor Rifle Division, the 205th Motor Rifle Brigade, the 136th Guards Motor Rifle Brigade, the 135th Motor

Rifle Regiment, the 291st Artillery Brigade (equipped with towed 152mm 2A65 guns); the 943rd Multiple Rocket Launcher Regiment (220mm *Uragan* MRLS); the 1128th Anti-tank Regiment; the 67th AA Rocket Brigade (first- and next-generation SA-11); and the 487th Helicopter Regiment (Mi-8 and Mi-24 *Hind* helicopters). The 19th Motor Rifle includes 3 Motor Rifle regiment (each with a tank battalion), a separate tank regiment (mostly T-72s), an *Akatsia* 152mm SP artillery regiment; and organic air defence. Prior to the conflict, apparently the 58th Army was reinforced with some of the newer weapon systems in the Russian arsenal (such as the S-300 long-range SAM), etc. The 4th Air Army has several regiments of Mig-29 and Su-27 fighters as well as Su-24, Su-25 and Tu-22 bombers and recon aircraft, plus Mi-24 *Hinds* and transport helicopters.

Finally, there were the peacekeeper battalions—500 Russians and 500 Georgians deployed in each "separatist region"—lightly armed, with only a few BMPs and transport helicopters in each.

Prior to 8 August, the Georgians moved two combat brigades with perhaps half the republic's total number of tanks and IFVs, and perhaps most of their artillery (certainly all of their MRLS systems) up from Gori and towards Tskhinvali. Additional light infantry forces were activated in the Georgian enclaves inside South Ossetia proper. By this time, there had already been sporadic exchanges of fire between Georgia, Abkhazia and Ossetia for roughly a week, though nothing serious; the Abkhazians did, however, shoot down at least three of the Georgians' unmanned reconnaissance aircraft. Meanwhile, the Russians, moved five battalions from the 19th Motor Rifle Division closer to the Russian entrance of the Roki Tunnel, and placed the remainder of the 58th Army on yellow alert. Apparently, several other Russian units were activated at this time, e.g. two ethnic Chechen battalions and certain air assault formations. In addition, about half of Russia's Black Sea Fleet, having recently conducted manoeuvres off the Abkhazian and Russian coastlines, remained in the area, within a few hours of the Georgian ports.

For their part, the Ossetians placed their forces on red alert and began evacuating civilians from the region (especially Tskhinvali) during the last few days before the war; while the Abkhazi activated their military units but did nothing else for the moment.

8

THE MILITARY CAMPAIGN

Setting the Stage

The region of South Ossetia is largely surrounded by nearly insurmountable mountains. Except for small groups of infantry without much by way of heavy equipment, the eastern and western sides of the roughly oval-shaped quasi-republic are quite impenetrable. In the south, a single pass leads into the region from the Georgian town of Gori. This pass eventually exits into a hilly countryside and empties into a bowl-shaped depression, in the middle of which lies Ossetia's capital city of Tskhinvali, with a pre-war population of between 20 and 30 thousand. Beyond Tskhinvali, a single road leads north towards the only route navigable across the region's northern border by any sort of transport—the Roki Tunnel, which had been cut through miles of rock during the Soviet days and connects directly with North Ossetia, an autonomous region of the Russian Federation. The remainder of South Ossetians are scattered in villages around Tskhinvali, although before the war several ethnic Georgian enclaves also remained.

To the west, across the mountains, lies Abkhazia. It, too, has only a single navigable route leading into it from both the north and south, although the region's western border is the Black Sea itself, easing navigation somewhat. The southern route crosses the Kodori Gorge into Georgia proper, where it first encounters the town of Sugdidi.

Georgia itself is also roughly oval-shaped; to the south and west of

Sugdidi are the main ports of Poti and, further south still, Batumi, which is especially vital to Georgia's oil transportation industry, while about 50 kilometres to the east of Gori is Georgia's capital, Tbilisi. From Gori to Tskhinvali to the Roki Tunnel is another 50 kilometres at the most—similarly from the regional centre of Kutaisi to Sugdidi, through the Kodori Gorge and into the Abkhazi capital of Sukhumi. Finally, it should be noted that much of Georgia proper, from Poti and Batumi in the west to Tbilisi in the east, the terrain is generally even and more suitable for mobile operations than the hilly Ossetia ringed by mountain ridges.

The Georgian-Abkhaz Conflict Zone

The steadily deteriorating political relationship between Georgia and the Russian Federation, between 2006 and 2008, was accompanied by rising political tension, particularly in the conflict zones in Abkhazia and South Ossetia.

In early 2008, a marked increase in military tension could be observed in the Georgian-Abkhaz conflict. One reason for this was the intensification of air activity over the conflict zone, including flights over the ceasefire line both by jet fighters and by unmanned aerial vehicles (UAVs). In the period of 18 March – 12 May, the United Nations Observer Mission in Georgia (UNOMIG) was able to verify five Georgian reconnaissance UAVs and two jet fighter (Su-25 type) flights over Abkhaz-controlled territory. A number of Georgian UAVs were reportedly shot down by Abkhaz and Russian forces.

The Georgians claimed that the purpose of the UAV flights was to monitor Russian military reinforcements in Abkhazia, but Sukhumi viewed them as a part of preparations for Georgian military operations in Abkhazia.

UNOMIG considered both the Georgian flights in the conflict zone as well as the actions taken by the Abkhaz and the Russian forces against Georgian UAVs as violations of the ceasefire regime since the Moscow Agreement on a Ceasefire and Separation of Forces prohibited the introduction and operation of heavy weapons in the zone of conflict. The involvement of the Russian air force, not part of the Russian-manned CIS peacekeeping force (CIS PKF), in the downing of a Georgian UAV on 20 April 2008 was inconsistent with the Moscow Agreement and was considered by the UN Security Council on 23 April and 30 May 2008. UAV

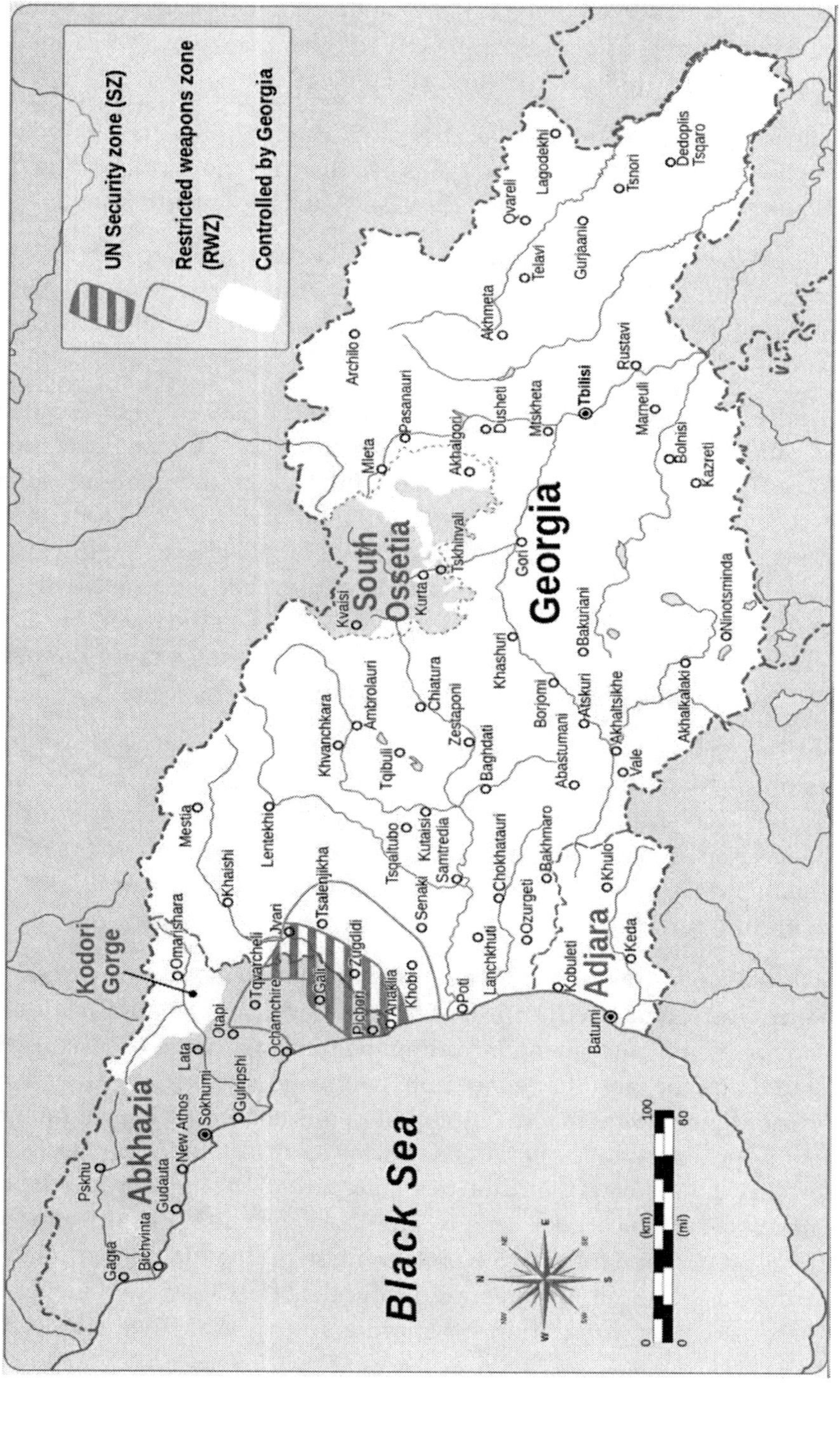

Map 8: Georgia Before 2008

flights were also observed in the Kodori Valley, both in its lower (controlled by Abkhazia) and its upper (controlled by the Georgia) parts. Neither side admitted to flying UAVs in the Kodori Valley.

During the period from 29 February to 5 March, Abkhazia conducted military exercises which involved tanks, small arms and mortar firing, in the Ochamchira area close to the Georgian-Abkhaz ceasefire line.

In mid-April, the Abkhaz side complained about an alleged build-up of Georgian forces along the ceasefire line. UNOMIG carried out extensive patrolling of the area, but found no evidence to substantiate the Abkhaz allegations.

At the end of April 2008, in consideration of the possibility of a further deterioration in the Georgian-Abkhaz conflict zone, the Russian Federation reinforced the CIS PKF with a 525-strong airborne battalion deployed in the Restricted Weapons Zone, while pointing out that the CIS PKF would still remain below the authorized threshold of 3,000 personnel. However, the new Russian battalion was reportedly equipped, *inter alia*, with 10 pieces of artillery, which do not traditionally belong to the inventory of a peacekeeping force. UNOMIG attempts to monitor the camp of the new CIS PKF contingent was obstructed by the Abkhaz.

At the end of May 2008, referring to a presidential decision on the provision of humanitarian assistance to the Abkhaz side, the Russian Federation also introduced a 400-man strong military railway unit to Abkhazia to rehabilitate the local railway south of Sukhumi up to the town of Ochamchira. At the end of July, the unit completed the repair work and was withdrawn.

The Georgian Government considered both these measures aggressive in nature and demanded an immediate withdrawal of all additional Russian forces and equipment, including the railway troops. The Georgian side stated that the lack of advance notification and the introduction of an airborne battalion were in clear violation of a number of CIS regulations governing peacekeeping operations. As far as the railway troops were concerned, the Georgian authorities stated that the reinforcement of infrastructure in the conflict zone by the Russian military could only be viewed as preparation for an armed intervention in Georgia. Russia's move was criticised by the US Administration and the NATO Secretary General, who assessed it as a violation of Georgia's territorial integrity. In its

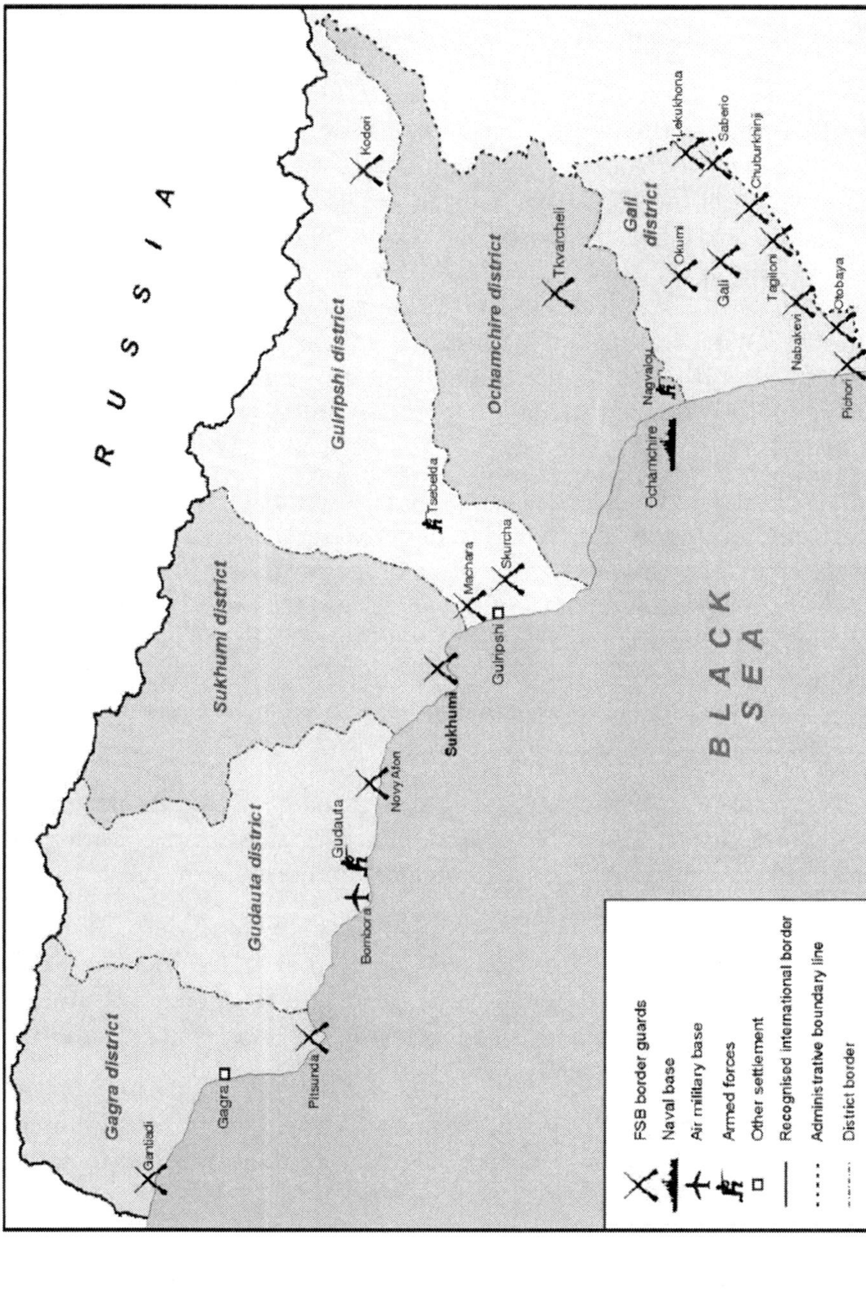

Map 9: Russian Military Presence in Abkhazia

resolution of 5 June 2008, the EU Parliament stated that the Russian troops could no longer be considered neutral and impartial peacekeepers and that the peacekeeping format should therefore be revised.

Additionally, the Georgian side argued that the military reinforcements confirmed that the Russian Federation was a party to the conflict and could no longer serve in either a mediating or a peacekeeping capacity. Georgia intensified its calls for a change of the peacekeeping format and in particular proposed the replacement of the existing peace operation with a joint Georgian-Abkhaz police force under European Union and OSCE supervision and training, without excluding the possibility that the Russian Federation might play a role. Georgia announced that if a substantial change in the peacekeeping format was not achieved, it was ready to make a formal request for the withdrawal of the CIS PKF.

For its part, the Abkhaz side insisted that the CIS PKF was strengthened in response to Georgian plans to carry out a military action. It reiterated its opposition to any change in the peacekeeping format and warned that a withdrawal of the CIS PKF would lead to a resumption of hostilities. The Abkhaz side also indicated that if Georgia should decide to withdraw its consent to the presence of the CIS PKF, it would propose an agreement on military cooperation with the Russian Federation to retain its military presence in Abkhazia.

From mid-May until July 2008, a number of incidents occurred involving personnel of the CIS PKF and the Georgian Ministry of Internal Affairs, reflecting an alarming state of tension in the area, as well as in the Georgian-Russian relationship.

In June, UNOMIG noted that the Georgian side had increased the number of trainees and training areas as well as the frequency of training conducted for its law enforcement agencies (in the Security Zone) and its military (in the Restricted Weapons Zone).

On 20 June 2008, Abkhaz *de facto* Vice-President Raul Khajimba publicly stated that the use of force might be needed in order to seize control of the Georgian-controlled upper Kodori Valley.

From the end of June until mid-July 2008, a series of bomb blasts occurred in public places on the Abkhaz side of the ceasefire line as well as roadside explosions on the Georgian side. The bombings resulted in four fatalities, including the head of the Gali branch of the Abkhaz *de facto* security service, and left 18 people injured (mostly civilians).

Referring to security considerations, on 1 July the Abkhaz authorities closed the Inguri bridge, a main communication link over the ceasefire line for the local, mainly Georgian, population.

On 9 July, there was a clash between Abkhaz and Georgian forces on the Achamkhara heights in the lower Kodori Valley, resulting in several personnel being injured on both sides. Tensions rose further after allegations by the Georgian side of mortar firing into the Kvabchara Valley, an area in the Georgian-controlled upper Kodori Valley, on 26 July. UNOMIG began conducting independent investigations into the incidents, but had to suspend them because of the August hostilities.

The Georgian-Ossetian Conflict Zone

In the summer of 2008, the main focus of tension shifted from the Abkhaz to the Ossetian conflict zone, accompanied by subversive attacks as well as by intensified exchanges of fire between the Georgian and South Ossetian sides, including mortar and heavy artillery fire.

Tension in the Georgian-South Ossetian conflict zone started to rise in mid-June 2008 with explosions and mine incidents close to the Georgian-administered villages of Kekhvi, Ergneti and Tamarasheni and the *de facto* South Ossetian militia post in Kokhati as well as with exchange of fire between the Georgian-administered villages of Sveri and Prisi and the South Ossetian-administered villages of Andzisi and Zemo Prisi respectively. Prolonged exchange of fire also took place in the southern environs of Tskhinvali and nearby Georgian villages. These incidents were a clear violation of the ceasefire agreement, resulting in a number of dead and wounded and caused collateral damage to houses on both sides.

The overall precarious security situation in the zone of the Georgian-South Ossetian conflict dramatically deteriorated in early July 2008. On 3 July, explosions in the Ossetian-administered village of Dmenisi killed Nodar Bibilov, leader of the *de facto* South Ossetian militia. A few hours later on the same day, another device was reportedly targeted against the pro-Georgian leader of the Temporary Administrative Unit of South Ossetia, Dimitri Sanakoyev (while he was travelling on the by-pass road linking the Small and Big Liakhvi Georgian enclaves), and causing injuries to three Georgian policemen.

An extensive exchange of small arms fire and mortar shelling occurred in Tskhinvali and its southern environs during the night of 3-4 July, causing several casualties and property damage. In a public statement, the South Ossetian leadership blamed the Georgian side for initiating the fire exchange and qualified it as an act of aggression against South Ossetia. In an official statement, the Georgian Ministry of Internal Affairs blamed the South Ossetian side for firing against Georgian villages and claimed that the Georgian side returned fire in order to protect the civilian population in the area.

The shelling on 3-4 July was followed by an exchange of fire between the South Ossetian-administered village of Ubiati and the Georgian-administered village of Nuli. Another exchange of fire erupted between the newly established Georgian and Ossetian peacekeeping posts on the strategically important Sarabuki heights, overlooking both the South Ossetian Geri bypass road as well as the Eredvi-Kheiti bypass road, the only functional road linking the Georgian enclave north of Tskhinvali, with a population of about 10,000, with the rest of Georgia.

On the night of 7-8 July, four Georgian soldiers were detained by the South Ossetian *de-facto* authorities. They were released with the assistance of the OSCE Mission to Georgia in the evening of 8 July. On the same day, four Russian military aircraft entered Georgian airspace around the zone of the conflict. These events took place at the time of a visit to Georgia by representatives of the Permanent Missions of the OSCE member-states from Vienna (6-10 July) and on the eve of a visit to Georgia by US Secretary of State Condoleezza Rice (9 July).

In a statement on 9 July, the Ministry of Foreign Affairs of Georgia stated that the incident was an open aggression directed against the country and a brutal and undisguised attempt to infringe on its sovereignty and territorial integrity. In statements on 10 and 14 July, the Ministry of Foreign Affairs of the Russian Federation explained the violation of Georgian airspace as a "forced extreme" measure aimed at preventing an "armed attack" on South Ossetia and an alleged attempt by Tbilisi to liberate its detained servicemen.

On 10 July, Georgia presented an appeal to the UN to probe the violation of its airspace by convening an extraordinary session of the UN Security Council. Also at Georgian request, a special meeting of the OSCE Permanent Council was convened in Vienna on 14 July to discuss the

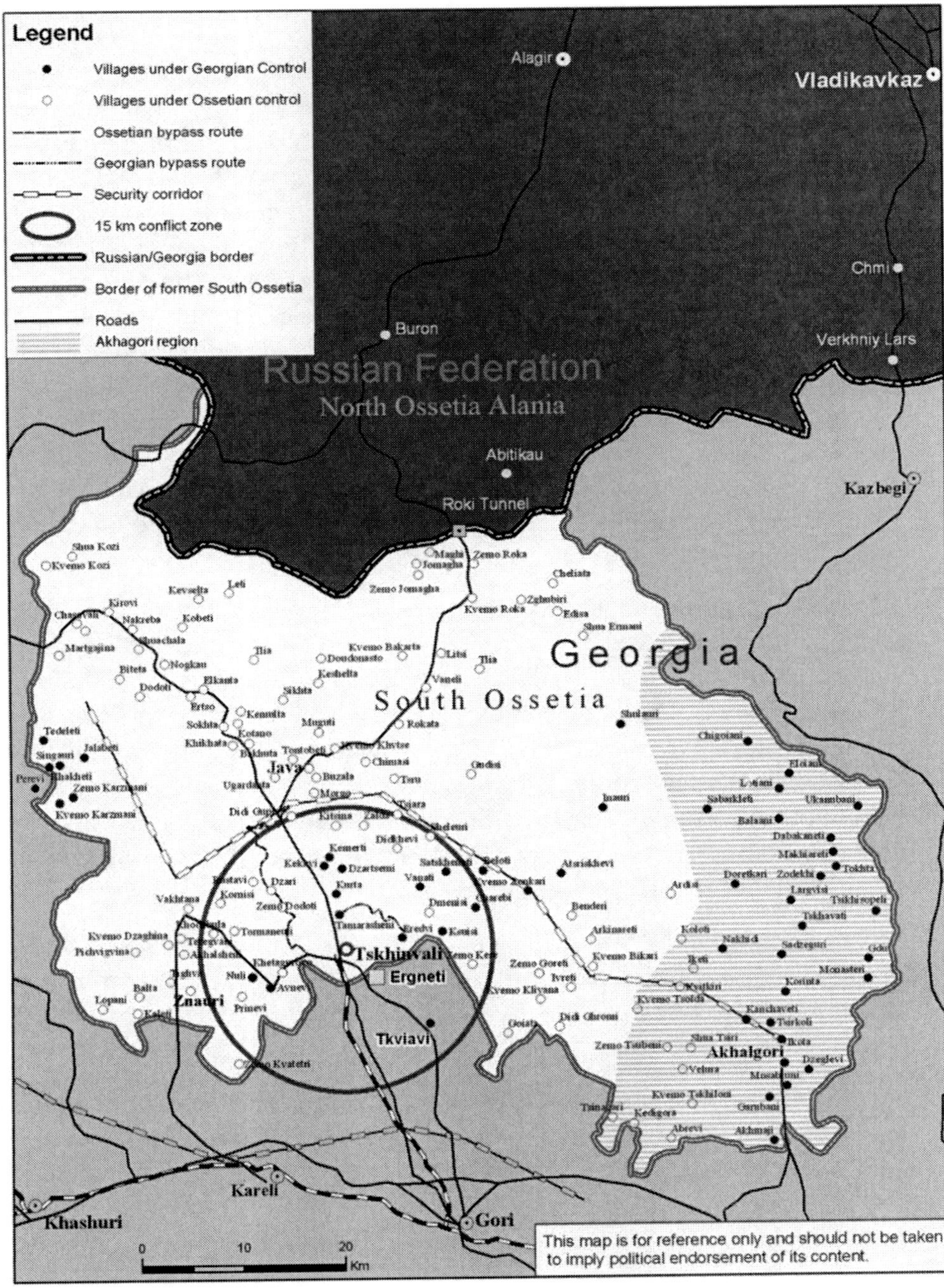

Map 10: The Georgian-Ossetian Conflict Zone

situation. These two events were indication of the seriousness of the situation in the region at that time.

The overall security situation in the zone of the Georgian-Ossetian conflict continued to deteriorate further in the second half of July. From 24 to 28 July, several explosions occurred in the southern environs of Tskhinvali and in the Georgian-administered village of Avnevi, close to the post of the Georgian Peacekeeping Force (PKF) battalion. From 29 to 31 July, exchanges of fire were reported between the Georgian-administered village of Sveri and the South Ossetian-administered village of Andzisi in the Sarabuki area, where the Georgian and Ossetian JPKF battalions established their posts after the events of 3 July. On the same day, exchanges of fire also took place in the area of Khetagurovo between the South Ossetian militia post and the Georgian police post on the Georgian Avnevi-Zemo Nikozi by-pass road. On 29 July, a Joint Monitoring Team of the Joint Peacekeeping Forces (JPKF) came under fire, but neither side admitted responsibility for the incident.

In the meantime, both sides started to strengthen their positions and to build new fortifications in various strategic locations in the conflict zone, including in the villages of Tliakana, Khetagurovo, Zemo Prisi, Didi Gromi, Kverneti, Kusireti, Chorbauli and the Tsunarishba reservoir on the Ossetian side and, on the Georgian side, in the village of Prisi and close to the Georgian bypass road running from Avnevi to Zemo Nikozi. Also reported were the completion of construction by a Russian company of a military base (Ugardanta) in the Java district and a military rehabilitation centre in the north-western part of Tskhinvali.

In early July, the South Ossetian authorities introduced restrictions on the freedom of movement of vehicles and people to and from the Georgian side. The OSCE observers encountered difficulties in visiting South Ossetian positions.

In mid-July, a yearly US-led military exercise called "Immediate Response" took place at the Vaziani base outside Tbilisi, involving approximately 2,000 troops from Georgia, the US, Armenia, Azerbaijan and Ukraine.

From 15 July to 2 August 2008, Russian troops carried out large-scale training exercises named "Kavkaz-2008" (Caucasus-2008) in the North Caucasus Military District, near the Russian-Georgian border and on the

Black Sea. The Russian exercise officially involved approximately 8,000 Russian troops. [Some analysts believe that the number of troops involved may have been intentionally understated]. Apart from the "Kavkaz-2008" exercise, there were a number of signals from the Russian side that it would intervene in case of a Georgian military operation in South Ossetia.

The beginning of August 2008 was marked by an even further deterioration of the security situation in the Georgian-Ossetian conflict zone. On 1 August, an IED went off on the Georgian Eredvi-Kheiti road bypassing Tskhinvali leaving five Georgian policemen injured. During the evening and night of 1-2 August, a series of intense and extensive exchanges of fire including sniper fire and mortar shelling occurred in the conflict zone, causing fatalities and casualties. The events on 1-2 August were assessed by the OSCE Mission to Georgia as the most serious outbreak of fire since the 2004 conflict. Exchanges of fire continued in the nights of 2-3 and 3-4 August.

In early August 2008, the South Ossetian authorities started to evacuate their civilian population to locations on the territory of the Russian Federation.

Beginning in the afternoon of 6 August fire was exchanged along virtually the whole line of contact between the Georgian and South Ossetian sides, with particular hotspots in the Avnevi Nuli-Khetagurovo area (west of Tskhinvali) and the Dmenisi-Prisi area (east of Tskhinvali). After a short break in the morning, firing, involving mortars and artillery, continued on 7 August, reportedly causing human casualties and fatalities. The same day, international observers could see significant movements of Georgian troops and equipment towards Gori from the east and west. Other troops and equipment were observed north of Gori, just outside the zone of conflict.

Diplomatic efforts were undertaken on 7 August, involving the Georgian State Minister for Reintegration, Temuri Yakobashvili, the Russian Special Envoy for the Georgian-Ossetian conflict, Ambassador Yuri Popov and the Commander of the JPKF, Major-General Marat Kulakhmetov. They aimed to arrange for high-level Georgian-South Ossetian peace talks but could not achieve any positive results. In the afternoon of 7 August, Georgian representatives left the JPKF Headquarters in Tskhinvali.

At 1900 hours (Tbilisi time) on 7 August, Georgian President Mikheil

Saakashvili stated in a televised address that he had just ordered Georgian troops to unilaterally cease fire. He called on the South Ossetian and Russian sides to stop the bloodshed and to meet at the negotiating table in either bilateral or multilateral format. For some hours, the ceasefire seemed to be stable and was also observed by the South Ossetian side, until firing was reportedly resumed again at around 2200 hours.

Outbreak of Large-scale Hostilities

The rising tension in South Ossetia in the period of June-early August 2008, which was characterized by some analysts as a low-intensity war, culminated in a large-scale Georgian military operation against the South Ossetian capital of Tskhinvali and the surrounding areas, on the night of 7-8 August 2008.

On 7 August at 2335 hours Georgian artillery units began firing smoke bombs and, subsequently, at 2350 hours, opened fire on both fixed and moving targets on the territory of South Ossetia. According to Georgian Government officials, this interval was supposed to allow the civilian population enough time to leave dangerous zones or to find protection/shelters.

In the early morning of 8 August, Georgian troops launched a ground attack against the city of Tskhinvali as well as operations on the left flank of the city (by the 4th Infantry Brigade coming from Vaziani) and on the right flank (by the 3rd Infantry Brigade coming from Kutaisi). The flank operations seemed to aim, *inter alia,* at occupying important heights surrounding Tskhinvali and then at moving further northwards to take control of the strategically important Gupta bridge and the roads, including the Ossetian-controlled Dzara bypass road, leading from the Roki tunnel to Tskhinvali to block movements of the Russian troops from the north.

After securing the heights in the vicinity of Tskhinvali, the Georgian forces, supported by artillery and tanks, moved into the town. By the afternoon of 8 August, the Georgian forces managed to seize control of a great part of the town of Tskhinvali (with the exception of its northern quarters and a part of its centre) and a number of villages, including Znauri, Muguti, Khetagurovo, Kokhati, Tsinagari, Orchosani, Didmukha, Gromi, Artsevi and Dmenisi.

However, the Georgian troops in Tskhinvali and vicinity started to

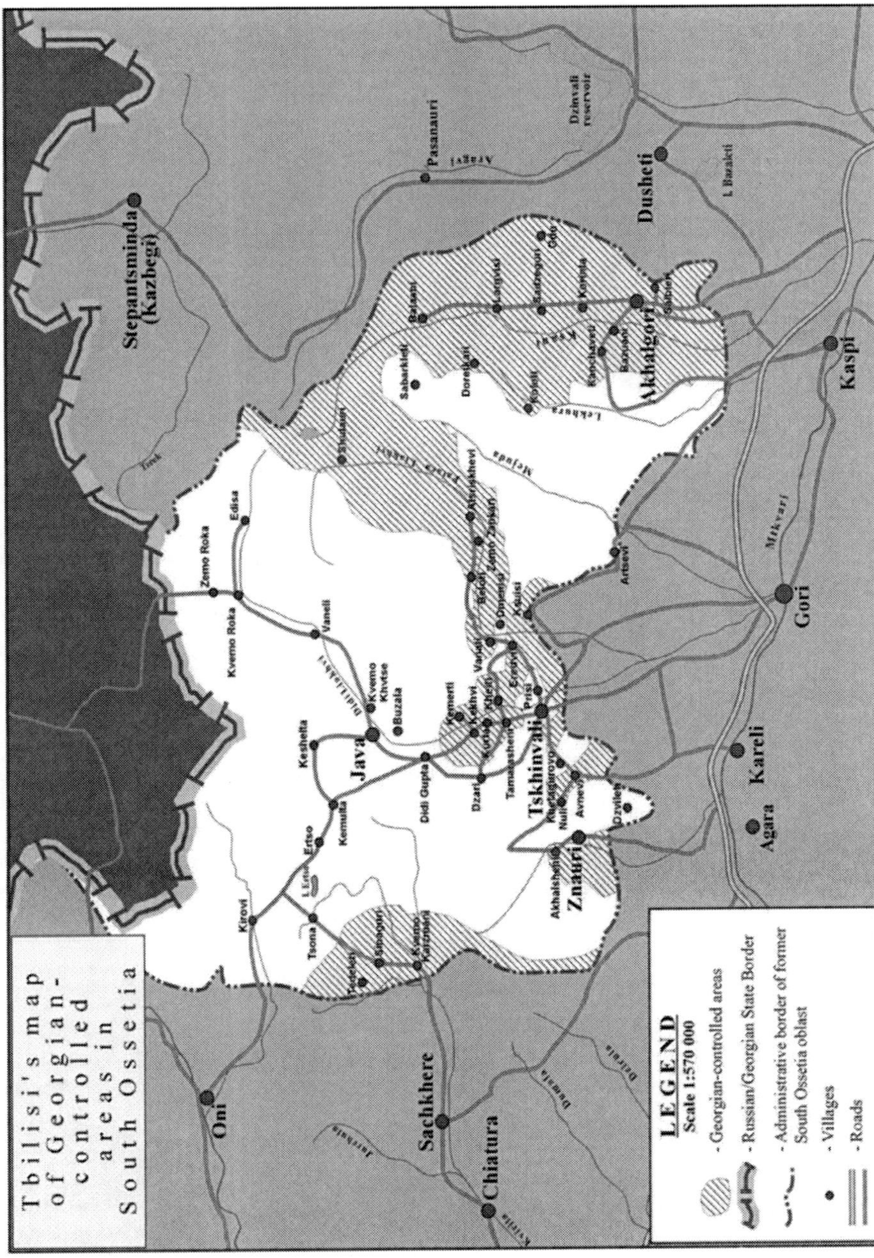

Map 11: Tbilisi's Map of Georgian Controlled Areas in South Ossetia

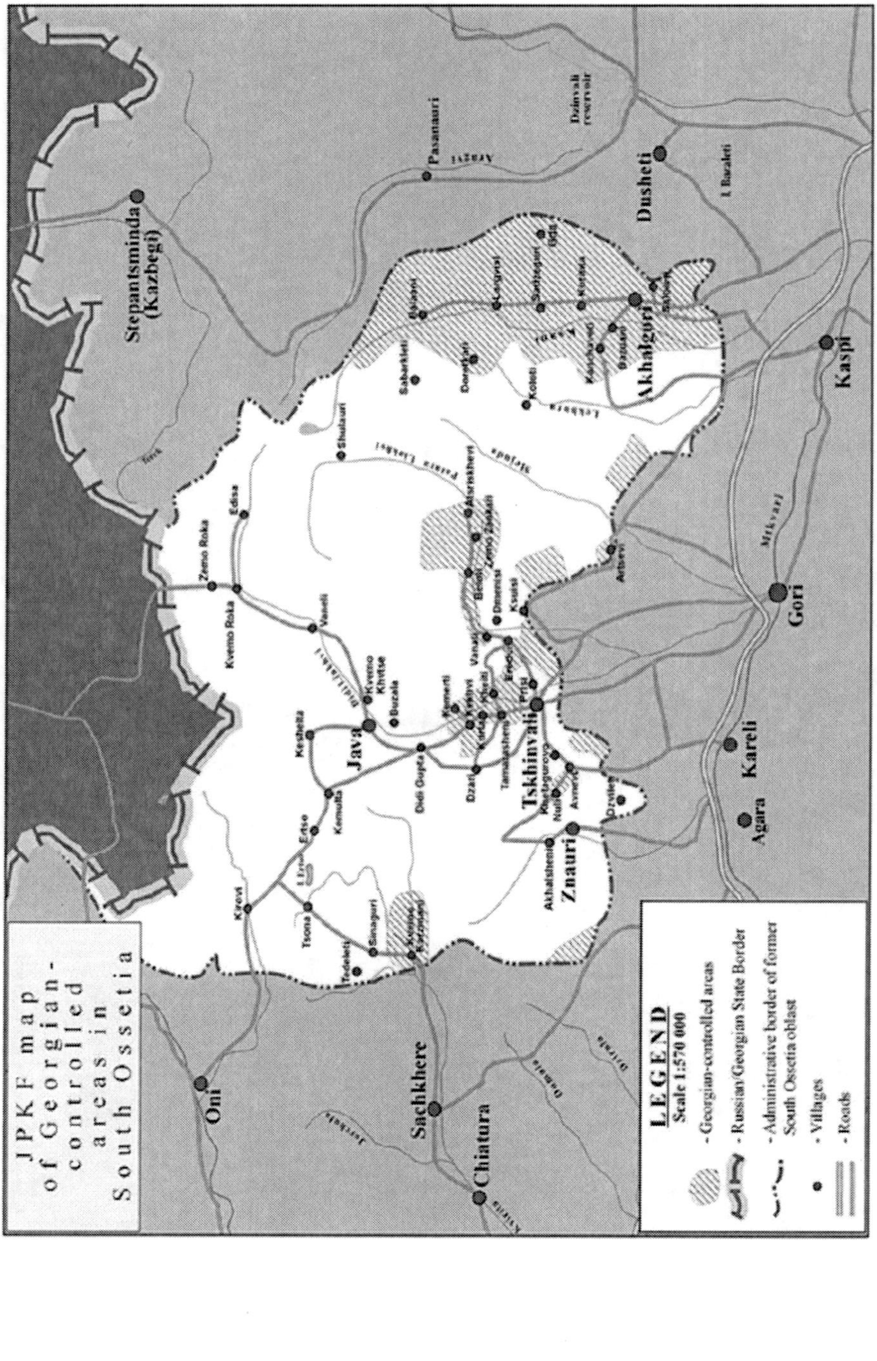

Map 12: JPKF Map of Georgian Controlled Areas in South Ossetia

encounter growing fire power from the opposite side, including from the Russian air force and artillery. The flank operations of the Georgian forces were generally not particularly successful and they did not manage to achieve their main objective of blocking the Gupta bridge and the main routes leading to Tskhinvali from the Roki tunnel and the Java base. In the meantime the Gupta bridge was targeted by Georgian artillery and aircraft (4 Su-25) and reportedly damaged, but the bridge was quickly repaired by the Russian and the South Ossetian forces.

Russian forces engaged in the armed conflict, including ground and air forces as well as the Black Sea Fleet, also attacked targets on Georgian territory outside South Ossetia. In the morning of 8 August, the Russian air force reportedly started attacks in central Georgia (Variani, Gori), gradually extending them to other parts of Georgia including the Senaki military base (9 August), military targets in the port of Poti and the capital of Tbilisi. Some civilian targets were also damaged.

Experiencing growing resistance, in the evening of 8 August the Georgian forces withdrew from the centre of Tskhinvali but still held their positions in the southern parts of the town. Then they were regrouped and reinforced by the 2nd Infantry Brigade from Senaki. The 4th Infantry Brigade was reinforced the Ministry of Interior special forces in Tskhinvali, while positions and objectives of the 4th Infantry Brigade on the left flank were transferred to the 2nd Infantry Brigade.

After regrouping, the Georgian forces undertook attempts to regain control of their position in Tskhinvali in the afternoon of 9 August but met with resistance, suffered losses and had to withdraw. Meanwhile, elements of the 2nd Infantry Brigade engaged a column of Russian armoured vehicles heading towards the north-western entrance of Tskhinvali with the Commander of the 58th Army, Army General Anatoly Khrulyov, who was injured in the ambush.

With Russia's intervention advancing and its forces gaining superiority on the ground, signs of collapse of morale seemed to appear among the Georgian troops by the afternoon of 10 August.

By the evening of 10 August, Russia had seven full regimental tactical groups (135th, 429th, and 503rd and 693rd Motorized Rifle Regiments of the 19th Motorized Rifle Division from North Ossetia, the 70th and 71st Motorized Rifle Regiments of the 42nd Motorized Rifle Division from

Chechnya, and one regiment of the 76th Pskov Air Assault Division), units of the 45th Reconnaissance Paratroop Regiment and the 10th and 22nd Special Forces Brigades, as well as significant artillery and air-defence forces. Two Chechen companies from the Zapad and Vostok battalions and regimental tactical groups of the 98th Ivanovo Airborne Division, deployed to the battle zone too. The total number of Russian forces in South Ossetia reached about 10,000 men and 150 tanks.

At the same time, Russia opened a "second front" in Abkhazia, deploying up to 9,000 men from the 7th Novorossiysk and 76th Pskov Air Assault Divisions, the elements of the 20th Motorized Rifle Division and two battalions of the Black Sea Fleet Marines. With their support, Abkhaz forces began to dislodge the Georgian forces from the Kodori Gorge.

On 10 August, the Georgian side declared that it would observe a unilateral ceasefire and would move its forces out of South Ossetia. The opposite sides did not follow suit. By midnight on 10 August, most Georgian troops had left the territory of South Ossetia in the direction of Gori. On 11 August, the Georgian forces withdrew from Gori to the town of Mtskheta, and started preparing a defensive line in the mountainous terrain for protection of Tbilisi, the capital. In the process of withdrawal, a significant quantity of military equipment was reportedly left behind.

The withdrawing Georgian troops were followed by Russian forces, who entered deeper into Georgian territory by crossing the administrative boundaries of South Ossetia and occupying a number of locations, including the town of Gori on 12 August. While in Gori, Russian forces reportedly destroyed installations and barracks at the local military base. The Russian forces were accompanied or followed by South Ossetian militia who committed serious human rights violations, particularly in the Georgian villages of South Ossetia.

Operations on the Abkhaz Front

In early August, tension also grew along the Georgian-Abkhaz ceasefire line, particularly in the Kodori Valley. The Georgian side repeatedly claimed that it had information about an impending Abkhaz and/or Russian offensive into the valley, whereas the Abkhaz side reported a build-up of Georgian troops there. Both sides also made claims that the other side was hiding heavy military equipment in the part of the valley under their control.

The dramatic escalation of hostilities in South Ossetia on 7-8 August and the Russian-Georgian military confrontation had profoundly affected the situation in the Georgian-Abkhaz conflict zone.

On 8 August, the Abkhaz side began moving heavy weapons into the Restricted Weapons Zone, in violation of the 1994 Moscow Agreement on a Ceasefire and Separation of Forces, disregarding protests by UNOMIG.

In the early morning of 9 August, several Russian vessels from the Black Sea Fleet deployed to the Ochamchira port, in Abkhazia, close to the Georgian-Abkhaz ceasefire line. The same day, the Black Sea Fleet set up a so-called "maritime security zone" along a large portion of the Georgian coast, including the port of Poti, to deny the area to Georgian and international maritime movement.

On the afternoon of 9 August, the Abkhaz authorities requested a UNOMIG team monitoring the Kodori Valley to immediately leave its base in Ajara in the Georgian-controlled upper part of the valley. After the departure of UNOMIG personnel, aerial bombardments of the upper Kodori Valley started on the same day.

On the night of 9-10 August, Abkhaz forces crossed the ceasefire line on the Inguri river and made incursions into Georgian-controlled territory for reconnaissance purposes and in order to cut Georgian communication and supply lines.

On 10 August, the Russian Federation continued its military build-up in Abkhazia, deploying additional ground forces by sea to the Ochamchira port and also by air to the Babushera airport near Sukhumi, with some 9,000 troops and 350 armoured vehicles. The troops were not part of the CIS peacekeeping force and therefore were clearly operating outside the 1994 Ceasefire Agreement. The same day, the Abkhaz authorities introduced martial law in the districts of Gali, Ochamchira and Tkvarcheli, adjacent to the Georgian-Abkhaz ceasefire line, and announced partial mobilisation.

In the late evening of 10 August, the Russian forces crossed the Georgian-Abkhaz ceasefire line on the Inguri river moving deep into Georgian territory and occupying a number of locations, including the towns of Zugdidi, Senaki and Poti by 12 August, without encountering any armed resistance from the Georgian side. The Russian forces destroyed installations in the military sector of Poti port and the Georgian navy vessels there, and plundered the Senaki military base.

The Russian military advances in the Zugdidi district and in other areas south of the Inguri river created a risk of encirclement for the Georgian security forces deployed in the upper Kodori Valley. On the night of 11-12 August, Georgian forces left the upper Kodori Valley with most of the local population. Abkhaz and Russian forces occupied the area on 12-13 August.

In an attempt to justify its armed incursion into the upper Kodori Valley, the Abkhaz side referred to the presence of the Georgian security forces in the area as a threat to the Abkhaz statehood. However, the Russian authorities acknowledged that the Abkhaz side had been planning its military operation in the upper Kodori Valley in case of Georgian military actions against Republic of South Ossetia. Indeed, the operation against the upper Kodori Valley seems to have been well-prepared in advance and the forces assigned to this operation had reportedly started their deployment in the lower Kodori Valley on 6 August.

On 12 August, Abkhaz armed personnel entered the Ganmukhuri and Kurcha pockets north of the Inguri river on the Georgian side of the ceasefire line, which the Abkhaz occupied till 9 September. UNOMIG patrols were denied access to this and other areas in the lower Gali district till 4 September. Up to 15 August, Abkhaz forces occasionally crossed the ceasefire line in other locations as well, entering Georgian villages on the southern side of the Inguri river.

Georgian Operations

Georgian ground forces engaged in the conflict consisted mainly of the following units: the 2nd, 3rd and 4th Infantry Brigades, 1st Artillery Brigade, 53rd Infantry Battalion, artillery and mechanized elements of the 1st Brigade, besides a Separate Tank Battalion, Separate Infantry Battalion and Air Defence Battalion. In addition to the forces under the Defence Ministry, anti-riot and counter terrorism battalion-size units of the Ministry of Internal Affairs (special police forces) also took part in the operations. The total strength was estimated at 10,000-11,000 personnel.

On 8 August, President Saakashvili declared a mobilisation of the reserve National Guard, assembling around 5,000 men, but they reportedly failed to play a noteworthy role in the conflict. Meanwhile, 2,000 of the best-trained Georgian soldiers of the elite 1st Infantry Brigade were deployed in Iraq. On 10-11 August, US transport facilities flew them back to Georgia but in the end they did not take part in combat, having arrived too late.

Having lost its control over the bulk of South Ossetian territory, Georgian forces began to regroup at Gori. Meanwhile, Georgian units and artillery continued to shell Tskhinvali from a number of dominating points, and displayed fierce resistance in a number of Georgian enclaves. However, by the end of 11 August, South Ossetia was completely cleared of Georgian forces, and Russian units had moved into Georgia proper by the next morning, establishing a demilitarized buffer zone as much as 25 kilometres wide to prevent any further artillery attacks on South Ossetia. Georgian units resisted stubbornly in the area around the village of Zemo-Nikozi, repelling the Russian attack for a short time, but were soon pushed out.

Georgian defences and the entire army soon began to collapse. From the morning of 12 August onward, the Georgian army began to retreat toward Gori, a retreat which soon grew into a panicked flight from Gori, almost all the way to Tbilisi. Along the way, the Georgians abandoned a significant quantity of ammunition and military equipment, especially the artillery brigade.

On 11 August, Russian forces entered Georgia proper from Abkhazia virtually unopposed. Having taken the city of Zugdidi, Russian units (paratroops from the 7th Division) spread across almost all of Western Georgia on raids aimed at destroying heavy weapons at Georgian military bases in Senaki and Poti.

Georgian artillery and air defence performed quite well and generally better than other units in the course of the August hostilities. However, the massive Russian military action caught the Georgians off-guard and unprepared both strategically and tactically. At the time, the Georgian military seems to have been more prepared for a mobile, mostly offensive war in either Abkhazia or South Ossetia, but not for simultaneous large-scale combat with superior, heavily armed, and air-supported enemy forces entering from Abkhazia and South Ossetia, i.e. on both fronts, at the same time.

Russian Operations

The official Russian records, submitted to the IIFFMCG in July 2009, holds that on 8 August, at 1430 hours, units of the 693rd and 135th Motorised Rifle Regiments of the 19th Motorised Rifle Division charged with the task of carrying out the peacekeeping mission entrusted to the Russian Federation and protecting Russian citizens were deployed from the territory of the Russian Federation to the territory of South Ossetia through the Roki tunnel and began to move into South Ossetia. The air force and artillery units launched strikes against Georgian military facilities to restrict movements of the enemy reserves, disrupt its communications, incapacitate base airfields, and destroy warehouses and bases containing fuel and lubricants and to seal off the areas of hostilities.

In addition to the two regiments of the 19th Motorised Rifle Division of the 58th Army, previous information provided to the IIFFMCG by the Russian authorities in mid-May 2009 stated that a number of other military units participated in the Russian operation on the eastern front (South Ossetia) including elements from the 42nd Motorised Rifle Division (from Chechnya), the 76th Assault Division (Pskov), the 98th Airborne Division (Ivanovo), the 20th Motorised Rifle Division (Volgograd), the 234th Assault Division, the 205th Separate Motorised Rifle Brigade, the 429th and 71st Motorised Rifle Regiments, the 104th Assault Regiment, the 331st Parachute Regiment and the 45th Special Purpose Regiment (Moscow district).

According to the Georgian official records submitted to the IIFFMCG the 33rd Motor Rifle Mountain Brigade (Dagestan), the 114th Rocket Brigade (Astrakhan district), the Separate Anti-Aircraft Rocket Brigade (Volgograd) and the 10th Special Forces Brigade (Krasnodar district) also participated in the Russian operation on the eastern front.

It is independently assessed that over 12,000 Russian troops were deployed on the eastern front, i.e. in South Ossetia and beyond, in the course of the August crisis. Separately, elements from the 7th Assault (Mountain) Division (Novorossiysk), the 34th Rifle Mountain Brigade (Karachai-Cherkessia), the 31st Separate Assault Brigade (Ulianovsk), the 526th, 131st and 15th Separate Motorised Rifle Brigades as well as the 2nd, 108th and 247th Assault Regiments deployed in Abkhazia and beyond its administrative boundaries (Zugdidi, Senaki, Poti) and some of these troops may have taken part in the Russian operations on the western front in Georgia.

According to some sources, Russia deployed up to 15,000 troops in Abkhazia in total. The overall number of Russian troops moved into Georgia in August 2008 amounted to 25,000–30,000 supported by more than 1,200 pieces of armour and heavy artillery. Also involved in the action were up to 200 aircraft and 40 helicopters. Several thousand armed Ossetians and volunteer militias from the North Caucasus supported the Russian forces on the eastern front as well as up to 10,000 Abkhaz troops and militia forces with armour and guns on the western front.

Russian military operations in Georgia in August 2008 appear to have been well-planned and well-executed. The operational planning had been validated in practice during the "Kavkaz-2008" military exercise (and previous similar exercises since 2005), which ended on 2 August 2008. After the exercise, some units returned to their garrisons, but others seem to have remained and deployed in a precautionary move near the Georgian border. Therefore, they could quickly move to South Ossetia through the Roki tunnel when ordered to do so.

Naval Operations

The Russian Black Sea Fleet, deployed in Georgian territorial waters and/or in its vicinity reportedly consisted of around 13 vessels, including its flagship, the guided missile cruiser "Moskva", as well as landing, anti-submarine and patrol ships, and minesweepers.

The Russian Black Sea Fleet left Sevastopol on the evening of 8 August and established a de-facto sea blockade of the Georgian coast. The Russian Task Force included the Moskva guide missile cruiser, the Smetlivy destroyer (Kashin class), the Mirazh (Nanuchka III class) guide missile corvette, the R-239 and R-334 (Tarantul III class) guide missile corvettes, the Aleksandrovets and Murmanets (Grisha V class) corvettes, three minesweepers, three large tank landing ships, a transport, and a rescue ship. On the evening of 9 August, the Mirazh corvette probably sank one Georgian patrol cutter with two Malakhit (SS-N-9) anti-ship missiles in what amounted to the Russian Navy's first real sea battle since 1945.

Air Operations

Russian air operations reportedly opened in the morning of 8 August with the first attacks targeting the Georgian air defence installations in the Gori district. Units employed during the armed conflict seemed to have come mainly from the 4th Air Force and Air Defence Army (Rostov district) and included Su-24, Su-25, Su-27 and Su-29 aircraft as well as Mi-8 and Mi-24 helicopters.

Targeting was focused on Georgian operational ground and air assets. Air defence radar sites and airbases were attacked, with regular repeat attacks against Marneuli, Vaziani and Bolnisi. These targets were well away from the main conflict zone. Hence, rather than to provide close air support to ground forces in contact, the Russian air attacks seemed to be strategically intended to support a broader military objective, including to deprive the Georgian brigades engaged in South Ossetia of any support from second echelon forces, particularly air support. Given this primary objective, the targets also included port installations along the Black Sea coast, air traffic radar sites, aircraft manufacturing and maintenance plants. As the Georgian withdrawal continued, Russian efforts were diverted to supporting Russian ground troops in order to accelerate Georgian withdrawal. In the course of the hostilities, the Russian air force reportedly lost several aircraft, including one strategic bomber and reconnaissance aircraft Tu-22M3.

Russia's Air Force carried out attacks on military targets all across Georgian territory, completing several hundred sorties using Su-24M bombers, and Su-25 attack planes, and the Tu-22M3 long-range bombers. That said, the use of air power was limited by political considerations. There were no attacks on Georgian infrastructure, transport, communications or industry, nor any on government buildings. The distance of targets from Russian bases also complicated matters. In addition, Russian helicopters had a hard time flying over the Caucasus passes, and thus extensive use of helicopters by Russia began only after 10-11 August, once a temporary landing/take-off strip was set up in South Ossetia. The overall losses of Russian Air Force amounted to one Tu-22M3 long-range bomber, one Su-24M frontal bomber, one Su-24MR reconnaissance plane, and four Su-25 attack planes. Moreover, the Russian Army launched 15 Tochka-U (SS-21) short-range ballistic missiles against military targets and a few new Iskander (SS-26) short-range theatre ballistic missiles.

The Georgian air force used Su-25 aircraft and Mi-24, Mi-8/17 and UH-1H type helicopters. However, due to its huge numerical inferiority vis-à-vis the Russian air force, it did not seem to play a significant role in combat and conducted a limited number of sorties, mainly in the morning of 8 August.

Cyber War

Reported cyber attacks were one of the particular features of the Russian-Georgian conflict in August 2008. It looks quite apparent that significant cyber attacks were launched against Georgia in the course of the conflict. Most Georgian Government and media sites were unavailable or defaced at some time during the first days of the conflict. A number of websites were then relocated to US, Estonian and Polish servers. Some analysts believe that these attacks may have reduced Georgian decision-making capability, as well as its ability to communicate with allies, thereby possibly impairing the operational flexibility of Georgian forces.

The most significant occurrences include the following:

- On 20 July, President Saakashvili's website was shut down for 24 hours;
- On 7 August, several Georgian servers and the Internet traffic were seized and placed under external control;
- On 8 August, large-scale cyber attacks against sites in Georgia began. The source of the cyber attacks was uncertain. Some reports attributed them to an organization called the "Russian Business Network".
- At this time, it was reported that all Georgian Government websites were unobtainable from US, UK and European cyberspace. The Turkish AS9121 TTNet server, one of the routing points for traffic into the Caucasus, was blocked, reportedly via COMSTAR;
- On 9 August, the Georgian Ministry of Foreign Affairs website was defaced by hackers, who replaced it with offensive photographs. Other Georgian websites which also suffered cyber or hacker attacks included those of the Ministry of Internal Affairs, the Ministry of Defence and the website of Sanakoyev's pro-Georgian Interim Administration of South Ossetia. In addition, reportedly the National Bank of Georgia was defaced and Georgian news portals were affected by DDoS (distributed denial of service) attacks.
- By 12 August, President Saakashvili's website and a popular Georgian TV website (www.rustavi2.com) were transferred to Tulip Systems. Tulip was then also attacked;
- On 12-13 August, the Ministry of Defence website experienced extensive cyber attacks and two periods of downtime.

More limited attacks of no particular significance may have been launched against some Russian sites, too. For example, the RIA Novosti website was offline because of DDoS attacks for over 10 hours.

If these attacks were directed by a government or governments, it is likely that this form of warfare was used for the first time in an inter-state armed conflict. However, the nature of defence against cyber attacks at this stage of its development means that such attacks are easy to carry out, but difficult to prevent, and to attribute to a source.

Georgia's Air Defence in the War

The Georgian air-defence system represents a symbiosis of what it inherited from the collapse of the Soviet Union and new acquisitions from former Warsaw Pact and Soviet successor states.

During Soviet times, the 19th Tbilisi Air-Defence Army of the Soviet Air-Defence Troops was deployed in Georgia (reduced to an Air-Defence Corps in 1991). It included three SAM brigades in Tbilisi, Poti, and Echmiadzin, armed with S-75 (SA-2) and S-125 (SA-3) SAM systems, a separate SAM regiment armed with S-75 SAM systems (SA-2, deployed in Gudauta, Abkhazia), and a separate SAM regiment near Tbilisi, equipped with S-200 (SA-5) long-range SAM systems, as well as two radar brigades. However, after the collapse of the Soviet Union, some of the Soviet Armed Forces, including air defence, did not fall under Georgian jurisdiction, but remained under Russian control. During the early 1990s, all of the air-defence divisions on Georgian territory were dismantled and their equipment transferred to Russia for scrapping. Nonetheless, Georgian forces seized some air-defence equipment from the Russian military, including at least one S-75 and two S-125 SAM battalions, as well as a few P-18 radars. These systems were put into service to form the nucleus of the air defences of the Georgian armed forces. The Georgians used the S-75 SAM battalions in the war with Abkhazia in 1992-1993 and shot down a Russian Su-27 fighter near Gudauta on 19 March 1993.

The S-75 battalion was removed from service in Georgia, but the two S-125 Neva-M low- to high-altitude SAM systems battalions was deployed in Tbilisi and Poti (a total of seven quadruple rail launchers) and those in service with the Georgian Air Force had been modernized by Ukrainian specialists by 2005.

The Georgian Army received several short-range air-defence systems in the first half of the 1990s from the arsenals of the former Soviet Army located in Georgia but transferred to Russian jurisdiction. These included KS-19 100-mm anti-aircraft guns, S-60 57-mm anti-aircraft guns, ZU-23-2 twin 23-mm anti-aircraft guns, ZSU-23-4 Schilka quad 23-mm self-propelled anti-aircraft gun systems, Strela-2M (SA-7), Strela-3 (SA-14), and Igla-1 (SA-16) man-portable SAM systems (MANPADS). However, a significant proportion of these arms were lost by Georgia during its unsuccessful war with Abkhazia. Some of the ZU-23-2 anti-aircraft guns were mounted on MT-LB armoured multipurpose tracked vehicles.

With Mikhail Saakashvili's coming to power in 2003, Georgia began the rapid development of its military capacities with the aim of acquiring the means to regain the separatist Abkhazian and South Ossetian regions. To neutralize Russia's potential to interfere in its operations against Abkhazia and South Ossetia, Georgia began to purchase modern air-defence systems.

(a) Georgia acquired a 9E3711 Buk-M1 (SA-11) battalion of low- to high-altitude self-propelled SAM systems composed of three batteries (each battery includes two self-propelled launcher mounts and one self-propelled loader-launcher) from Ukraine in 2007. These were delivered together with 48 9Ì38Ì1 surface-to-air missiles. Georgia noted this transfer in its official report for 2007 to the UN Register of Conventional Arms. Other than Russia and Ukraine, only Finland, Cyprus, and Egypt possess Buk systems in several different versions. According to subsequent internet reports from Ukraine, the Buk-M1 systems were delivered by sea to Georgia on 7 June 2007. On 16 July 2008, photos of Georgian Buk-M1 systems used during tactical training in Western Georgia dating from August 2007 appeared on the Internet. According to a Ukrainian source, on 12 June 2008, another battery of Buk-M1 systems was delivered to Georgia.

(b) Ukraine delivered eight self-propelled launcher vehicles 9K33M2 Osa-AK (SA-8B) low-altitude SAM systems (two batteries) and six (ten, according to some sources) 9K33M3 Osa-AKM self-propelled launcher vehicles update SAM systems. The Buk-M1 and Osa-AK/AKM systems were deployed by the Georgian Air Force in Gori, Senaki, and Kutaisi.

(c) Ukraine sold Georgia two modern 36D6-M radars that were deployed in Tbilisi and Savshevebi near Gori. The 36D6-M is a mobile, 3-D air surveillance radar, developed by the Iskra company in Zaporizhzhya, Ukraine. The 36D6-M radar is a deep modernization of the ST-68U (19Zh6) Tin Shield radar, taken into service in 1980 and used with the S-300P (SA-10) SAM system. The 36D6-M radar has a range of up to 360 kilometres.

(d) Ukraine delivered the Kolchuga-M passive electronic monitoring radar system, capable of passively detecting modern aircraft, including those using stealth technology. It is possible that another four Kolchuga-M and one Mandat electronic warfare systems, all produced in Donetsk at the SKB RTU and the Topaz Company, were delivered to Georgia in May 2008. Earlier, Ukraine was severely criticized by the United States for having sold Kolchuga systems to China, Iraq, and Iran.

(e) The Ukrainian company Aerotekhnika upgraded the obsolete Georgian P-18 *Spoon Rest* radars to the P-180U version, which amounts to a qualitatively new and modern 2-D air surveillance radar system. At the time when it attacked South Ossetia, the Georgian Air Force had four P-180U radars deployed in Alekseyevka (near Tbilisi), Marneuli, Poti, and Batumi.

In 2006, the company *Aerotekhnika* united Georgian military and four civilian air-traffic-control radars and the Kolchuga-M system into a single Air Sovereignty Operations Center (ASOC) early warning and command control tactical system. The central command centre of the ASOC was located in Tbilisi, and in 2008 was connected to a NATO Air Situation Data Exchange (ASDE) through Turkey, which allowed Georgia to receive data directly from the unified NATO air-defence system.

According to the Russian Defence Ministry, Ukraine either delivered or planned to deliver 50 9K310 Igla-1 (SA-16) man-portable SAM systems and 400 9M313 surface-to-air missiles, with missile seekers, upgraded by the Ukrainian Arsenal plant.

Several East European states also participated in the renewal of the Georgian air defence system. According to the Russian Defence Ministry, Bulgaria delivered 12 ZU-23-2M twin 23-mm anti-aircraft guns and 500 9Ì313 surface-to-air missiles for Igla-1 man-portable SAM systems. According to the UN Register of Conventional Arms, Poland delivered 30 Grom man-portable SAM systems (improved Igla-1) and 100 surface-to-air missiles, and it is possible that such deliveries took place in 2008 as well. Georgia acquired Soviet era man-portable SAM systems from other countries as well.

Finally, there are reports that Georgia acquired one battery of the Israeli Spyder-SR short-range self-propelled SAM system in 2008. The Spyder-SR SAM system, developed by *Rafael*, uses Python 5 and Derby air-to-air missiles in a surface-to-air role.

The Russian Ministry of Defence also reported that the Georgian Army acquired the Skywatcher army air-defence early-warning and command control tactical system produced by the Turkish *Aselsan* Company in 2008.

Thus, by the time Georgia invaded South Ossetia, its air defences had acquired significant capability to detect, locate, and destroy air targets. The Georgian forces that advanced into South Ossetia were the equivalent of about a large division (nine light infantry and five tank battalions, up to eight artillery battalions, plus special forces and Ministry of the Internal Affairs troops), were protected by an air defence echelon that included one Buk-M1 SAM system battalion, up to three Osa-AK/AKM SAM system batteries, a large number of man-portable SAM systems, as well as a few C-60 57-mm anti-aircraft guns, ZU-23-2 twin 23-mm anti-aircraft guns, and ZSU-23-4 Schilka quad 23-mm self-propelled anti-aircraft gun systems. Thus, the air-defence system of Georgian attack groups was about the equivalent of best frontline Soviet divisions during the late 1980s - early 1990s.

The confrontation with Georgia's air-defence system proved to be a serious trial for Russia's military aviation, especially since it seems that its capabilities were initially underestimated. Meanwhile, Georgia's air defences reportedly relied on data received from the Kolchuga-M passive electronic monitoring radar systems, minimizing the use of active radar, while the Georgian Buk-M1 and Osa-AK/AKM self-propelled SAM systems used ambush tactics. This made it more difficult to defeat the Georgian air-defence systems. According to unofficial reports, the Georgian Buk-M1 SAM systems shot down four Russian aircraft on the first day of battle on 8 August: three Su-25 attack planes and one Tu-22M3 long-range bomber.

According to unofficial sources, Russia lost another three airplanes (one Su-24MR reconnaissance plane on 8 August, one Su-24M frontal bomber on 10 or 11August, and one Su-25 attack plane on 9 August) as well as perhaps one Mi-24 attack helicopter. Both the Su-24 were probably shot down by Georgian Osa-AK/AKM SAM systems or man-portable SAM systems, and the Su-25, according to several reports, fell victim to friendly fire from a MANPAD wielded by Russian servicemen. According to the Sukhoi Company, three Russian Su-25s also were hit by Georgian SAM and MANPAD missiles but were able to return safely to base. For their part, Russian Army air-defence forces claimed to have shot down three Georgian Su-25 attack planes.

From the crews of the downed planes, two Russian pilots (of the Su-24MR and the Tu-22M3) were taken hostage, and exchanged for Georgian prisoners on 19 August. According to unofficial reports, another five Russian pilots (of the Su-25 shot by friendly fire, the navigator of the Su-24MR, and three crew from the Tu-22M3) died. The Russian Defence Ministry officially recognized the loss of only three Su-25 attack planes and one Tu-22M3 long-range bomber, and considered them downed by Buk-M1 SAM systems. The training of Georgian personnel in the use of the Buk-M1 SAM systems took place in Ukraine, and Ukrainian military instructors may have supervised their use in combat.

One can conclude that following the unpleasant surprise arising from Georgia's effective use of Soviet-made SAM systems on 8 August, the Russian armed forces deployed all the resources at their disposal against Georgia's SAM and radar systems. Both S-125M SAM battalions, the majority of Georgia's military and civilian radars, as well as the most part Buk-M1 and Osa-AK/AKM SAM systems were destroyed. It would appear that the only remaining threat to Russian planes and helicopters in the last days of combat came from Georgian MANPADs.

Russian forces were able to capture five Osa-AKM self-propelled launch vehicles, a few ZU-23-2 anti-aircraft guns and a few ZSU-23-4 Shilka self-propelled anti-aircraft gun systems from the retreating Georgian forces. Near Gali and Senaki, Abkhaz and Russian forces captured minimum one Buk-M1 battery, as witnessed by published photos. Russian forces were able to capture or destroy almost all of the self-propelled launcher mounts for the Georgian Buk-M1 SAM systems.

The war in South Ossetia marked the first time when air power faced off against new-generation SAM systems, like the Buk-M1, which were brought into service in the 1980s. In all previous military campaigns, such as the War in Vietnam, the Arab-Israeli Wars of 1967, 1973, and 1982, combat actions in Chad and Libya in the 1980s, the NATO campaigns in the former Yugoslavia of 1994 and 1999, and the Wars in the Persian Gulf of 1991 and 2003, the air-defence systems in question were all designed in the 1950s and 1960s (this excludes, of course, the use of modern MANPADs). Moreover, in Georgia, the Russian Air Force for the first time in its history fought against modern air-defence systems, and relatively modern and numerous SAM systems.

Ceasefire Agreement

On 12 August, French President Nicolas Sarkozy, in his capacity as President of the Council of the European Union, visited Moscow and Tbilisi in a move to end the military hostilities. A six-point ceasefire plan was agreed upon, providing, *inter alia*, for cessation of hostilities and withdrawal of forces to the positions occupied prior to the armed conflict. On the same day, the ceasefire arrangement was publicly confirmed by Russian President Dmitry Medvedev. Russian troops were to stop military activities at 1500 hours on 12 August. However, Russian and South Ossetian forces reportedly continued their advances for some time after the 12 August ceasefire was declared and occupied additional locations, including Akhalgori/Leningori on 16 August.

At midday on 12 August, Russian President Dmitry Medvedev decided to cease the active phase of the peace-enforcement operation. That evening, Saakashvili signed a preliminary ceasefire agreement that French President Nikolas Sarkozi had just brought from Moscow. Russian formations concentrated along the southern borders of South Ossetia and Abkhazia, exercising partial control of the demilitarized zone. Meanwhile, active raids on Georgian territory to capture and destroy Georgian weapons, and the "demilitarization of the Georgian armed forces," continued. From August 13 to 15, Russian paratroops raided Poti again, destroying almost all of the docked ships and boats of the Georgian Navy, and took away a quantity of military equipment. The same day, Russian forces entered Gori and began to raid Georgia's military bases. Other Russian raiding units neared within 20 kilometres of Tbilisi. This all occurred in the context of the complete paralysis of a demoralized Georgian Army, and the conclusion of individual agreements with local Georgian authorities and commanders on non-resistance against the Russian forces. The remaining combat-capable units of the Georgian Army (including the 1st Infantry Brigade hurried back from Iraq) concentrated at the northern approach to Tbilisi in expectation of a Russian attack on the capital. The morale of even these troops was reportedly extremely low.

Most of the Russian troops withdrew from their positions beyond the administrative boundaries of South Ossetia and Abkhazia after 22 August. Some of them remained in the so-called buffer zones and withdrew much later, after an implementation agreement, as a complement to the 12 August ceasefire agreement, was reached on 8 September 2008 in Moscow. On

9 October 2008, the Russian Foreign Ministry officially confirmed the completion of the withdrawal of the Russian forces from the zones adjacent to South Ossetia and Abkhazia. However, the issue of full compliance by the parties with the above two agreements have remained a subject of diverging interpretations and remain contentious.

Contentious Issues

At an early stage of the operation, the Commander of the Georgian contingent to the Joint Peacekeeping Forces (JPKF) Brig. Gen. Mamuka Kurashvili publicly stated that the objective of the operation was to restore "constitutional order" in the territory of South Ossetia. Somewhat later the Georgian authorities refuted Kurashvili's statement as unauthorised and, as justification of the operation, emphasized a countering of the Russian incursion. The official Georgian information provided to the IIFFMCG says in this regard that "in order to protect the sovereignty and territorial integrity of Georgia as well as the security of Georgia's citizens, at 2335 hours on 7 August, the President of Georgia issued an order to start a defensive operation with the following objectives:

(a) Protection of civilians in the Tskhinvali Region/South Ossetia;
(b) Neutralization of the firing positions from which fire against civilians, Georgian peacekeeping units and police originated;
(c) Halting of the movement of regular units of the Russian Federation through the Roki tunnel inside the Tskhinvali Region/ South Ossetia.

The Georgian allegations of a Russian invasion were supported, *inter alia*, by arguments of illegal entry into South Ossetia of a large amount of Russian troops and armour, prior to the commencement of the Georgian operation. According to the official Georgian position, the process of the build-up of Russian forces in South Ossetia started in early July 2008 and continued in the course of August, including troops and medical personal, tents, armoured vehicles, tanks, self-propelled artillery and artillery guns. This process allegedly intensified in the night of 6-7 August and in the late evening of 7 August. Georgian allegations concerning a Russian military build-up in South Ossetia prior to 8 August 2008 were denied by the Russian side. According to Russian official information, the first Russian units entered the territory of South Ossetia and the Russian air force and artillery started their attacks on Georgian targets at 1430 hours on 8 August, i.e. immediately after the decision on an intervention was made by the leadership of the Russian Federation.

Most analysts are not in a position to consider the Georgian claim concerning a large-scale Russian military incursion into South Ossetia before 8 August 2008 as substantiated. However, there are a number of reports and publications, including of Russian origin, indicating the provision by the Russian side of training and military equipment to South Ossetian and Abkhaz forces prior to the August 2008 conflict. They also indicated an influx of irregular forces from the territory of the Russian Federation to South Ossetia in early August as well as the presence of some Russian forces in South Ossetia, apart from the Russian PKF battalion, prior to 1430 hours on 8 August 2008. Also, it seems that the Russian air force started its operations against Georgian targets, including those outside South Ossetian administrative boundaries, already in the morning of 8 August, i.e. prior to the time given in the Russian official information.

In the course of the armed conflict, subsequently named "the five-day war" (7–12 August 2008), and its immediate aftermath, the Russian side justified its military intervention in Georgia by the intention to stop an allegedly ongoing genocide of the Ossetian population by the Georgian forces as well as to protect Russian citizens residing in South Ossetia and the Russian contingent of the Joint Peacekeeping Forces, deployed in South Ossetia in accordance with the Sochi Agreement of 1992. In this connection, the Russian side claimed that in the morning of 8 August 2008 two Russian peacekeepers were killed and five wounded by the Georgian attacks on the peacekeepers' premises in Tskhinvali, which casualties "gave the right to the leadership of the Russian Federation to take a decision on the introduction of troops into South Ossetia". The Georgians denied their deliberate attacks on the Russian peacekeepers, arguing that the Georgian troops entering Tskhinvali were fired at from the Russian peacekeepers` compounds and that they had to return fire. Taking into account the existing situation on the ground, casualties among the Russian PKF personnel were likely. There were no reports on clashes between the Georgian forces and the Russian peacekeepers outside Tskhinvali.

As far as the Russian accusations of genocide are concerned, they became less frequent in later months as the casualties among the Ossetian civilian population turned out to be much lower than initially claimed. Russian officials stated initially that about 2,000 civilians had been killed in South Ossetia by the Georgian forces and eventually the figure of overall civilian loses in the course of the August 2008 conflict was reduced to 162.

A number of foreign politicians and international analysts have criticised the Russian military operation in Georgia in August 2008. In particular, the crossing by the Russian forces of the administrative boundaries of South Ossetia and Abkhazia and their advance deep into Georgia's territory were qualified as an unjustified and disproportionate use of force. Moscow called its military actions in Georgia a "peace enforcement operation", while Tbilisi characterized it as an "aggression". The Russian side justified its military advances/attacks deep into the Georgian territories by operational needs on the eastern front (prevention of possible Georgian counter-attacks from the Gori region) and by the alleged danger of an imminent Georgian attack on Abkhazia in the west. Notwithstanding the legal aspects of the issue, the following comments are relevant:

(a) The Georgian armed forces were hardly ever able to conduct military operations on two fronts at the same time, i.e. South Ossetia and Abkhazia simultaneously. Certainly, such operations were even less feasible after the commencement of the large-scale Russian intervention in the region;

(b) In practical terms, there were no Georgian combat troops in western Georgia when the Russian operation there started, since the Georgian 2nd Infantry Brigade from Senaki and the 3rd Infantry Brigade from Kutaisi were deployed on the eastern front and were already largely defeated by the Russian forces by that time. The Georgian security forces in the upper Kodori Valley (2,800-strong according to the Russian official assessment and 500-800-strong according to independent assessments) with their fortified positions there seemed to have defensive tasks in August 2008. Taking into account the mountainous terrain, most military analysts also believe that any operation against the Abkhaz-controlled territories initiated from the upper Kodori Valley could have only a supportive role to a larger operation across the Inguri river and from the Black Sea, but such Georgian operations in August 2008 were not at all feasible.

Casualties and Losses

Killed, Wounded, Missing, POWs

According to official sources of the parties to the conflict, about 850 persons were killed in the course of the August armed conflict, and 2,300–3,000 were wounded. On the Georgian side, 160 Georgian military personnel were reportedly killed, 10 missing in action and 973 wounded. Also 11 Georgian policemen were killed, 3 were missing in action and 227 wounded. Among the Georgian civilian population, 228 persons were killed and 547 wounded. Among civilians, 2 local journalists and 1 foreign journalist were killed and 4 wounded.

The Russian casualties reportedly consisted of 67 military personnel killed, 118 missing in action and 283 wounded. According to the Georgian authorities, the Russian loses in the August war amounted to 400 servicemen killed.

The South Ossetian side presented a list of 365 South Ossetian residents killed in the fighting between 7 and 12 August 2008, but it is unclear how many civilians and servicemen were among them.

Reportedly 42 Georgian POWs were exchanged for 12 Russian POWs. As announced on end of August, the Russian armed forces sustained official losses of 71 dead, five POW (including two pilots) and 356 injured. However, these figures do not include losses to Ossetian forces and various volunteers (probably, up 150 died). Russian and Ossetian forces lost a few tanks and infantry combat vehicles. Losses to the Georgian side are not yet clear, but estimated at over 500 killed and up to 1,500 injured, with more than 100 POW (though the Russians have acknowledged taking only 15).

Georgia entirely lost its air and naval forces and air-defence systems. Reportedly, Russian forces captured and destroyed a significant portion of the Georgian army's arsenals. The Russians seized up to 150 units of Georgian heavy weaponry, including 65 T-72 tanks (including 44 in operational condition), 15 BMP armoured infantry fighting vehicles, a few dozen armoured personnel carriers, vehicles, guns and SAM systems. Russia seized a large quantity of automobiles and small arms, including American M4A3 carbines. Several Georgian tanks, armoured vehicles, and guns were completely destroyed in battle.

Refugees, IDPs

In his report of 15 May 2009, the Commissioner for Human Rights of the Council of Europe estimated that a total number of approximately 138,000 people were displaced in Georgia by the August 2008 conflict. Most of them returned to their homes. According to the Georgian Government estimates, however, about 38,000 IDPs did not return. The figure includes 19,000 IDPs from South Ossetia, nearly 2,000 from the upper Kodori Valley and over 11,000 from the areas adjacent to South Ossetia, who cannot return for reasons such as security or destruction of property, and some 5,000 IDPs from Akhalgori district.

According to Russian sources, about 2,000 refugees remained in North Ossetia out of estimated 30,000–35,000 who fled South Ossetia in August 2008.

In addition to the hardship of the new IDP population, in Georgia alone approximately 220,000 IDPs from territories of Abkhazia and South Ossetia have been living in protracted displacement for the last three decades as a consequence of the armed conflicts there in early 1990s.

Material Losses

According to an official Russian source, during the armed conflict on the territory of South Ossetia 655 houses were fully destroyed, and 2,139 damaged. The Georgian material losses were reportedly estimated at USD 1 billion by the Georgian Government.

Conclusion

Not only did Saakashvili's adventure end in total failure, but Georgia suffered a heavy military defeat. The new Georgian Army clearly did not live up to the ambitious hopes of its leaders. While Georgian servicemen displayed an adequate level of military training and perseverance at the tactical level, at higher levels of command the performance of the Georgian Army was less than satisfactory. The tenacity of the Georgians in South Ossetia can be explained by local and ethnic motivation, typical of interethnic conflicts. But once the ethnic motivation is gone, servicemen quickly lose morale. Typical Caucasus emotionality quickly turned into panic and demoralization when faced with a clearly superior enemy. The unit command of the Georgian Army was unable to maintain discipline,

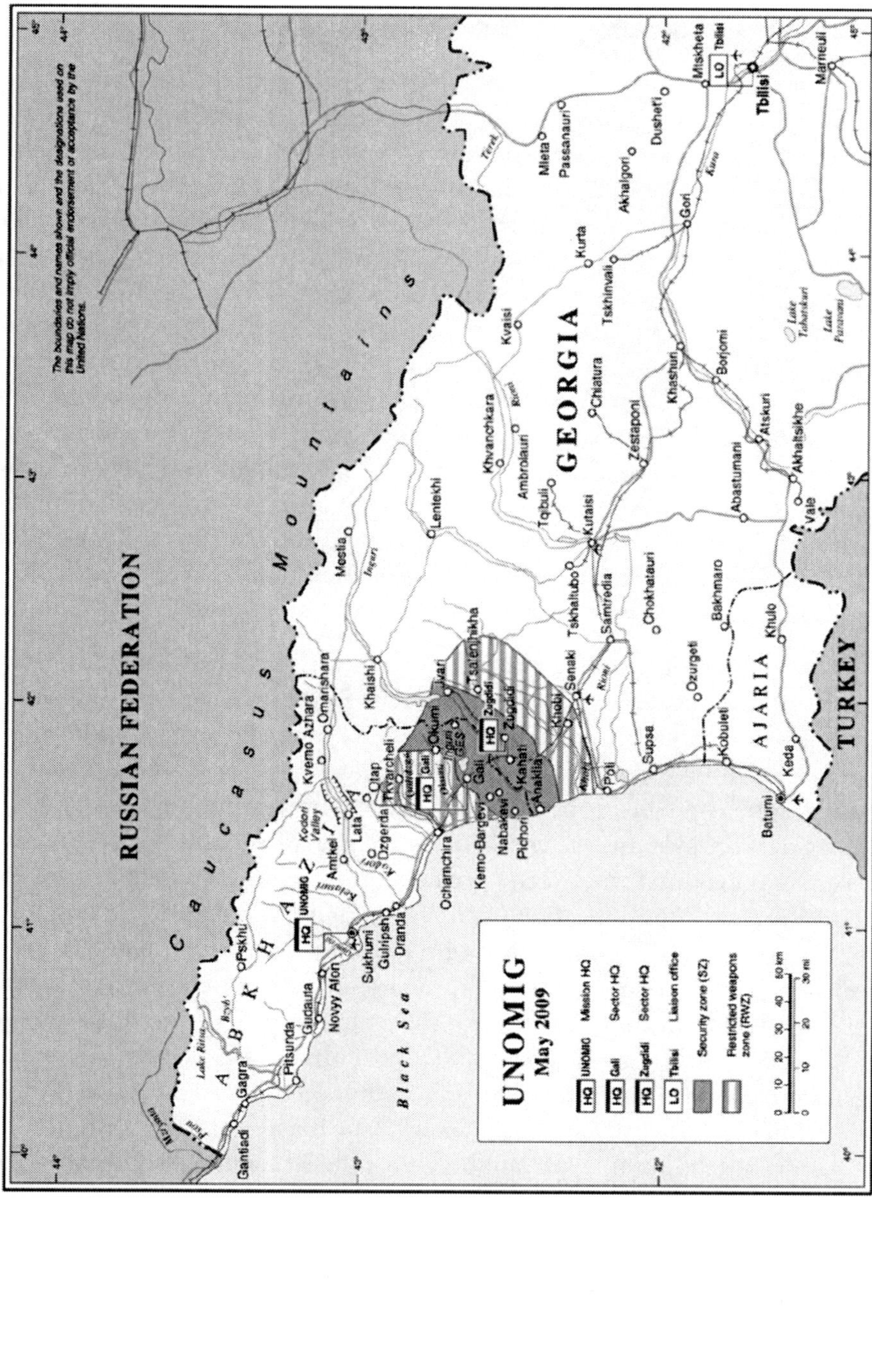

Map 13: UNOMIG Map – May 2009

and lost control when under stress and when its communications were attacked. A widespread sense of the futility of fighting against the powerful Russian Armed Forces may also have contributed to the collapse of morale.

A clear analogy can be drawn between the fate of the Georgian Army and the collapse of the armed forces of South Vietnam in 1975. Like the Georgian Army, the South Vietnamese Army was built, trained, according to the American model and was well-equipped. However, when they fought against the forces of North Vietnam, which combined local combat techniques with Soviet and Chinese organization and tactics, the outwardly impressive South Vietnamese forces proved to be much less effective than expected and fell apart after several defeats. In Georgia, as in South Vietnam, the imitation of Western methods of organization and force generation failed to match Western levels of military effectiveness. The creation of an effective national military machine requires long-term work on the part of the state, and an ability to take national characteristics into account. In and of themselves, "Western" standards of force generation do not guarantee superiority over "non-Western" armies. Those who believe in the *a priori* superiority of the West in military affairs have learned yet another unpleasant lesson from the Georgian conflict.

One should not, however, discount the strength of the Georgian Army, in spite of what occurred. On the whole, the Saakashvili regime developed Georgia's military capacity in a sensible manner, showing an admirable concern for the armed forces. From a technical point of view, the focus on acquiring heavy, self-propelled artillery, multiple-launch rocket systems and air-defence systems proved to be entirely justified, and it was precisely these weapons that inflicted the greatest damage on the Ossetian and the Russian forces. The acquisition of UAVs was similarly justified, along with night vision, modern communications, radio-technical reconnaissance and electronic warfare equipment. In these categories, the Georgian Army was perhaps even better equipped than Russian Army. The emphasis placed by Western military instructors on the individual training of soldiers also seems to have paid off. But, on the whole, the Georgian Army needed more time to ripen. Saakashvili's rash decision to throw this army into battle prematurely, leading to confrontation with the Russian Armed Forces, led to its fateful demise.

As for the performance of the Russian Armed Forces, the speed of their reaction was clearly unexpected, not only by the Georgians, but by the West as well, not to mention a few pessimistic observers within Russia itself. Three tactical battalion groups from level-ready units were introduced into South Ossetia in a matter of hours. Within three days, a powerful alignment of forces and equipment was assembled under extremely difficult natural conditions, capable of effective action and inflicting quick defeat on a numerically equivalent enemy. The Russian forces may have demonstrated insufficient coherence at the tactical level, but their superiority over the Georgian forces in terms of combat capability and effectiveness is indisputable. Russia has thus demonstrated that it has units and groups ready for combat operations, as well as an effective military command. The traditionally weak aspects of the Russian Army, such as night operations, reconnaissance, communications, and rear support, remained as before, though in view of the enemy's weakness these weak points did not play a significant role. There is no doubt that these issues will have to be examined as a first priority in view of the results of the campaign, as well as issues concerning counter-battery combat.

9

CYBER WARFARE ASPECTS

During the August 2008 war, Russian military forces, supported by cyber attacks, rapidly defeated opposing Georgian forces and seized territory later traded in exchange for Georgia's granting greater autonomy to pro-Russian governments in South Ossetia and Abkhazia.

Cyber power is the ability to exploit cyberspace to create advantages and influence events, and cyberspace is the interdependent and interconnected networks of electronics and the electromagnetic spectrum where information is created, stored, modified, exchanged, and exploited.

The 2008 Russia-Georgia war marks the only public incidence of cyber power integrated with traditional kinetic military operations. To date, however, little attention has been paid regarding how to integrate cyber power into conventional military operations. Rather, research has tended to focus on the independent use of cyber power for espionage and as a means of strategic attack to punish and/or compel a state to do one's will.

Cyber power has evolved similarly to early airpower and will likely make contributions to joint warfare now and into the foreseeable future, i.e. to conduct cyber reconnaissance, gain and maintain cyber superiority, and conduct cyber interdiction.

Estonia Cyber Attack 2007/2008

There were a series of cyber attacks Estonia that began 27 April 2007 and swamped websites of Estonian organizations, including the Estonian parliament, banks, ministries, newspapers and broadcasters, amid the country's row with Russia about the relocation of the *Bronze Soldier of Tallinn*, an elaborate Soviet-era grave marker, as well as war graves in Tallinn. Most of the attacks that had any influence on the general public were distributed denial of service (DDoS) type attacks ranging from single individuals using various low-tech methods like ping floods to expensive rentals of botnets usually used for spam distribution. Spamming of bigger news portals commentaries and defacements including that of the Estonian Reform Party website also occurred.

Some observers reckoned that the onslaught on Estonia was of a sophistication not seen before. The case is studied intensively by many countries and military planners as, at the time it occurred, it may have been the second-largest instance of state-sponsored cyber warfare, following *Titan Rain*. The Estonian Foreign Minister accused the Kremlin of direct involvement in the cyber attacks. However, on 6 September 2007 Estonia's defence minister admitted he had no evidence linking cyber attacks to Russian authorities. Russia called accusations of its involvement "unfounded," and neither NATO nor European Commission experts were able to find any proof of official Russian government participation.

Cyber Power in the 2008 Russia-Georgia War

The 2008 Russia-Georgia war helped focus attention on cyber power and its utility in war in a way that previous cyber power uses had not. That conflict's high profile caused it to become the subject of much study, so it is a rich source of information for analyzing the dynamics of cyber power in a joint military campaign.

On the surface, cyber power would not appear to be particularly useful in a war with Georgia. Only 7 percent of the citizens used the Internet daily, which might cause one to overlook Georgia's critical cyber vulnerability—more than half of 13 connections to the outside world via the Internet passed through Russia, and most of the Internet traffic to Web sites within Georgia was routed through Turkish or Azerbaijani Internet service providers, many of which were in turn routed through Russia. Georgia's Internet infrastructure suffered from a dearth of internal connections known as Internet exchange points. Consequently, a Georgian user's request for a Georgian Web site would likely be routed through Russia. As a result, pro-Russian forces could employ cyber power to affect a large percentage of Georgia's access to, and use of, the portion of cyberspace known as the Internet. Lacking control of the infrastructure required for external or internal Internet use, Georgia could neither disperse network traffic nor cut Internet connectivity from abroad as defensive measures without ceding the cyber advantages of Internet access if the state came under cyber attack.

The Russia-Georgia war officially started on 7 August 2008, after Georgian military forces responded to alleged Russian provocation with a massive artillery barrage on the town of Tskhinvali in South Ossetia. Moscow seized the opportunity to further solidify South Ossetia's and Abkhazia's independence from Georgia. It immediately deployed troops to South Ossetia and initiated aerial bombing raids on Georgian territory. It also deployed its navy to blockade the Georgian coast and landed marines on the coast of Abkhazia. After Russian mechanized forces and South Ossetian militia defeated the lightly armed Georgian military around Tskhinvali, they invaded Georgian territory uncontested. Georgia was not able to offer even a modicum of additional resistance because of the advantage cyber power created for the Russian forces.

The concentration and advanced preparation of cyber attacks in the war suggest that cyber superiority and cyber interdiction operations against Georgia were the product of cyber reconnaissance and intelligence preparation of cyberspace well in advance of the conflict. The cyber interdiction campaign against Georgia included both Web site defacements and DDoS attacks. The botnet assault was precise in scope and concentration, never exceeding 11 targets, and the same Web sites continued to be attacked throughout the war. Most of the cyber attacks were customized for Georgian targets with at least one Web site defacement prepared more than two years prior to the conflict. The cyber attacks were also sophisticated in their targeting.

Government and news media Web sites were struck first, helping sow confusion by hindering Georgians and their officials from determining what was actually happening and delaying any international response. In addition to Georgia's two major banks, cyber attacks targeted commercial entities that could have been used to communicate or help coordinate a response to Russian forces writ large and the cyber attack specifically. The concentration of botnet cyber attacks on 11 targets, the years-long cyber attack development, and the sophisticated appreciation of how Georgia would likely use the Internet to operationally respond all indicate that the cyber superiority the pro-Russian cyber forces held over Georgia was the product of excellent pre-conflict cyber reconnaissance and intelligence preparation of cyberspace.

To assert cyber superiority, pro-Russian cyber forces suppressed Georgia's cyber defences through diversion and direct attack. Educational institutions devoted to science, technology, and medicine were among the initial 11 botnet cyber targets struck. At the time, Computer Emergency Response Team Georgia (CERT Georgia) was chartered solely to provide cyber security for higher education institutions within the Georgian Research and Educational Networking Association (GRENA). By attacking educational institutions, cyber attackers focused CERT Georgia on its charter mission of protecting GRENA's cyberspace and away from responding to the larger national crisis. By attacking what the opponent must succour—the GRENA—pro-Russian cyber forces used CERT Georgia's natural response against it to divert and suppress the state's best cyber defences. Also, a popular Georgian Internet hacker forum was among the initial 11 cyber attack targets, impeding some of Georgia's more capable cyber experts from coordinating an organized response. Pro-Russian forces achieved cyber superiority to gain command of the air—through disruption, dislocation, and disorganization of the opposing force.

Pro-Russian cyber power maintained cyber superiority throughout the conflict, and as a result Georgia never mounted a successful cyber defence or cyber counterattack. For example, Georgia attempted to manoeuvre around the cyber attacks by filtering them out based on their origin (that is, their originating Internet protocol [IP] address). However, the cyber attackers' intelligence preparation allowed them to easily defeat this tactic. Cyber attackers routed their assault through foreign servers to mask their real IP addresses and created false IP addresses to spoof Georgia's cyber defence filters. Still, Georgia preserved the use of some government Web sites by moving them to US-based servers. Despite the failure of Georgia's cyber defence, it did attempt at least one major counterattack, but it also failed. Georgia posted cyber attack tools and instructions in Russian-language Internet forums to deceive pro-Russian cyber forces into unwittingly attacking Russian Web sites instead of Georgian sites. This Georgian counterattack appears to have had a negligible effect on the Russian Web sites targeted. Overall, the cyber defence efforts were too little too late.

With cyber superiority in hand, pro-Russian forces used cyber interdiction to choke Georgian communications by leveraging the generic properties of transportation networks. After the first wave of botnet cyber attacks on the initial 11 targets, an ad hoc cyber militia joined the assault. Cyber attack tools and a list of suggested targets were posted on Web sites for Russian supporters to launch their own strikes. The instructions were simple enough for people with limited computer skills to follow. This ad hoc cyber militia was so effective that it shut down or defaced 43 Web sites beyond the 11 original botnet targets. In total, 54 Georgian Web sites related to communications, finance, and government were struck, and Georgians could not access these sites for information or instructions. The cyber attacks thus denied Georgian forces access to a key portion of their information network, the Internet, reducing their overall information network's useful capacity.

As a result, the cyber attacks dislocated Georgian data flows, shunting data that normally would have travelled over the Internet into more traditional conduits such as telephone and radio communications. Additionally, land, sea, and air combat operations created a dramatic spike in the data volume and data rate demands on Georgia's overall information network. For example, in the town of Gori, government and news Web sites were disabled with DDoS attacks just prior to a Russian air attack, which would predictably drive information demands up. A subsequent spike in information communication demands combined with the dislocation of Internet communications to more traditional forms—such as cell and land phones—appear to have created a bottleneck.

Georgians were trying to transmit more data at a higher rate than the useful capacity of their information network could accommodate because a large proportion was being consumed by cyber attacks injecting extraneous data into the network. The cyber attacks effectively jammed Georgia's overall information network during the early stages of the war when rapid and organized action by Georgian defences, cyber and kinetic, could have had the greatest impact. Cyber interdiction created a Russian military advantage at the operational and tactical levels by hindering the Georgian military's ability to organize and conduct effective operations to thwart kinetic Russian military operations. Cyber interdiction created conditions such that Georgian forces could not help but to act mistakenly.

Furthermore, cyber interdiction likely multiplied the effectiveness of cyber attacks conducted to achieve cyber superiority by interfering with CERT Georgia's ability to gain situational awareness and orient itself to more effectively respond. Because all Georgian information communications were essentially jammed by the cyber interdiction attacks, CERT Georgia would have had an extremely difficult time simply gathering enough data to understand the cyber attacks' effects, much less mitigate them. By jamming all Georgian communications, cyber interdiction not only interrupted Georgia's traditional military response but also likely stifled Georgia's cyber defences, prolonging pro-Russian cyber superiority.

In the war, cyber attacks for cyber superiority and cyber interdiction were mutually reinforcing. The result was a situation where Georgian communications—its system of information supply—were gummed up, preventing timely delivery of data and commands to Georgian forces. The Georgians had to choose whether to yield superiority in decision speed or decision quality. The effect with either option was an unqualified Russian military advantage that Georgia could not overcome.

Implications

Cyber power today is critical to victory, but it probably cannot win wars alone if for no other reason than its inability to create much violence, although this shortcoming will likely fade in the future. Consequently, it is imperative to understand how best to employ cyber power in concert with land-, sea-, and air-power. Two principles to guide cyber power strategy at the operational level are: securing the enemy's freedom of action, and confronting him with a choice between at least two bad options. Cyber superiority satisfies the first principle, while cyber interdiction satisfies the second. The example of the 2008 Russia-Georgia war demonstrates the truth of these principles, but how should one go about gaining and maintaining cyber superiority and conducting cyber interdiction?

With securing cyber superiority being the first priority for military cyber power, initially focusing on neutralizing the adversary's capability to prohibitively interfere with friendly operations via cyberspace seems most logical. Consequently:

(a) The enemy's cyber attack, cyber reconnaissance, and cyber defence capabilities should be among the highest priority targets for cyber reconnaissance and all-source intelligence preparation of cyberspace, as well as among the highest priority targets for suppression or destruction (via cyber or kinetic attack) once hostilities begin.

(b) Cyber attacks directed at those portions of cyberspace irrelevant to the war but which an opponent must succour, such as the cyber attack on the GRENA that diverted CERT Georgia from the larger conflict, are valuable in that they focus the enemy's cyber defence forces away from decisive points.

(c) Cyber attacks should be used to interdict data required by enemy cyber repair, recovery, and quick reaction defence forces to disrupt the adversary's ability to effectively parry cyber strikes. Together, these actions should neutralize, divert, and disorganize an opponent's cyber power to gain and maintain cyber superiority.

Cyber interdiction targets are the next most important cyber objectives in joint military operations, first at the operational level and then the tactical and strategic levels. At the operational level, analogous to the rail marshalling yards that were the primary air interdiction targets of World War II, data marshalling yards (also known as data fusion centres) are the logical focal points for cyber interdiction. Data fusion centres are few in number compared to the combat systems they support (for example, fighters, tanks, and submarines), and they are the nodes where raw materials (data) are marshalled and transformed into information, a coherent understanding of the situation to be shared across military forces. Data fusion centres are centres of gravity in cyberspace because they are where orientation happens. Fusion centres at the operational level include enemy command and control nodes and intelligence, surveillance, and reconnaissance processing, exploitation, and dissemination nodes. By destroying, degrading, or neutralizing these data marshalling yards, cyber interdiction caps an adversary's operational effectiveness by limiting his ability to orient and concentrate effects in time and/or space. Regardless of an enemy's camouflage, concealment, and deception capability to foil kinetic strikes, data fusion centres must advertise their location in cyberspace (for example, IP address) to some degree to receive data and distribute information. Data fusion centres are almost certain to be vulnerable to cyber attack because their utility heavily depends on their connectivity—the power of a network grows exponentially with the number of users. If these nodes are not widely connected, they are irrelevant to the enemy's warfighting effort and can be ignored. Degrading data fusion capabilities creates greater uncertainty at the operational level and compels an adversary to rely more on his ability to adapt at the tactical level. In turn, an enemy's ability to adapt at the tactical level depends on the effectiveness of his tactical network and communication/data links. Thus, cyber interdiction at the operational level magnifies the significance and impact of cyber interdiction and electronic attacks to disrupt data links at the tactical level.

An opponent's tactical data links are the next most important cyber interdiction target set after data fusion centres. At the tactical level, each node (for example, fighter plane, platoon, and destroyer) on the tactical network has some level of data fusion capability, so information is rarely concentrated to the point that attacking those nodes in cyberspace will have widespread effects. However, tactical data is so perishable that even temporary disruptions to the data link network can have significant negative impacts on the ability of each tactical unit to derive information before the data are no longer a valid basis for decisions. As a result, disrupting tactical network data links, not disabling nodes, is the appropriate objective of cyber interdiction at the tactical level. Interrupting these links can cause brief but meaningful delays and misperceptions in an opponent's decision cycle to create or magnify a "first look-first shot-first kill" tactical advantage. By focusing military cyber power on gaining and maintaining cyber superiority and cyber interdiction at the operational and tactical levels, joint forces can maximize their capabilities and gain a significant decision advantage difficult for an opposing force to overcome.

Conclusion

Cyber power is critically important in joint warfare. Military cyberspace operations should have as their priority the attainment and maintenance of cyber superiority and cyber interdiction in support of kinetic operations with a focus on supporting the air campaign. Additionally, operations to gain and maintain cyber superiority should concentrate on neutralizing enemy cyber attack and cyber reconnaissance capabilities, followed by suppressing enemy cyber defences. Cyber interdiction attack operations should focus on the cyber equivalent of rail marshalling yards—data fusion centres—and tactical data links. Together, cyberspace superiority and cyber interdiction yield a powerful decision-making advantage in joint warfare, the cumulative effect of which is to compel an enemy to make mistakes that will likely prove fatal in due course.

10

RUSSIAN OPERATIONAL ART IN THE RUSSO-GEORGIAN WAR OF 2008

During the brief Russo-Georgian War of August 2008, the Russian military in a quick and decisive campaign overwhelmed Georgian forces to gain control of two breakaway republics, destroyed much of Georgia's armed forces on land and sea, and caused NATO to reconsider its offer of membership to Georgia.

Overview of Soviet and Russian Operational Art

For over a century, Russian and Soviet military thinkers have developed the operational art and have produced quality works on the subject. They have prepared for and practiced operational art in a series of wars under widely varying conditions over the last 80 years. These wars are rich in lessons of success and failure in operational art. The campaigns and major operations within these wars reveal both the Russian military's conception of operational art as well as their capacity to craft it to achieve strategic objectives at that time. The Russo-Georgian War of August 2008 is no exception. It reflects the current state of operational art within the armed forces of the Russian Federation. Furthermore, the reforms announced immediately following the war by the president and other senior leaders reflect the nation's and military's intentions to improve their capacity to effectively wage campaigns in the near future and present additional insights into some of Russia's strategic objectives.

In the 1920s and 1930s, Soviet thinkers developed the theory of operational art through an in-depth analysis of the lessons of World War I and the Russian Civil War. They discovered that the then extant theory of war that divided war into strategy and tactics no longer accurately reflected the conditions of war. The industrial and French revolutions had fundamentally changed how wars were fought. Countries now fielded massive, mobilized armies equipped with large quantities of high quality weapons that increased the lethality and range of battle. New machines and weapons such as the railroad, trucks, airplanes, and tanks provided new capabilities as well as extended the reach of forces engaged in operations. These Soviet thinkers posited that a new domain of warfare existed between strategy and tactics and they named it "operational art".

They defined operational art as:

> a component part of military art, concerned with the elaboration of the theory and practice of preparing and conducting front and army operations of the different services of the armed forces. Operational art is the connecting link between strategy and tactics. Proceeding from the demands of strategy, operational art determines the methods of preparing and conducting operations for the achievement of strategic goals and serves and the point of departure for tactics, which organizes the preparation and conduct of the combined arms battle in accordance with the operation's goals and tasks.

These Soviet thinkers understood that operational art should not be an abstract concept, but rather, could be the product of any number of historical, economic, political, cultural, geographic, and other factors existing in the society. It was important for these thinkers to develop a concept of operational art that was consistent with the Soviet Union's geostrategic situation, economic weakness, as well as its political aspirations. Amidst these ideas, two great debates developed on the appropriate way ahead for the Soviet Union. The first debate was between M.V. Tukhachesky and A.A. Svechin over which strategy best suited the Soviet Union, one of annihilation verses one of attrition. Tukhachevsky won this contest and then championed the second debate, the mechanization of a mass army as the means to conduct decisive operations in a total war.

For these Soviet thinkers the lessons of the First World War were quite stark. New concepts were needed to not only explain war, but also to enable the Soviets to win with their limited resources. To these thinkers, the fundamental operational challenge seemed to be how to build success from tactical victories. Recent wars indicated that a force could defeat the enemy in a battle, but could not exploit success before enemy reserves arrived, leaving the offensive to whither and stall at the tactical level short of decisive victory. The key problem to be solved was how to sustain the offensive until strategic objectives were achieved.

The Soviet thinkers, especially V. K. Triandafillov, developed concepts within operational art of successive or sequential operations, simultaneous operations, and later, deep operations. Each of these operational concepts was an attempt to avoid the challenges faced when attacks bogged down after penetrating an enemy's tactical defences. Additionally, to overcome this challenge the Soviets sought and developed new technologies to overcome tactical stalemates and attrition war. Armoured forces, airborne forces, long-range artillery, air power, and forward logistics played a decisive role in allowing penetrations and envelopments to continue into the operational depth of the enemy.

The experience of World War II codified these ideas into a cogent operational concept that dexterously wove together simultaneous and sequential front and multi-front operations to drive the German Army out of the depths of the Soviet Union and back to Berlin, leading to the defeat of Germany. The Second World War also had another significant impact on Soviet thought on operational art. The disastrous experience of the first two years of the war burned into the Soviet military culture the necessity of being prepared for theatre war in Europe. The Soviet Union geared their military theory, organization, and training towards a large-scale, high-intensity war in Europe. Other types of more limited or unconventional wars were largely ignored in terms of theory, doctrine, and the institutionalization of specialized organizations. This overbearing focus on theatre war in Europe would severely impede the development of appropriate concepts for operational art as well as appropriate force structure after the fall of the Soviet Union.

After the development of nuclear weapons, the Soviets briefly modified their theory of operational art to fit their view of the chaos of the nuclear battlefield. However, the desire to be capable of fighting without nuclear weapons was strong and from the 1960s through the 1980s the military sought ways to fight on a modern battlefield conventionally. The focus in conventional war centred on the initial period of war when Soviet theorists thought it was necessary to execute those missions that would decisively influence the course or outcome of the war. Theorists believed that it was important to achieve operational and strategic surprise through deception, higher tempos, and the development of operational manoeuvre groups that could operate deep in the enemy's rear, collapsing the enemy's ability to resist. These thinkers wanted to avoid the creation of mobilization signatures prior to a war that indicated an impending offensive. They sought ways to skip mobilization yet still generate the necessary force ratios for a successful operational offensive. Emphasis was placed on rapidly closing forces into a region at the start of a campaign or through the airlift of airborne forces into the combat zone. In the waning years of the Soviet Union, new concepts emerged, especially in response to the dramatic victory of US forces in the Gulf War of 1991. Ideas focused on tailoring forces to achieve maximum flexibility for specific missions, changing land only actions into air-land operations, establishing unified commands on a geographic basis, creating rapid deployment forces, and developing concepts for fighting on non-linear, non-contiguous battlefields.

When the Soviet Union dissolved in 1991, so did the Soviet military. Russia inherited a military that was in a terrible condition and struggled in the difficult economic and political trials of the 1990s. Although many of these new ideas of the 1980s remained alive, attempts at reform were hampered by the conditions of the time and by the convictions of the military's senior leadership, which still clung to the seminal lesson of World War II. The result was a military that was still focused on massive theatre war with large, conscription-based mechanized armies requiring a huge industrial base to support. The Russian government was unable to support such a strategy, leaving the military ill-prepared for its wars, which the operations in Chechnya depicted to the world.

After the breakup of the Soviet Union, several attempts were made at military reform, each ending in failure. Under Yeltsin, weak attempts were announced, but each failed due to a lack of political will and the poor economic condition of the country. With Putin's rise to power, small steps were attempted initially with little meaningful progress, especially after the military's performance in Chechnya. Yet the military remained wedded to its concepts of large-scale, high-intensity conflict. The war in

Georgia would help change that focus because it would give the Russian military a vision and an experience of what future war would look like.

Russia's Strategic Objectives in Georgia

Russia's strategic objectives in the war with Georgia can be divided into two categories:

(a) Those objectives that do not relate directly to planning a military campaign. With these objectives, Russia was signalling interests and intentions to other players in the international arena. Clearly, Russia wanted to send a strong signal to the West that Russia has returned to the world as powerful player, is capable of effectively acting in its periphery, and is willing and able to use military force to protect its interests. Russia desired to send the West and Georgia as well as the former Soviet states that the former Soviet states are within Russia's sphere of influence. NATO expansion into these states is not without risk. A strong message was sent to Ukraine as well as other former Soviet states that have ethnic Russian populations that Russia will take steps to protect them and could use them as a means for expanding its influence and control in the region.

(b) Those that pertain directly to operational art since they articulate military requirements for the war. The Russian military took these objectives and designed a campaign to achieve them. First, Russia wanted to gain control of the two breakaway regions of South Ossetia and Abkhazia.

Russia wanted to demonstrate the tenuous authority of the Georgian government as well as Georgia's economic dependence on Russian cooperation by shaking up and humbling Georgia's government through a war and demonstrating that Russia could interdict Georgia's economy at will. Third, Russia wanted to destroy Georgia's armed forces in order to eliminate the threat to the two breakaway regions. Last, one could argue that Russia wanted to punish Georgia for its overall Western orientation.

From the operations in August 2008, it is clear that the military analyzed these strategic goals and crafted an operational plan that would establish the military conditions necessary to support the strategic objectives. Additionally, it appears likely that the military was given some restrictions for the use of force so as not to overly provoke the international community. For example, although Russian armoured formations approached the capital of Georgia, Tbilisi, they did not attempt to enter the city. The Russian approach towards the capital and the anticipation of an assault caused great stress within the city as well as a flurry of diplomatic activity, indicating the utility of the military's position. Additionally, the Russian army did not seize control of the Baku-Tbilisi-Ceyhan or the Baku-Supsa pipelines, but rather, placed forces close enough to it to threaten them. Finally, in the face of international condemnation and pressure but after achieving their strategic objectives, Russian forces withdrew from Georgia proper and back into South Ossetia and Abkhazia with the exception of small buffer zones south of those regions.

The military planners probably thought that the following problems were key to achieve the strategic objectives. Gaining control of the two breakaway republics was a straightforward military task, if not without its challenges. To decisively influence the Georgian economy, military force would need to be applied along the coast of Abkhazia to control the ports and isolate the country. Additionally, key communications and transportation infrastructure would need to be cut to fracture the country, and the two pipelines threatened. Transit fees from this pipeline are a considerable portion of Georgia's economy. Chastening the regime was more problematic, especially without a direct assault on the capital. Essentially, the Russians would need to place their forces where they could threaten the capital and create a crisis, use information operations to discredit President Saakashvili, and employ cyber attack to put the government in disarray and create confusion. By creating a political crisis in the capital within the government and by demonstrating that the international community could not save Georgia, the Russians intended to achieve their goal of a humbled Georgian regime, less willing to pursue a Western orientation and more willing to acknowledge Russia's interest in its near abroad.

The Russian military campaign in Georgia was a skilful blend of classical Russian operational art melded with new Russian ideas and lessons learned from observing Western armies at war. The sequencing of multiple operations to achieve strategic objectives by keeping the enemy off balance and preventing his concentration is wholly within the classical concepts of Russian operational art. Additionally, the Russian operations demonstrate that they developed some new innovations of their own and by observing the US military in action. The war was a return to

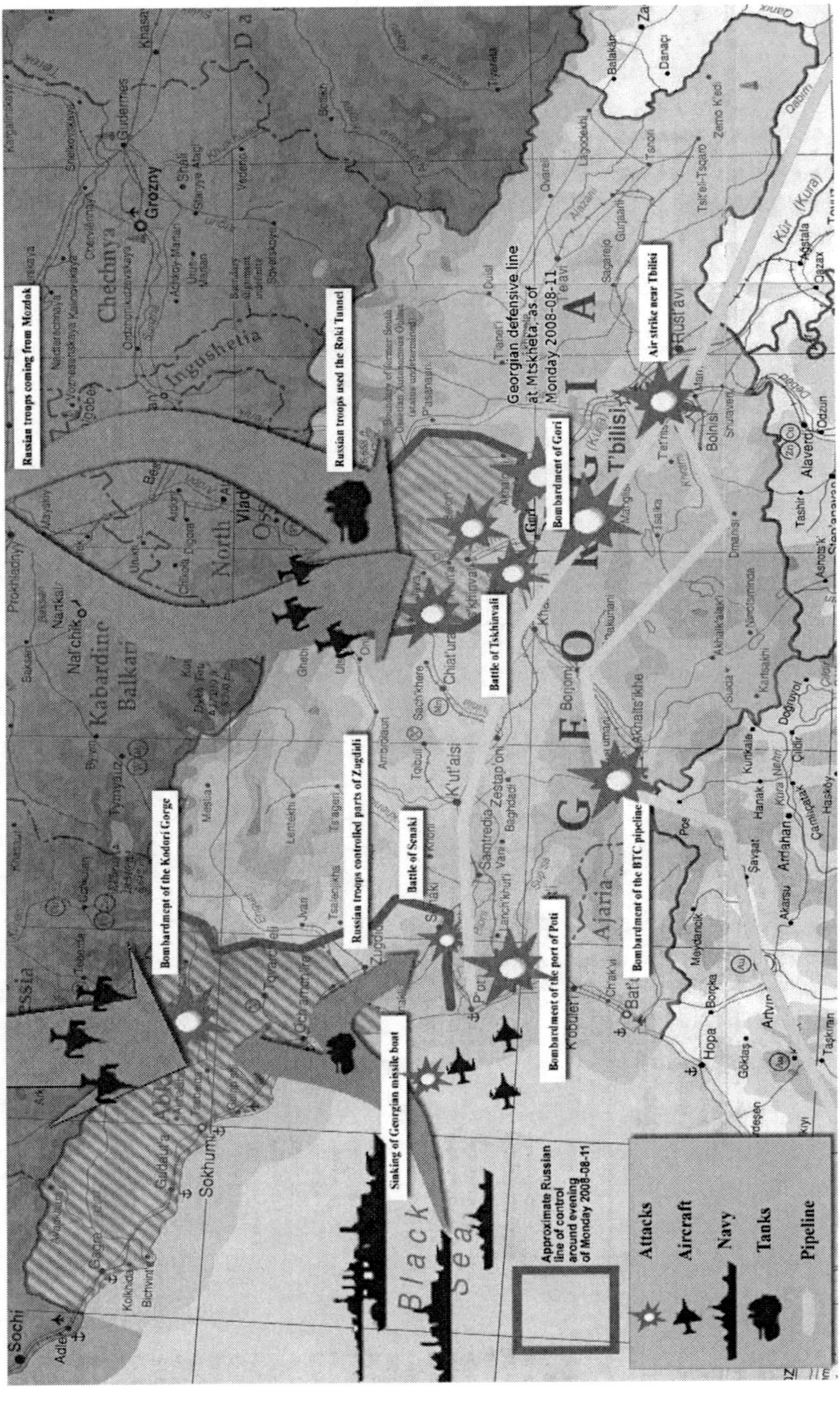

Map 14: Russian Military Actions in Georgia

conventional 20th century warfare with cyber attacks and information warfare integrated into the concept, both for operational as well as strategic purposes. The Russians were able to execute a combined arms offensive, integrating air, naval, paratrooper, and ground forces into one campaign under the control of a single headquarters.

Preparation

The rapidity of advance to objectives beyond the two breakaway regions, level of combined arms activities, accuracy of targeting, and scale of operational and logistical preparations strongly point to detailed preparation for the war. It is believed that the decision to initiate the war was made in April of 2008 during a crisis in Abkhazia when the Russian air force shot down two Georgian drones that were monitoring Russian peacekeeping forces. Thus, the Russian military had at least three months to prepare.

In addition to the preparations, the Russians leveraged other historical factors to their advantage. Soon after the Soviet Union broke apart in 1991, separatists wars broke out in various locations in the former Soviet states, Abkhazia and South Ossetia included. Russian forces participated in peacekeeping in those areas and ultimately ended up as members of the peacekeeping forces in both regions. Through these forces, Russia worked with local ethnic Russians to influence the region against Georgia and to build irregular security forces loyal to Russia. During the late spring and summer months probably after the decision to go to war, the Russians were able to add approximately an additional thousand troops to the peacekeeping forces in Abkhazia in April and May of 2008, obviously providing them with more forces already within their future area of operations who would know the area. These additional thousand were paratroopers—some of the best trained and prepared forces within the Russian military. These forces brought with them tanks, artillery, and air defence weapons, equipment not normally associated with the norms of peacekeeping missions.

The Russians even sent a battalion of railway troops into Abkhazia during the summer months to repair a disused railroad between Sukhumi, the capital of Abkhazia, and the coastal town of Ochamchire. Ostensibly there to improve the railroad infrastructure in advance of the 2012 winter games to take place at Sochi, the Russian troops entered Abkhazia without the permission of the Georgian government and worked from 30 May to 30 July, ending their work just a week prior to the invasion. The Russians staged an exercise in the North Caucasus from 15 July to 2 August that presented an opportunity for a military build-up adjacent to South Ossetia. Included in the exercise, "Kavkaz-2008" ("Caucuses 2008") were airborne formations from distant bases in Ivanovo, Pskov, and Novorossysk. The exercise focused on the relief of Russian peacekeepers in South Ossetia and offered an opportunity to organize their force, prepare their equipment, and rehearse the mission. The timing of the exercise, whether intentional or serendipitous, allowed some of the forces from distant places to remain in place for the invasion.

Another key factor in preparing the battlefield was the introduction or hiring of spies within South Ossetia and the Georgian government. It appears that this individual or group were able to determine that President Saakashvili intended to send the Georgian Army to seize Tskhinvali as well as all of South Ossetia. The time of the Georgian attack was probably also passed on. These key pieces of information gave the Russian military several opportunities. First, they were able to conduct final preparations and marshal their forces for movement. Secondly, the Russians probably alerted the South Ossetian irregular forces, enabling them to not only bolster their defence of Tskhinvali but also to secure the vital Roki Tunnel. Thirdly, it allowed the Russian 58th Army to move into Georgia and through the Roki Tunnel while the Georgian army was occupied in Tskhinvali, gaining operational momentum and allowing additional echelons to being moving. The 58th Army was able to generate approximately 70,000 troops into the operation in South Ossetia, roughly twice the size of Georgia's entire armed forces.

On 4 August, the 58th Army positioned about five battalions in vicinity of the Roki Tunnel. Additionally, the Russian government publicly admitted that Russian aircraft were overflying Georgia. This announcement gave Russia the cover to conduct more detailed reconnaissance over flights. Lastly, the Black Sea Fleet was made ready for operations along the coast of Georgia and Southern Russia.

Strategic Surprise

The Russians achieved surprise at all levels with this conventional operation, a goal that they had long desired in operational and strategic planning but had been unable to reach in previous conventional wars, most notably, in Afghanistan. When reviewing Russian press releases as well as actions from April through July 2008 with the perspective of hindsight, it seems that Russia was signalling its strategic intentions, if not its operational intentions. Lieutenant General Yurii Netkatchev, a former commander of the 58th Army, stated on 18 July during an interview about the exercise, "Kavkaz 2008", that the numbers of Russian troops participating in the exercise were greater than officially announced so as not to attract additional foreign observers. Additionally, he stated that when the exercises were complete, the additional forces may remain in the area for an unspecified period of time.

While world leaders were watching the Olympic Games in China, the Russians invaded Georgia and within five days, overwhelmed the Georgians through a series of operations designed to inflict shock on the Georgian government and military, making both unable to effectively or coherently respond to the offensive. Surprise was necessary not only for the ability to attain strategic and operational shock on the Georgian forces, but also for other important reasons. Strategic surprise along with an effective information operation allowed the Russian forces, using a high tempo of operations, to seize key objectives and areas before the world could react. At the operational and tactical levels, surprise enabled the Russians to seize and maintain control of the Roki Tunnel, which connects Russia with South Ossetia, before the Georgians could respond.

The Russians used strategic communications in an attempt to further the lifespan of their strategic surprise and create more time for operational manoeuvre before other countries, especially the United States and European countries could respond. Amidst the confusion of which country started the war, the Russian governments continued accusations in the international press about Georgian acts of genocide in South Ossetia and the Russian response to safeguard the population assisted in providing time for Russian ground units to attack deeper into South Ossetia.

Worth noting is that the Russians probably intentionally inflated the size of the Georgian attack on Tskhinvali on the 7 August, providing a rationale to the world for entering South Ossetia with a larger invasion force than necessary to secure the breakaway region. The larger force allowed Russia to move deeper into Georgia to achieve other strategic goals such as threatening the government in Tbilisi, rupturing the economy, and taking steps to further isolate Georgia from the outside world by cutting the east-west highway linking Tbilisi to the port of Poti as well as the railroad that carried oil from Azerbaijan to Poti.

To achieve strategic and operational surprise in their attack in South Ossetia, the Russians solved three problems in operational art. The first was the movement through the Roki Tunnel that connects South Ossetia with Russia. This critical transportation link was a single point of failure for Russian operations in South Ossetia since it sits on the only viable road between the two countries. If the Georgians could have blocked movement through it, the Russians formations would have faced enormous difficulties. Although the Russians have the largest amount of airborne forces in the world, to have staged an airborne assault deep to overcome this barrier may have proved too difficult logistically. Although there are airfields of sufficient size and capacity near Tbilisi, there are none in South Ossetia. Even if the airborne assault would have occurred, Russians typically want to open a ground line of communication to those forces as soon as possible for logistics reasons. The second problem solved was the throughput of forces from Vladikavkaz, the capital of North Ossetia in Russia, where operations began to Tskhinvali, the capital of South Ossetia and the site of the first major battle. The Russians were able to double the size of their force in Tskhinvali in 24 hours along this 167 kilometres long mountainous road. The third problem solved was the deployment of a large number of forces, mostly paratroopers, from throughout Russia in order to achieve sufficient force ratios for offensive operations without creating a large mobilization signature prior to initiating the war.

Initial Operation into South Ossetia

Russian forces entered South Ossetia through the Roki Tunnel on the night of 7-8 August as the Georgian forces were fighting an intense battle in Tskhinvali with Russian peacekeepers. Russian forces painstakingly infiltrated into Georgia prior to the invasion secured the tunnel prior to the arrival of the first echelon out of North Ossetia. Elite formations of paratroopers followed by Spetsnaz spearheaded the column that included the equivalent of a motorized rifle division (MRD) of the 58th Army and supporting artillery. The armoured battalions were actually combined arms battalions, consisting of armoured personnel carriers, tanks, and artillery. These organizations, formed in advance of the invasion and providing much greater tactical flexibility, reflected lessons learned in Afghanistan but later rejected as a standing organization by the Soviets and Russians. The column linked up with South Ossetian irregulars and continued to Tskhinvali, the capital of South Ossetia. In three days of fighting, the Russians successfully integrated the different capabilities of these forces as well as a battalion of Chechens, the "Vostok" battalion, to seize the city. As Russian armoured forces moved further into Georgia towards the capital Tbilisi, South Ossetian irregulars and the "Vostok" Battalion, a unit of Chechen nationals in Russia's Main Intelligence Directorate (GRU), remained in Tskhinvali to "mop up."

Operation into Abkhazia

On the following day, 9 August, the Russians began massing forces along the border with Abkhazia in preparation for a combined arms operation conducted between the army, air force, and navy and including irregular forces from Abkhazia. Abkhazian authorities had reported Georgian forces moving into the peacekeeping zone. This violation gave Russia the pretext for manoeuvring into Abkhazia. The air force attacked several targets in Abkhazia including the Kodori Gorge, where aircraft supported the attacks of Abkhazian irregular forces against Georgian troops. The railway between Tbilisi and Zugdidi in western Georgia was bombed and destroyed, assisting in isolating western Georgia and Abkhazia from reinforcements from the capital. The Black Sea Fleet sortied from its base in the Crimea towards the coast of Abkhazia.

On 10 August, Russian forces moved from Southern Russia into Abkhazia opening a second front along the coast of the Black Sea. The Black Sea fleet, consisting of 15 to 16 warships as well as three landing craft, arrived off the coast of Abkhazia and landed approximately 4,000 paratroopers at Ochamchire. These paratroopers linked up with their heavy equipment which had been transported down the recently repaired railroad from Russia and participated in the offensive in the Kodori Gorge – a remarkable act of operational manoeuvre. Forward moving Russian armoured columns linked up with Russian peacekeeper troops previously in the region as well as Abkhazian irregular forces to secure the province. Additional peacekeeper reinforcements were air landed in Sukhumi as well, helping swell the ratio of forces well to Russia's advantage with a dominating force of 9,000 men and 350 armoured vehicles.

The operation in Abkhazia has some classic characteristics of deep battle. First, the Russians inserted the forces deep into Abkhazia. In doing so, they appear to have cut the fastest route between the Kodori Gorge in Abkhazia and Georgia itself. The operational manoeuvre that landed paratroopers at Ochamchire not only had the advantage of dislocating any potential enemy north of Ochamchire, to include the Kodori Gorge, the area of severest fighting in the past, the move also enabled Russian forces to bypass the UN Peacekeeping headquarters located at Sukhumi, thus avoiding observation, and possibly, reporting to Tbilisi of the size and nature of the operation.

Moving the equipment down by rail at night further inhibited reporting. Lastly, the use of paratroopers instead of marines had one distinct advantage when it comes to remaining unobserved. The paratroopers that were part of the peacekeeping force wore the same uniforms as the paratroopers that were landed, making it extremely difficult for the UN Peacekeepers to differentiate between the two groups.

Overall, when one combines the operation in Abkhazia with the one in South Ossetia, one sees the practice of classic Soviet operational art: attacking with operations from multiple directions so that the enemy is faced with overwhelming challenges on where to concentrate its effort. The operation met little resistance as the Georgian Army was committed between South Ossetia and the capital, Tbilisi. Having successfully achieved their first strategic objective by securing the two breakaway provinces with their initial, nearly simultaneous operations on a non-contiguous front, the Russians now were poised to conduct sequential operations to attack deeper into Georgia to achieve other strategic objectives.

Follow-on Offensives into Georgia

On 11 August, the Russians attacked along two axes into Georgia proper (beyond the two dispute regions of South Ossetia and Abkhazia). Russian forces attacked out of South Ossetia towards the town of Gori with three operational goals. The first goal was to move towards Tbilisi to threaten the capital and the government. This operation directly supported the strategic goal of overthrowing Saakashvili. The second goal was to cut the East-West running highway and railway, denying the Georgian military forces in the East and West from supporting one another and also cutting the Western regions of Georgia off from the capital, Tbilisi. By cutting these means of communication and trade, Russia gained a strong position to affect Georgia's economy. The third goal was to create operational depth around Tskhinvali in order to protect that city from indirect fire attacks and the threat of ground attack by Georgian forces, allowing more effective control not only in the capital of South Ossetia, but the entire breakaway region.

In the West, Russian forces executed a simultaneous operation along the Black Sea coast. Armoured forces moved from Abkhazia into Georgia proper towards Senaki with related operational objectives, meeting little resistance. The first objective was to cut the East-West highway and railroad connecting the Western region to the capital (this was the second location for cutting these vital pieces of infrastructure). The second objective was to seize and control the Georgian Black Sea port of Poti, Georgia's largest port, giving Russia control not only of Georgian exports and imports, but also denying any other country the potential to reinforce. Thirdly, the Russian army was now positioned within an hour of the key, western Georgian city of Samtredia, which sits astride the Baku-Tbilisi-Supsa oil pipeline. Additionally, this city is where roads diverge to Georgia's other key ports, Supsa and Batumi. If Russia controlled Samtredia, it would essentially establish a blockade of the country from the land. The army was in a great position not only to further disrupt Georgia's economy, but also to send a strong signal to the West that Russia can control Caspian Sea basin energy routes. Lastly, the move also provided Russia with operational depth for securing Abkhazia.

Combined Arms

Combined arms operations, a classical Russian concept of operational art, were very evident in the campaign. The campaign included armoured forces, airborne forces, attack, bomber, and reconnaissance aircraft, irregular forces, and the Navy. Each played a role that, when combined, helped achieve the operational end-state necessary for the strategic goals. One may even be able to add cyber warfare to this concept. The Russian Air Force was an integral part of the campaign plan. Aircraft conducted reconnaissance, close air support, air superiority missions, and interdiction missions to spoil Georgia's ability to respond militarily. With the initial phase of operations in South Ossetia and Abkhazia, Russian aircraft attacked airfields east and south of Tbilisi, command and control facilities, and military bases to achieve depth to the operation, attack follow-on

Map 15: Russian Invasion Routes and Forces

echelons, and assist in isolating the battlefield. The radar at the international airport in Tbilisi was attacked to reduce Georgia's ability to track Russian aircraft. Additionally, attacks on the air infrastructure as well as the port of Poti on the first day of the war assisted in making Georgia more difficult to access by a country wishing to intervene. The Russian air force's counter air operations forced the Georgians to disassemble their aircraft and hide them, not attempting to wrest control of the air from the Russians. Transport aircraft assisted in moving a large number of forces, equipment, and supplies from around Russia into the zone of military action, enabling Russia to achieve strategic and operational surprise and also developing overwhelming combat power against the Georgians.

Russia's Black Sea Fleet significantly contributed to the mission, providing operational manoeuvre and fires, establishing a blockade, landing paratroopers at Ochamchire, and fighting a short naval battle. A guided missile cruiser fired into the Kodori Gorge during fighting there, providing operational fires. Also on 10 August, the navy fought a short battle with four Georgian vessels, sinking one. The fleet established a blockade or at least remained in the waters, deterring reinforcement of men or equipment from third-party countries into Georgia during the conflict.

Cyber Warfare

The newest Russian innovation in operational art demonstrated in this campaign was the inclusion of cyber attack. Indeed, one can argue that this began not on the ground with armoured formations or in the air with bombers, but rather, in cyberspace with distributed denial of service attacks. Although cyber attacks are difficult to attribute and the Russian government denied involvement in the attacks, the crescendo of attacks that began on 7 August against the Georgian government leaves little doubt to some experts that the cyber attacks were of Russian origin.

Although the cyber attackers themselves may not have been members of the military, the Russian government has demonstrated in the past some ability to "herd its domestic hackers as well as bringing its own resources to bear in these scenarios". Some of the attacks appear to have originated from within the Russian government while others originated in a Russian hacker network. In one expert's opinion, the cyber attacks in Georgia "were too successful to have materialized independent of one another." For example, the means to attack "proliferated on Russian websites in a user-friendly form" for anyone desiring to participate. One expert stated that he found 'copies of the attack script' posted in the reader comments section at the bottom of virtually every story in the Russian media that covered the Georgian conflict, complete with instruction on how the script could be used to attack a specific list of Web sites.

During the ground war, distributed denial of service (DDOS) attacks overwhelmed the Georgian government's websites, causing them to crash. The attacks, many from hundreds of thousands of "zombie" computers or "bots" unknowingly infected with viruses, generated hundreds of millions of requests, attacking websites of the Georgian government, president, parliament, news agencies, and banks. Although attacks began prior to the 7th of August, the intensity of attacks during the initial phases and even throughout the campaign was a significant challenge for the Georgian government.

It is important to recognize that the Russians not only used cyber attack against an opponent as they did with Estonia the preceding year, but they also appear to have attempted to integrate cyber attack with manoeuvre and deep fires. Russian aircraft attacked telecommunications infrastructure during the war, further inhibiting the ability of the Georgian government to communicate and get its message out. It also should be noted that although the cyber attacks were successful from the perspective of intruding into the information systems of the Georgian government, it is not clear that they had any impact on Georgia's ability to fight. The pictures of Hitler that were placed on Saakashvili's website may have been embarrassing, but these attacks as well as the denial of service attacks did not have any known operational or strategic impacts on Georgia. Control was not gained over the Georgian military or the population through these actions. Also, although the level of integration between cyber and conventional operations is not clear, it appears that the Russians may have attempted to link the two together to produce effects. It is also clear that if the Russians *did* plan the integration of cyber attack with conventional warfare, they have gained some valuable experience as well despite the shortcomings.

Information

The Russians did not achieve success in their information campaign, although the operations in Georgia reflect some new aspects of Russian thinking. Strategically, Russia was unable to convince the world, mainly the West, that its operations were justified and purely within the realm of peacekeeping. Russia was pilloried by the international community for its actions as well as its recognition of the two breakaway republics. At home, the Russian government was very successful in convincing its population of the rightfulness of the war, gaining large amounts of approval and little dissent.

Operationally the Russian military attempted a few new steps in support of an information campaign. Russian journalists were brought along to share with domestic and international audiences the progress of Russian troops in protecting Russian citizens and of propagandizing Georgian atrocities. The Russians were able to use television footage to achieve some psychological affect as well with the local population in the breakaway regions. The Russians were able to show on local television footage of their advancing forces liberating the local ethnic Russian population. Georgia, on the other hand, was unable to show any footage of its troops in action. The Russian government also used a military spokesman in daily television interviews to provide information and answer questions on the conduct of the campaign, a first for Russia. Altogether, Russian information operations were mildly successful, but the attempts made demonstrate a Russian military that is aware of the need to conduct operations in the information domain.

Command and Control

During the campaign, all of Russian forces involved in operations within Georgia were under the command of a single headquarters, the North-Caucasus Military District, located in Vladikavkaz, Russia. From reports, it appears that the ground, air, naval, and airborne as well as Ministry of Interior forces were all organized into one grouping and received their direction from the local, regional headquarters, under the command of an army general. The forces were specifically tailored for the mission assigned to them – a quick campaign in Georgia with limited aims.

A unified command is a major step in Russian operational thought that was discussed in the 1980s in the waning years of the Soviet Union, but only recently experimented with and put into effect. The Soviet command structure that the Russian Federation inherited focused on massive, combined arms formations optimized for large-scale, prolonged wars. Such organizations not only did not meet the demands of the new geopolitical environment Russia found itself in, but they also did not reflect the extant capabilities of the Russian army after 1991, which was largely incapable to fighting such operations. In recent years, a requirement for a more localized, tailored command and control system maintained in peacetime as well as wartime emerged. This system also included troops from other ministries or government agencies, so as to better defend Russian interests, especially against terrorist attacks. The military has conducted experiments with these regional groupings of forces to include using rapid reaction forces to quickly deploy and begin cooperating with local law-enforcement agencies to counter terrorist threats.

Consolidation and Achievement of Strategic Objectives

On 12 August 2008, President Dmitry Medvedev accepted a peace plan brokered by French President, Nicolas Sarkozy and announced a halt to the fighting in Georgia. The Russian military had established such a strong position in Georgia that the Russian government was able to call the shots on when to end the war, despite international political pressure that grew with each day since the initiation. In five days of fighting, Russian forces were 65 kilometres from the Georgian capital and had split the country into three parts. The Georgian army was defeated and the air force and navy destroyed. Russia had occupied, destroyed, or blockaded most of Georgia's Black Sea ports and the army was postured along the coast to prevent, or at least dissuade, intervention from a third country in the war. Reinforcements had not come from outside the country, other than the redeployment of a Georgian Brigade from Iraq too late to participate in the fighting.

Russian forces controlled much of "Georgia's most critical economic and transportation junctions" to include the east-west highway and railroad, the only land links that unite the country. Air links were blocked as well through the domination of the skies by Russian jets. In the west, Russian forces controlled the approaches to the port of Poti, the Senaki airfield, and the Kulevi oil export terminal, which is owned by Azerbaijan. Russia's Black Sea Fleet patrolled off the coast, essentially an undeclared blockade, controlled both from the land as well as the sea. The port of Poti was incapacitated through aerial bombing during the fighting, sinking three coast guard cutters in the harbour, and the destruction of a critical railroad bridge.

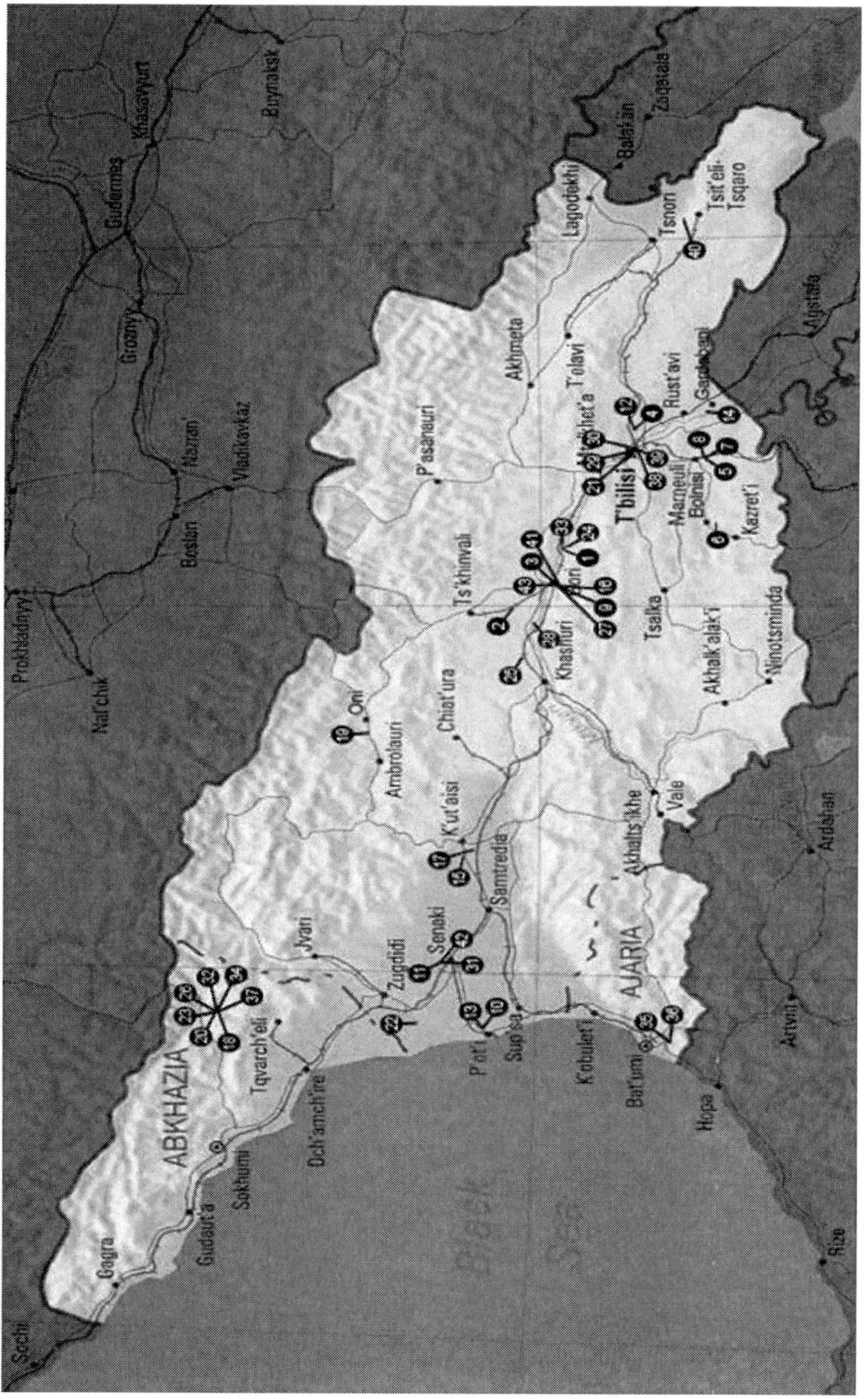

Map 16: Russian Bombing Targets

Russian forces and indigenous irregulars controlled South Ossetia and Abkhazia and were reportedly conducting ethnic cleansing to remove Georgians from the territories. Soldiers and irregular forces pillaged and terrorized the local Georgian populations. Cumulatively, this position attained by the Russian military enabled Moscow to threaten to dismember Georgia as a means to force a change of government in Tbilisi.

After the Georgian Army stopped resisting and after Russian President, Dmitrii Medvedev, announced the end of operations, Russian forces continued to implement their strategic goal of the destruction of the military potential of Georgia. The Russians were able to do this because of their dominating position within Georgia. Russian forces damaged or destroyed most of Georgia's military bases. Russian forces confiscated and transported back to Russia over 150 large pieces of equipment, to include tanks, air defence weapons, small arms, and captured American-made HMMWVs. Additionally, the Russians destroyed fifteen vessels of the Georgian navy and its coastal defence command point. The total materiel loss suffered by the Georgian forces was considered to be $250 million.

The military had achieved all of its strategic objectives. Georgia and its president had been chastened in their western ambitions and agenda. The Russians understood that a prolonged occupation of Georgia proper would probably result in a guerrilla war. Having experienced such a war in Chechnya, the Russians did not want to face one here. Facing greater international pressure and seeing no further strategic gains to be obtained by keeping Russian troops on Georgian soil, the Russians began withdrawing on 22 August. Buffer zones were established between the two breakaway regions southward into Georgia up to 40 kilometres. Additionally, Russian peacekeeping forces within the two regions were strengthened to solidify Russian control after the war. The strength of the Russian military's positions within South Ossetia and Abkhazia contributed directly to the political conditions necessary for President Medvedev to recognize the two breakaway republics as independent states on 26 August 2008.

Failures and Shortcoming of the War

One should not think that the Russian campaign in Georgia was perfect and without blemishes. This is far from the truth – and the Russian military and government recognized this as well shortly after the war in announcing major military reforms. Noteworthy in both the Russian as well as foreign press were the problems with soldier discipline during the war. Soldiers rode exposed on top of armoured vehicles instead of protected within. Soldiers looted and terrorized the local Georgian population. And there were reports of public drunkenness.

Significant shortfalls were identified during the fighting in the ability of weapons and equipment to perform to desired expectations, many of these shortfalls are traditional areas of weakness in the Russian army. Russian forces proved incapable of suppressing Georgian artillery in the fight for Tskhinvali. Units went into battle without their reactive armour. Some tanks that appeared on TV to be covered with such armour, actually had empty tiles installed. The quality of as well insufficient quantity of night vision goggles led to an avoidance of night operations, providing opportunities to the Georgians to break contact under the cover of darkness. Operations lacked cohesion due to an inadequate amount of Global Satellite Navigation Systems (GLONASS) to provide situational awareness. Effective command and control was impeded by poorly functioning radios that led to challenges in the close coordination of tank and infantry forces resulting in incidents of fratricide. At times, Russian soldiers used their cell phones to communicate and a Russian general allegedly once used the satellite phone of a Pravda correspondent. The commander of the 58th Army, General Anatoly Khrulev, was wounded when his column ended up in an ambush vicinity of Tskhinvali, apparently unaware of the enemy in the vicinity.

Air forces and air ground integration also had their deficiencies. Electronic warfare systems performed poorly and were unable to effectively suppress Georgian air defence systems leading to the loss of six aircraft. The tactical forces failed to sufficiently use rotary and fixed wing aircraft and even when they did, manoeuvre units had challenges effectively integrating fixed and rotary wing aircraft into the tactical fights. A lack of experts in the air force who knew how to integrate rotary wing aviation, which had been removed from the ground forces and placed in the air force, into ground operations led to a lack of coordinated action between the two. Although the Russians had introduced air controllers for close air support into the ground forces, there were insufficient numbers to be everywhere needed, leading to poor air-ground coordination. A lack of precision munitions was evident in addition to a lack of unmanned aerial vehicles, leaving commanders unable to neither find the enemy nor attack it with accuracy. Possibly this lack of reconnaissance and precision bombs contributed to the large amounts of firepower employed on Tskhinvali during the battle there.

One could also note that despite the participation of air assault, airmobile, and airborne units, the 58th Army did not attempt a vertical envelopment to gain operational depth, seize key transportation nodes in advance of attacking forces, or to dislocate Georgian forces. One wonders if these forces were not employed in this manner due to the challenges of the terrain, inadequacies in command, control and communication systems, readiness levels of the airmobile and air assault units, the requirements for close and detailed coordination between services, or a matter of training proficiency.

Conclusion

The Russian military overwhelmed a third-rate power by placing roughly four times as many soldiers in the combat zone than in the entire Georgian army. The Georgian military made some key mistakes, not the least of which was the failure to block the Russian advance through the strategic choke point of the Roki Tunnel. If the Georgians had blocked the tunnel, it is interesting to speculate whether the Russians had a feasible alternative plan that would achieve in a timely manner the same strategic objectives before international condemnation increased to such a level that Russia would have chosen to cease using its military to achieve its goals. Additionally, assertions that the Georgian army should have fought better because it had American equipment and trainers miss the point of that assistance. The Americans, tragically for Georgia, were training the Georgian military for a different type of war, a counter-insurgency in Iraq which Georgia was participating in with one brigade. The Georgian military lost its focus on its vital task, to secure itself from foreign aggression and was unable to defend itself against a looming, resurgent adversary. The Georgian leadership underestimated the threat and possibly overestimated the assistance that the United States or NATO would provide if a conflict with Russia were to break out.

Most Western analysts see the war as a breakdown of Russian policy or a harbinger of Russia's further withdrawal from accepted norms of international behaviour. The strategic costs of the war far outweigh the gains that were achieved. However, there is another way to look at this war – at the operational-strategic level. In this view, it appears that Russia was successful. The armed forces, given a limited aim and clear, strategic tasks, were able to craft a campaign plan that integrated combined arms to achieve all of the strategic objectives with minimal cost in life and equipment. Moreover, they achieved these goals in five days, something they were unable to do in either war in Chechnya. The Russian military proved to be an effective means of national power in assisting its government in achieving its geopolitical goals in the near abroad.

The Russian military appears to be on a path to becoming even more operationally viable as a means of national power. It is taking valuable lessons learned in operational art from its Soviet past and slowly sloughing off the entrenched beliefs that hinder optimization for its present geopolitical situation. It is observing other militaries and trying to blend its operational thought and capability into an emerging, Russian way of waging war that is effective in achieving tasks proportionate with its geostrategic aims. And it is experimenting with new capabilities in operational art, mainly cyberwar, to grow its capacity and capability. This emerging combination of cyber and conventional war could be something for which most countries of the world are unprepared. As Moscow continues to aspire to the role of a great power, it will be interesting to observe how Russia further develops its version of operational art.

11

COMMENTS AND OBSERVATIONS

Analysis of the Russia-Georgia War of 2008

On 7 August 2008, war broke out between Georgia and Russia in response to the secession of the breakaway regions of Abkhazia and South Ossetia. The conflict, which is called the *Five Day War*, cost the lives of over 850 persons, resulted in a massive exodus of civilians, and made once-thriving villages and towns into battlegrounds for the two warring nations. The Russian military moved into the separatist regions in what Moscow claimed was an act of duty to protect the Russian citizens who were persecuted by the Georgian military. The Russians claimed they were only protecting the freedoms and rights of the over 35,000 Russian citizens in Ossetia. However, Georgia claimed that it was protecting its territorial districts in a time of a national crisis. Georgia is seeking to unify its nation despite strong resistance from the separatist regions while Russia seeks to re-establish itself as the regional hegemon in the Caucasus.

Could this war have been avoided? If Saakashvili's optimism could have been checked, then war could have been avoided. In this connection, the role of the US needs more scrutiny. The US stood firm in support of Saakashvili in spite of the fact that his regime became increasingly authoritarian. The US military assistance to Tbilisi continued at a time when its leaders were employing increasingly bellicose rhetoric towards the breakaway regions. Georgia's unilateral 'peace plans' also got unconditional US support although Saakashvili did little to promote peace and reconciliation. And most surprisingly, the US did nothing to stop

Saakashvili from starting a military strike against South Ossetia that ultimately dragged Russia into the war.

From a larger perspective, the cause of the August war is also a product of the type of regimes that both Russia and Georgia have. The root cause of the Georgia-Russia war of August 2008 can, therefore, be attributed to the nature of their democracies. Nevertheless, the causes of the war were complex and multi-faceted. From Russia's perspective, the war was necessary, not only to show that it is capable to act as a great power, but also to advance its geostrategic interests. From Georgia's perspective, the war failed to bring about the expected outcome that Saakashvili wished for. Domestic politics, especially the nationalist rhetoric of the leaders and growing militarism in both Russia and Georgia played a crucial role in the decision of a military solution to the conflict. The failure of the Western nations, particularly the US, in deescalating the tension also contributed to the outbreak of this limited war with far-reaching consequences for the security and stability of the region.

After the conflict was over, the Council of the EU established an Independent International Fact-Finding Mission on the Conflict in Georgia (IIFFMCG) on 2 December 2008. It was the first time in the history of the EU that it collaborated to arbitrate and investigate the causes of an inter-regional armed conflict. Swiss diplomat and peacekeeper Heidi Tagliavini was appointed as the head of the IIFFMCG to investigate the origins and the course of the conflict in Georgia, including with regard to international law, humanitarian law and human rights, and the accusations made in that context. Although the IIFFMCG was the most extensive and comprehensive investigation on the conflict in Georgia, its report cannot claim veracity or completeness in an absolute sense. It incorporates what was available to it at the time of writing.

Two international legal issues related to the conflict were the self-determination of the Abkhazians and South Ossetians as well as their right to unilateral secession from the Republic of Georgia. The South Ossetians and the Abkhazians envisaged their right to self-determination as the legal foundation for their pursuit of sovereignty and self-governance of the two regions. International law does not recognize the right to form new states or declare independence for reasons of self-determination or desired emancipation—outside of the colonial context in developing nations as a response to apartheid. No instance of attempted secession other than unprecedented circumstances such as genocide had ever found acceptance in the international community.

Direct Consequences of the War

The war officially ended on 12 August 2008, when Moscow and Tbilisi agreed to a mutual cease-fire. The preliminary ceasefire agreement took place on the eve of 12 August, signed by Russian President Dmitry Medvedev, Georgian President Mikheil Saakashvili, and French President Nicolas Sarkozy, who was acting on behalf of the EU. Despite the six-point ceasefire plan, Russian and South Ossetian forces continued their military advances for many more days after the Georgians had agreed to halt their military action. The coalition of Russians and South Ossetians occupied additional territories, including the Akhalgori district. A partial withdrawal of Russian troops did not occur until 22 August, while some troops did not withdraw until after an implementation agreement was reached on 8 September, and the remaining forces did not leave until the month of October.

The greatest effect of the Russian invasion has been economic for both sides. Also, the IIFFMCG confirmed that both nations violated international law and human rights. Nstances were:

(a) Despite being warned and advised against shelling Tskhinvali, Georgia went ahead and started the conflict;
(b) Russian and South Ossetian persistent military advance deep into Georgian territory, and their excessive use of disproportionate force, was in violation of international law.
(c) Georgia triggered an unnecessary war by shelling Tskhinvali and shooting at Russian peacekeepers, and
(d) Russia responded with a disproportionate, unjustified measure of military force in clear violation of international law.

The August war between Russia and Georgia is a watershed event in the post-Soviet history of the Eurasia. The war marked a significant departure from the foreign policy the Russian Federation had pursued since the collapse of the Soviet Union. By invading Georgia Russia, had shown a willingness to use its economic and energy leverage to pursue a restoration of its power, and a willingness to use military force to that end. Guessing correctly that the Western reaction to the invasion would be limited in scope and only partially coherent, Russia then raised the stakes by almost immediately recognizing the independence of Georgia's two separatist regions, Abkhazia and South Ossetia, thus throwing down a diplomatic gauntlet alongside the military one. How the West, and in particular the US, responds to this crisis will play a large part in determining the geopolitical future of Eurasia. The Russian military blitzkrieg took many by surprise. Moscow was evidently signalling the exhaustion of its capacity to stomach any more insults.

It was an equally unambiguous message to the nations of the Caucasus, Baltic, Central Asia and Eastern Europe that Russia still retained the power and the will to protect its influence in its "backyard", however close they may be to the US. In the process, the Kremlin succeeded in putting aside any doubts that the EU might have had about any security arrangement without Russia as an equal partner to guarantee the security of nations in the region.

The swiftness with which Russia moved into Georgia suggests that it may have been preparing for such a contingency months before the war. Russia's issuance of passports to its citizens in South Ossetia only months before the outbreak of conflict lends credence to such doubts. The immediate provocation for ordering the Russian military against Georgia was of course the thoughtless Georgian military foray into South Ossetia. The proverbial straw that broke the camel's back was the eagerness with which Ukraine and Georgia were pushing their case for membership in NATO, fully supported by the US. To the Kremlin this was post-Cold War encirclement taking its final form.

It is not that Russia had willingly allowed the erosion of its prestige and power in the region since 1991. It was then fettered by the chaos and economic meltdown that followed the dissolution of the Soviet Union. When NATO and the US moved into Kosovo and humiliated Yugoslavia, a nation considered close to Russia, in 1998-99, Moscow was helpless and it had to swallow its pride. When the Czech Republic, Hungary and Poland became full members of NATO in 1999, it could do nothing but watch. Later, in 2004, seven more nations, all either former republics of the USSR or falling within the dismantled Warsaw Pact including Poland and the three Baltic countries, joined the Western alliance. It brought the US through NATO to the borders of Russia. If Georgia and Ukraine were inducted, it would mean that NATO would border Russia through half of the 14 nations (Norway, the three Baltic countries and Poland being the others) that share land boundaries with it. Russia would decidedly resist this.

Cyberattacks during the Russo-Georgian War

The Russian-Georgian war was quite historic and precedent setting for several reasons. This appears to be the first case in history of a coordinated cyberspace domain attack synchronized with major combat actions in the other warfighting domains (consisting of Land, Air, Sea, and Space). The cyber scenario of the Russo-Georgian War suggests that, in future, conflicts will not take place only on the open battlefield, but also on the Internet, fought with the aid of information warriors. Thus, a small force of hackers would be an important component of military power.

On 19 July 2008 an Internet security firm reported a distributed denial of service (DDoS) cyber attack against Web sites in Georgia. Three weeks later, on 8 August, there was a second, more substantial round of DDoS attacks against Georgian Web sites. These additional DDoS attacks appeared to coincide with the movement of Russian troops into South Ossetia in response to Georgian military operations launched a day earlier in the region. By 10 August the DDoS attacks had rendered most Georgian governmental Web sites inoperative.

As a result of these attacks, the Georgian government found itself cyber-locked, barely able to communicate on the Internet. In response, the government took the unorthodox step of seeking cyber refuge in the US. Without first obtaining US government approval, Georgia relocated critical official Internet assets to the US, Estonia, and Poland. These attacks had an impact on the availability of government websites and denied access to public services such as electronic banking through the National Bank of Georgia. While not officially attributed to the Russian government, these attacks appeared coordinated with indications of government guidance and support to private individuals and groups.

The underlying implications of the overall issue should be of great concern to defence analysts and strategists. There is little, if any, modern legal precedent. The fact that American IT companies provided assistance to Georgia, a cyber belligerent, apparently without the knowledge or approval of the US government, illustrates what is likely to become a significant policy issue. Although nations still bear ultimate responsibility for the acts of their citizens, applying that dictum to the modern realities of cyber conflict is a complex challenge.

Russia is one of the earliest exponents of 'information warfare' so it is not surprising that the conflict demonstrated the use of computer network attack in support of an extensive 'perception battle'. Russia sought to establish and control the narrative, both in the traditional media and in cyberspace. This activity reflected complete disregard of national borders or sovereignty. The Internet has thus become a battleground in which information is the first victim.

The Russian attacks on Georgian websites used all the success factors for total outsourcing of the bandwidth capacity and legal responsibility to the average Internet user. The Russian government denied that it was behind the attacks, stating that it was possible that "individuals in Russia or elsewhere had taken it upon themselves to start the attacks". It was asserted that the Saint Petersburg-based criminal gang known as the Russian Business Network (RBN) was behind many of these cyber attacks. RBN was considered to be among the world's worst spammer, child-pornography, malware, phishing and cybercrime hosting networks.

It is clear that anyone who wished to take part in the cyber-attack on Georgia could do so from anywhere with an internet connection, by visiting one of pro-Russia websites and downloading the software and instructions needed to perform a DDoS attack. One website, called StopGeorgia, provided a utility called DoSHTTP, plus a list of targets, including Georgian government agencies and the British and American embassies in Tbilisi. Launching an attack simply required entering the address and clicking a button labelled "Start Flood". The StopGeorgia website also indicated which target sites were still active and which had collapsed. Other websites explained how to write simple programmes for sending a flood of requests, or offered specially formatted web pages that could be set to reload themselves repeatedly, barraging particular Georgian websites with traffic. There was no conclusive evidence that the attacks was executed or sanctioned by the Russian government and also there was no evidence that it tried to stop them.

The cyber-attacks against Georgia launched by Russian hackers in 2008 demonstrated the need for international cooperation for security. The organizers of the cyber-attacks were aware of Russia's military plans, but the attackers themselves were believed to have been civilians. The first-wave of cyber-attacks launched against Georgian media sites were in line with tactics used in military operations. Most of the cyber-attack tools used in the campaign appear to have been written or customized to some degree specifically for the campaign against Georgia. While the cyber attackers appeared to have had advance notice of the invasion and the benefit of some close cooperation from the state institutions, there were no fingerprints directly linking the attacks to the Russian government or military.

Cyber attacks and cyber weapons are strategic arms and in effect are real offensive weapons. Cyber-attacks can harm or even paralyze a country and therefore have equivalent implications as that of physical military attacks. Most cyber attacks leave behind forensic evidence that can be used to assess the capabilities of the attacker. Once again, warfare capabilities have outpaced legal and political systems. Three developing trends that extend across the levels of warfare from strategic to tactical are:

(a) The increasing ability of network intelligence operatives at all levels to exfiltrate critical information from potential opponents and neutral players that is valuable for military, economic, diplomatic, and social/cultural purposes;

(b) The increasing value of controlling and degrading/denying an opponent's media and publicity message (Information Operations) through denial/disruption/degrading and subversion of targeted information conduits such as web sites, voice over IP (VOIP), chat rooms, social networking sites (Twitter, FaceBook, etc.), and other cyberspace technology-based communications mediums; and

(c) The time-sensitive nature of cyberspace warfare—a nation cannot engage in cyberspace warfare from a cold start, it must have well-developed tactical, operational, and strategic capabilities developed well in advance of any conflict. These capabilities are represented by trained human capital supported by doctrine, organization, command and control, and technology that has been developed, tested, and refined in strenuous cyberspace combat exercises. Cyberspace intelligence capabilities and situational awareness also need to be developed long before any potential conflict involving the cyberspace domain.

Georgia and Kosovo: A Single Intertwined Crisis

The Russo-Georgian war was rooted in broad geopolitical processes. In large part it was simply the result of the reassertion of Russian power. The Russian empire collapsed in 1992. The Western powers wanted to make the disintegration permanent. It was inevitable that Russia would, in due course, want to reassert its claims. That it happened in Georgia was simply the result of circumstance.

There is another context to this, i.e. Russian perceptions of US and European intentions and of US and European perceptions of Russian capabilities. This shaped the policies that led to the Russo-Georgian war, which can be understood over the question of Kosovo.

Yugoslavia broke up into its component republics in the early 1990s. The borders of the republics did not cohere to the distribution of nationalities. Serbs, Croats and Bosnians found themselves citizens of republics where the majorities were not of their ethnicities and disliked the minorities intensely for historical reasons.

One conflict became particularly brutal. Bosnia had a large area dominated by Serbs. This region wanted to secede from Bosnia and rejoin Serbia. The Bosnians objected and an internal war in Bosnia took place, with the Serbian government involved. This war involved the single greatest bloodletting of the Balkan wars, the mass murder by Serbs of Bosnians.

At the time, the US and Europeans did nothing about these crimes, which became a political issue only when the magnitude of the Serbian crimes became clear. In this context, the Clinton administration helped negotiate the Dayton Accords, around the principle that there could be no adjustment in the borders of the former Yugoslav republics. Ethnic Serbs would live under Bosnian rule. The principle that existing borders were sacrosanct was embedded in the Dayton Accords.

A crisis then began to develop in the Serbian province of Kosovo. Over the years, Albanians had moved into the province in a broad migration. By 1997, the province was overwhelmingly Albanian, although it had not only been historically part of Serbia but also its historical foundation. Nevertheless, the Albanians displayed intentions of moving toward either a separate state or unification with Albania. Serbia moved to resist this, increasing its military forces to crush the Albanian resistance.

NATO launched a campaign designed to stop the killings which was carried out without UN sanction because of Russian and Chinese opposition. The Russians were particularly opposed, arguing that major crimes were not being committed and that Serbia was an ally of Russia and that the air assault was not warranted by the evidence. The US and other European powers disregarded the Russian position. Far more important, they established the precedent that UN sanction was not necessary.

This transformed NATO from a military alliance, when it took on the role of peacemaker, empowered to determine if intervention was necessary, allowed to make the military intervention, and empowered to determine the outcome. Thus a military and security alliance transformed, into a regional multinational grouping, with responsibility for maintenance of regional order, even within the borders of states that are not members.

The bombing campaign against Kosovo created a crisis in relations with Russia. It did not force capitulation and NATO was not prepared to invade Kosovo. The air campaign continued inconclusively as the West turned to the Russians to negotiate an end. The Russians sent an envoy who negotiated an agreement consisting of three parts. First, the West would halt the bombing campaign. Second, Serbian army forces would withdraw and be replaced by a multinational force including Russian troops. Third, implicit in the agreement, the Russian troops would be there to guarantee Serbian interests and sovereignty.

As soon as the agreement was signed, the Russians rushed troops to the Pristina airport to take up their duties in the multinational force. However, they were never seen as part of the peacekeeping operation or as part of the decision-making system over Kosovo. The Russians felt doubly betrayed, first by the war itself, then by the peace arrangements.

Thus, the expansion of NATO into the former Soviet Union and the promise to include Ukraine and Georgia into NATO were seen in terms of the Kosovo war. From the Russian point of view, NATO expansion meant a further exclusion of Russia from decision-making, and implied that NATO reserved the right to repeat Kosovo if it felt that human rights or political issues required it. The UN was no longer the prime multinational peacekeeping entity. NATO assumed that role in the region and it was expanding all around Russia.

On 17 February 2008, Kosovo declared independence and was recognized rapidly by a small number of European states and countries allied with the US. For the Russians, the transformation of NATO from a military alliance into a regional UN was the problem. The West argued that NATO was no longer just a military alliance but a political arbitrator for the region. It was Russia's worst nightmare. In the history of the coming period, the war in Kosovo stands out as a turning point. It set the stage for the rise of Putin and the future crises.

Lessons and Losses of Georgia

The Georgian Government, defeated in the five-day war with Russia, has been adopting a two-pronged approach in its information strategy: trying to prove that the war was initiated by Russia on 7 August, and frequently praising the might of the Georgian Army, which inflicted 10 times more on damage Russia than Russia did on it. Georgian TV stations have no footage showing the capture of Tskhinvali, destroyed Russian forces, or shots of actual battles. Although Russia does not have chronological footage of combat either, it does have war trophies as the Russian Army removed large amounts of military equipment, arms, and ammunition from Gori, Senaki, Poti, and Upper Abkhazia.

The Russian 58th Army with up to 70,000 personnel was engaged in the military activities against Georgian forces. The number is twice the size of the entire Georgian armed forces. Furthermore, the 58th Army was well prepared for the war. Military exercises, Caucasus 2008, were conducted in the Northern Caucasus at the end of July, using the theme of resistance to Georgian military aggression over South Ossetia and the destruction of the opponent on its own territory.

At the same time, the Georgian Army never conducted any exercises pitting its military forces against the potential adversary—the 58th Army. The Georgian Army was not ready to occupy the city of Java, the most fortified bastion of the Ossetian separatists. It had no plans to block the Roki Tunnel, connecting North and South Ossetia. Furthermore, the bulk of the Georgian Army, its elite brigade of 2,000 personnel, was in Al-Kut, Iraq; and their return to Georgia was not completed until 12 August, when hostilities had already ended.

It was a serious strategic mistake to carry out a full-fledged offensive against Tskhinvali, which the Georgia Army maintained only for one day and with serious losses. On the very first day of the war, the Georgian Army's communications system failed—it was later found to be useless in mountainous regions. Army officers were receiving and transmitting orders via mobile connections, which were easily tapped by Russian radio-electronic radar. Their coordinates were transferred to the aviation forces, which carried out targeted bombing of the Georgian positions.

Georgian artillery was quite efficient in the five-day war with Russia, although the Georgian air force was hardly used. Georgia's small fleet of Su-25 jets flew only once in the direction of the Roki tunnel, but they were later dismantled and hidden away, so that they would not fall into Russian hands.

The arrival of 10,000 Georgian reservists to Gori on 9 August was poorly organized. The aim of their actions was not defined. In the end Georgia reservists returned to Tbilisi on 10 August. At the company and battalion levels, Georgian soldiers indeed fought well, but the Georgian government did not ensure proper news coverage of the war. There are nearly no video materials of the military actions, prompting Georgian journalists to call this the war "that was hidden from history."

From 11 to 20 August, after the Georgian Army had stopped resisting, the Russian Army started destroying Georgia's military potential. Russian forces confiscated 65 tanks. 20 tanks were destroyed on the site, while 44 tanks were sent to Russia. The Georgian people watched live pictures on television of the Russians transporting five units of the 2nd Ground Brigade's Osa air defence systems. The Russians took 1,728 firearms, including 764 American–made M-4 fully automatic assault rifles, 28 M-40 machine guns, and 754 Russian Kalashnikov machine guns. Russian trophies also included American Humvees—armoured vehicles that the American military took to Georgia for military exercises. As a result of the aerial bombardment in Senaki, two Georgian helicopters were destroyed and the runway of the military airport was blown up along with several hangers.

The Russian forces destroyed the military capacity of the marine forces and command centre of the coastal defence. Up to 15 navy vessels belonging to the Georgian navy were destroyed, while nine Amfibia speed boats were transported to Abkhazia.

As a result of the Russian military aggression, the Georgian Army suffered material losses worth $250 million. 270 soldiers died in the five days of fighting and more than 1,000 were wounded. The Georgian Army suffered the heaviest casualties on 8 and 9 August as a result of Russian air raids.

The US announced that it would supply Tbilisi with a $1 billion aid package for reconstruction and humanitarian aid, but it is moot to what extent will it contribute to rebuilding Georgia's military potential.

Russian forces had struck Georgia to cripple it strategically. Russia bombed the commercial port of Poti, and installed its military on the East-West highway at Gori, and blew up the railway bridge that links Baku to the Black Sea. The railway network serves as an additional outlet for Kazakh oil shipped across the Caspian, and its extension into Turkey at Kars. On 23 August, a train loaded with Azeri oil was blown up near Gori. Russia (or Abkhazia) also blew up or mined bridges along the single road into the Svaneti region of high mountain peaks bordering Russia, and which separate Abkhazia from South Ossetia.

The war shattered any remaining illusions over the frontiers of the normative map of Europe. In this first European war of the 21st century, both Georgia and Russia in turn chose to use force to settle a separatist conflict.

All the primary parties have to be criticised: Russia for setting a trap for Saakashvili to fall into, Georgia for its astounding military and political blunder in falling into it, the US for having failed to restrain its protégé, and Russia again for invading and occupying Georgia proper under the bogus pretext of 'peace-keeping'. As a secondary actor, France in its capacity as EU Presidency, rushed in to mediate a defective peace plan that left Russia with an excuse to continue its occupation of Georgia proper. This has had the following consequences:

(a) Georgia has paid the price of Saakashvili's folly. The Russian parliament unanimously voted for the independence of both South Ossetia and Abkhazia on 25 August, thus following the model of Kosovo. These territories are now irrecoverable for Georgia.

(b) Russia's continued occupation of strategic points in Georgia (port of Poti and close to the East-West highway near Gori) does not mean peacekeeping but rather, threatens strangulation of the Georgian economy and its role in the transit of oil and gas from the Caspian to the West.

Domestic Economic and Political Implications

Energy

Georgia is an important transit country for oil and gas and the only significant route for taking Caspian oil to world markets that does not pass through Russia. About 1.4 per cent of world oil production (1.2 million barrels per day flows through Georgia. Oil produced in Azerbaijan is transported by the Baku-Tbilisi-Ceyhan (BTC) pipeline and rail to Georgian ports. The Baku-Tbilisi-Erzurum pipeline takes gas produced in Azerbaijan to the Turkish city of Erzurum. The South Caucasus pipeline has a capacity of about 8.4 billion cubic metres per year, with flows of only about half that. Georgia also imports gas from Russia and transits Russian-sourced gas to Armenia. Armenia imports about 1.7 billion cubic metres per year via Georgia, with Georgia obtaining under 1 billion cubic metres from Russia as a transit fee, and Russia provides additional gas to Georgia if Azeri-sourced gas is insufficient for all consumption. Georgia imports about 12 per cent of its electricity from Russia and Armenia, and much of its electricity network is owned by Russian companies.

Energy transit is an important contributor to Georgia's economy (fees, facilities, employment) and helps it obtain the oil and gas that it needs for its own consumption. For Azerbaijan, the shutdown of its three main transit routes simultaneously has severe effects. Its other options – to use a pipeline through Russia to the Black Sea port of Novorossisk or to ship to the Iranian port of Neka – are politically and financially less palatable and cannot provide enough capacity to make up for what has been lost with BTC and the Georgian ports. As there are tight limits on the storage capacity of its terminal, the capacity of domestic refineries and the size of the Novorossisk pipeline, Azerbaijan had to substantially reduce its oil production. This is enormously costly for the government and oil producers there.

The EU, via the Nabucco project that it supports, has looked to Azerbaijan and Central Asia as new sources of gas to increase supply and diversify sources. The US has favoured this as a way to reduce Russian leverage in both Europe and Central Asia. This gas, according to plans, would transit Georgia, skirting the other options of Russia or Iran. Azerbaijan and Kazakhstan are expected to increase their oil production in the near future and will need increased transit capacity, which has been expected to be met in part by Georgia.

Russian interests will benefit if Georgia can no longer serve as a key energy transit route. Russia certainly would prefer that energy transit from Central Asia and Azerbaijan not use the Caucasus as an alternative for several reasons:

(a) Russia loses potential transit fees if non-Russian routes are used;

(b) The more energy transit Russia controls, the more leverage it has with the Central Asian republics and Azerbaijan;
(c) If Russia can restrict supply growth coming from its neighbours, it can keep energy prices higher and make more money on its own exports; and
(d) Gazprom would like to be able to purchase gas at large price differentials from European market prices, thus making a larger profit and reducing its need to invest in Russia's own stagnant gas output. If Central Asia were to export some of this gas through non-Russian routes, however, this option could be lessened.

Economy

The damage to civilian infrastructure in Georgia (not including South Ossetia) has been estimated at up to $400 million. Georgia is particularly dependent on foreign direct investment to finance its large current account deficit, and a decline in investor confidence is likely to have a sharp impact on the currency (the lari), especially given the government's limited foreign exchange reserves. If depreciation is severe, it will cause real problems for those who have borrowed in foreign currency-denominated loans, including major banks, large businesses and the government.

Politics

With thousands of Russian troops still present in his country, Saakashvili, despite the signs of unrest, had a strong domestic position, benefiting from outrage over Moscow's attacks and a rally-round-the-flag atmosphere. Even figures often bitterly opposed to the president acknowledge this. But hawks inside the ruling elite who were more inclined to risk a military confrontation with Russia will likely be pushed aside. Though many of them expected Russia to intervene, they did not expect the massive scale of its incursion.

Saakashvili's government will have to explain how it allowed itself to be lured into a direct confrontation with Russia. It was impossible to imagine that Russian tanks would be 20-25 minutes drive from Tbilisi, that there would be so many refugees and displaced persons and so many casualties among civilians.

Implications for Russia

The intervention in Georgia is a turning point for Russia's relations with both its neighbours and the broader international community. It has been marked by self-confidence and aggressiveness, a willingness to push confrontation to the limit and disregard for international opinion. Buoyed by the rapid oil-driven growth in its national wealth, Russia believes that it should exercise a decisive influence on global processes.

For nearly two decades, the Kremlin expressed interest in cooperation and integration with Western institutions largely on their terms, but it is now returning to the more characteristic great power behaviour of insisting on playing by special rules. There is a strong risk that it is prepared to accept a degree of international ostracism and confrontation if it deems these the costs necessary to achieve its goal of re-creating a security zone around its borders, in which its neighbours accept or are forced to accept limitations on their choice of relations with the EU and the US.

Russian Strategy in the War against Georgia

Although Russia claimed to be protecting Russian citizens and peacekeepers in South Ossetia, it entered this war in pursuit of the following larger objectives:

(a) End Georgia's presence in and sovereignty over both South Ossetia and Abkhazia.
(b) Damage Georgia's military capability.
(c) Undermine Georgia's chances of NATO accession by demonstrating to Europe and the US both the "unreliability" of the Georgian government and the danger of extending NATO's protection to Georgia.
(d) Punish the Georgian government for its refusal to give up its NATO aspirations.
(e) Punish the West for its support of Georgia and its recognition of the Kosovo Unilateral Declaration of Independence.
(f) Give pause to other post-Soviet states—especially Ukraine and Azerbaijan—with Euro-Atlantic leanings and NATO aspirations.

How did the situation erupt from a frozen conflict to a military confrontation?

The war began after a long period of Russian actions designed to either provoke Georgia into conflict—the end result of which would be Russian control over Abkhazia and South Ossetia—or to result in a de facto annexation of both Abkhazia and South Ossetia if Georgia failed to respond to Russia's actions. Some of these Russian actions were the following:

(a) Attacking Georgian-controlled territory in Abkhazia with helicopter gunships in March 2007.
(b) Attacking Georgian territory in South Ossetia with attack aircraft in August 2007.
(c) Unilaterally withdrawing from military and economic sanctions against Abkhazia, allowing for transfer of armaments to the separatist military there in March 2008.
(d) Issuing instructions for Russian government authorities to deal directly with the separatist authorities in Abkhazia and South Ossetia instead of using the Georgia government as an interlocutor in April 2008.
(e) Shooting down an unarmed Georgian reconnaissance drone over Abkhazia in April 2008.
(f) Deploying additional Russian forces to Abkhazia and subsequently deploying railroad troops to repair the rail line from Russia into Abkhazia in April to May 2008.
(g) Overflying South Ossetia with multiple Russian fighter aircraft in July 2008. Whether the direct cause of the war was a Georgian operation to retake Tskhinvali after the separatists there refused to respect a Georgian-declared ceasefire or a Georgian dash to secure Tskhinvali after Russian armored and mechanized forces entered South Ossetia from Russia may never be clear. If the former was the case, we can argue that the war resulted from a miscalculation by a Georgian government that was under considerable stress and in considerable confusion after a series of Russian or Russian-backed provocations. If the latter was the case, it is a clear and premeditated invasion of Georgia by Russia. We may never have an unambiguous picture of how the initial conflict unfolded.

Why did Russia announce a suspension of its operations in Georgia?

Russia announced a suspension of its operations on 12 August because it substantially achieved all but one of its objectives. The only objective not achieved was the removal of the Saakashvili government, which Russia determined was not crucial to the success of a short, limited war against Georgia.

Another factor leading to Russia's suspension of its operations was the imminent arrival of the French-Finnish delegation with a peace agreement that would return the situation to the status quo of 6 August. Russia probably did not want to get drawn into negotiations—it would rather let the facts on the ground speak for themselves. While President Medvedev accepted the terms of the EU six-point peace plan, Russia is unlikely to reduce its forces in Abkhazia and South Ossetia to the levels authorized under the existing peacekeeping agreements (i.e., the levels of pre-6 August) without significant concessions from Georgia. Russia's continued military presence in the regions and its diplomatic strategy will be designed to ensure that both Abkhazia and South Ossetia are lost to Georgia for good, that Georgia's NATO chances are significantly degraded, and that Russia's power is respected both within and outside the post-Soviet space.

Summation

Analysis of Russia's disproportionate military response to Georgia's aggression against South Ossetia must consider the Russian national security identity and the Western political and military expansion following the collapse of the Soviet Union. While the latter fuelled rising expectations of smaller countries hoping to obtain additional Western security guarantees through the NATO's expansion, the former put the idea of war with Georgia into a logical design. The strong embrace by Georgia, Azerbaijan and the Ukraine of the western political course following the wave of purportedly democratic revolutions sweeping Eastern Europe and the Caucasus threatened Russia's perceived national security interests. Rooted in the premise of having stable and "friendly" borders, these interests did not, and as the war demonstrated will not, at least in Georgia, tolerate excessive foreign political and military presence Russia perceives as hostile to its national interests in the region.

It is important to recognize that the EU, dependent on Russian gas, did not fully or homogenously serve as the US agent in the developments preceding and following the war in Georgia. Germany, France, and Italy, which are Russia's traditional partners, differed markedly from other EU member-states in their stance on the war and Russia's actions, calling for the importance of maintaining regional security and closely working with Russia on common outstanding security concerns based on rather objective assessment of Russia's intervention. The EU's Eastern members, however, understandably, yet short-sightedly and vigorously, propagated NATO's military expansion and Western political orientation, standing in solidarity with Georgia's leaders in the aftermath of the war. Working in cooperation with the "New Europe," the US failed to deliver on its earlier non-expansion promises, increasingly preparing the ground for clashes between Russia on the one hand and Georgia and the Ukraine, on the other. The war in Georgia clearly demonstrated Russia's intentions to defend its perceived national interests, while also showing Russia's unwillingness to proceed with the Soviet-type occupations. Signalling to the nearby countries its pre-eminence in the traditional "backyard," Russia's military response also sent a message to the Western counterparts to be wary of political and military expansion in Russia's "zone of privileged interests."

Apart from the strategic objectives of containing the Western political and military expansion, Russia's intervention in Georgia certainly sought to defend the interests of its citizens and South Ossetians during the conflict, as well as to provide regional security under the established regional peace treaty, Russia's domestic law and international legal framework. While instrumental in painting a more comprehensive picture of Russia's motivations during the war, Russia's humanitarian concerns were less important in causing its intervention in Georgia. However, they were a necessary component for providing Russia with moral, legal and legitimate grounds for what might later more clearly appear to be a well pre-mediated invasion of Georgia in pursuit of larger strategic objectives.

12

LESSONS AND IMPLICATIONS

Russia launched the war against Georgia in August 2008 for highly-valued strategic and geo-political objectives, which included *de facto* annexation of Abkhazia, weakening or toppling the Mikheil Saakashvili regime, and preventing NATO enlargement. The Russian politico-military elites had focused on Georgia since the days of the presidency of Eduard Shevardnadze, whom they blamed, together with Soviet president Mikhail Gorbachev, for the dissolution of the Soviet empire and the dismantlement of the Soviet Union itself.

Russian post-communist security establishments also viewed the attractive Abkhaz coast line and illicit business opportunities provided by lawless Abkhazia and South Ossetia as additional incentives for deep involvement along the metropolitan periphery. Russian military and covert action support of secessionist movements there starting in 1992 should be seen along this continuum. Since 2006, the military operation rapidly became the matter of "when," not if.

The war also demonstrated the weaknesses of NATO and the EU security systems, because they provided no efficient response to Russia's forced changing of the borders and occupation of an OSCE member state.

Despite negative assessments of the Russian military performance both in and outside the Russian Federation, its war goals were mostly achieved. From Russia's geo-political perspective, the war was a success. The military performance is more difficult to define and evaluate.

Russia's Geopolitical Goals

Moscow formulated far-reaching, carefully prepared goals when it prepared—over a period of at least 2 ½ years, and possibly longer—for an invasion of Georgia. These goals included:

(a) Expelling Georgian troops and effectively terminating Georgian sovereignty in South Ossetia and Abkhazia. Russia prepared the ground for independence and possible eventual annexation of these separatist territories. These goals seem to have been successfully achieved.

(b) Preventing Georgia from joining the NATO and sending a strong message to Ukraine that its insistence on NATO membership may lead to war and/or its dismemberment.

(c) The Russian assault eroded the effectiveness of the NATO umbrella in Eastern Europe, even though Georgia is not yet formally a member, since it became apparent that Moscow can use force against its neighbours with relative impunity.

Russia's long-term strategic goals included:

(a) Increasing its control of the Caucasus, especially over strategic energy pipelines. If a pro-Russian regime were established in Georgia, it would have brought the strategic Baku-Tbilisi-Ceyhan oil pipeline and the Baku-Erzurum (Turkey) gas pipeline under Moscow's control. By attempting to accomplish regime change in Georgia, Moscow is also trying to gain control of the energy and transportation corridor that connects Central Asia and Azerbaijan with the Black Sea and ocean routes overseas—for oil, gas, and other commodities. In 1999, Western companies reached an agreement with Central Asian states to create the BTC pipeline. This corridor has allowed Azerbaijan and partly Kazakhstan and Turkmenistan, to bypass Russian-controlled pipeline networks and transport oil from the Caspian Sea basin straight through Georgia and Turkey, without crossing Russian territory. The growing output of the newly independent Central Asian states has been increasingly competing with Russian oil. By 2018, the Caspian basin, including Kazakhstan and Azerbaijan, could export up to 4 million barrels of oil a day, as well as a significant amount of natural gas. Russia would clearly like to restore its hegemony over hydrocarbon export routes that would considerably diminish sovereignty and diplomatic freedom of manoeuvre in these newly independent states.

(b) Recreating a sphere of influence in the former Soviet Union and beyond, if/when necessary by use of force.

Pre-Conditions for the War

Pro-Russian Separatists inside Georgia. Russian relations with Georgia were the worst among the post-Soviet states. In addition to fanning the flames of separatism in South Ossetia since 1990, Russia militarily supported separatists in Abkhazia, which is a part of Georgian territory, to undermine Georgia's independence and assert Russia's control over the strategically important South Caucasus. Despite claims about oppressed minority status, the separatist South Ossetian leaders are mostly ethnic Russians. Abkhazia and South Ossetia have become Russia's protectorates, their population largely militarized and subsisting on smuggling operations. Moscow granted the majority of Abkhaz and South Ossetians Russian citizenship and moved to establish close economic and bureaucratic ties with the two separatist republics, effectively enacting a creeping annexation of both territories. Use of Russian citizenship to create a "protected" population residing in a neighbouring state to undermine its sovereignty is a slippery slope that is leading to a redrawing of the former Soviet borders in Russia's favour.

Sending a Message to other former Soviet-bloc Nations. Aggression against Georgia also sends a strong signal to Ukraine and to European states along Russia's borders. Today, up to 50 percent of Ukrainian citizens speak Russian as their first language, and ethnic Russians comprise around one-fifth of Ukraine's population. Yet, Ukraine's pro-Western leaders, have expressed a desire to join NATO, while the pro-Moscow Ukrainian Party of Regions opposes such membership. NATO opponents in Ukraine were greatly encouraged by Russia's action against Georgia. Beyond this, Russia demonstrated that it can sabotage American and EU declarations about integrating the CIS members into Western structures such as NATO.

Military Performance

The Russian and Georgian performances in the war were in many ways mirror images of each other. Russian strategy was well-thought-out and properly resourced, giving Russia significant advantages at the operational level of war and allowing it to overcome shortcomings at the tactical level. The Georgian military, by contrast, was reasonably well-trained and well-equipped at the unit level and fought well in tactical engagements, but the reactive nature of Georgian strategic and operational planning and the often haphazard way in which plans were conceived and implemented undercut the tactical advantages the Georgians enjoyed, thus undermining their entire effort. Georgian operations were "spontaneously" planned, with no reserve designated, no fire support or engineer plans, and the main effort commander selected only hours before the war began. There was also significant intervention by the civilian leadership of Georgia in the planning and execution of the operation.

At the strategic level, Russia was able to execute a combined political-military strategy that isolated Georgia from its western partners while setting the conditions for military success. At the operational level, these advantages were parlayed into success by the early commitment of a decisive amount of forces to the theatre of operations and sufficient, if not especially elegant, operational coordination. At the tactical level, despite disadvantages in capabilities at the unit level and use of tactics that exposed its forces to the risk of higher casualties, the offensive-mindedness, superior numbers, and speed of Russian forces committed to the fight overwhelmed their enemy and translated into battlefield victory.

Forces Deployed

Any assessment of the performance of the Russian armed forces in the war with Georgia must begin with a comparison of Russian and Georgian forces committed to the fight. What is clear is that the war resulted in a military victory for Russia; what is less clear is whether the origin of the victory lies on the strategic, operational, or tactical level, or on some combination of these levels. In other words, was the cause of the Russian victory a superior strategic plan that allowed Russia to use overwhelming force to subdue Georgia; was it superior operational art that consistently maximized Russian firepower and manoeuvre capabilities while integrating these with other military capabilities; or was it simply greater tactical skill that allowed Russia to consistently win tactical engagements, eventually causing the defeat of the Georgian forces?

One clear fact that emerges from an examination of the forces committed by both sides is that despite significant geographic challenges to the introduction of forces into the theatre of combat, Russia managed to assemble, relatively quickly, a force that possessed a significant numerical superiority over its Georgian foe. In South Ossetia, Russia committed the 58th Army, based in the Russian city of Vladikavkaz. Russian military transportation aircraft provided the needed support as the forces deployed and engaged in the theatre. In all, Russian transport aircraft flew more than 100 sorties to move men, equipment, and supplies to theatre before and during the war. Alongside Russian forces fought South Ossetian militias and volunteer forces from the Russian North Caucasus, including the Chechen battalions, dreaded and feared by Georgians due to memories of atrocities they committed during Georgia's civil wars of the 1990s, when they also fought on the side of the Abkhaz separatist forces.

In Abkhazia, where Russia opened a second front on the third day of the war, elements of the 7th Airborne Division from Novorossisk and the 76th Air Assault Division from Pskov landed from the Black Sea alongside naval infantry of the Black Sea Fleet, while elements of the 20th Motorized Division from Volgograd deployed by way of a railway line from Russia that Russian troops had repaired earlier that year. As in South Ossetia, in Abkhazia Russian forces were augmented by Abkhaz military forces, which were substantially more capable than their South Ossetian counterparts.

Accurate estimates of the total number of Russian and allied forces committed in the war are elusive, but most analysts agree on a figure in the 35,000-40,000 range.

The Russian air force demonstrated decisive air superiority over its Georgian foe. For the air campaign, they flew 200 total combat sorties over the 5 days of the war. Russia enjoyed an overwhelming advantage in aircraft of all types, with some 14 times as many combat aircraft in theatre as Georgia.

Moscow committed itself to making the Georgia war a combined forces operation, ordering the Black Sea Fleet into action for the first time since World War II. Russian naval forces arrived in theatre late on the second day of the war in the form of Black Sea Fleet ships led by the cruiser *Moskva* and the destroyer *Smetlivy*, along with troop ships and support ships. Given that the distance between their base in Sevastopol and the Georgian Black Sea coast is 400 nautical miles, these ships must have left base immediately upon the outbreak of the war or even before. Their mission was two-fold: to land Russian troops in Abkhazia, and to seize and destroy Georgian naval facilities and forces.

Arrayed against the Russian and allied forces were some 12,000-15,000 Georgian troops, along with a small number of special police forces. Initially, Georgia committed the 3rd and 4th Infantry Brigades to the operation, along with a task force composed primarily of Ministry of Defence and Ministry of the Interior Special Forces units, which together were designated as the main effort. When Georgia's forces in South Ossetia found themselves increasingly outnumbered by their enemy, the Land Forces Command committed the 2nd Infantry Brigade to the fight as well. Georgia's small air force consisted of eight Su-25 attack aircraft and around 25 helicopters, but it played no role in the war after the first day, as the Georgian leadership decided to ground the air force to preserve it from destruction. Beyond an incident in which the Russian side claimed that four Georgian patrol boats came out of the port of Poti to attack them and were destroyed, the Georgian Navy and Coast Guard had minimal capability and played no role in the war.

Thus, the war between Russia and Georgia saw some 35,000-40,000 Russian and allied forces, augmented by significant air and naval forces, confront some 12,000-15,000 Georgian forces with little air and no naval capability. While it is tempting to assume that any Russia-Georgia war would result in a significant numerical advantage for Russia simply due to the differing sizes of their military forces, this view is not necessarily accurate. First, it underestimates the geographical challenges for Russia in rapidly inserting significant numbers of forces into South Ossetia and Abkhazia, the former of which is separated from Russia by the Greater Caucasus mountain range and accessible only by the Roki Tunnel, and the latter which is most accessible from Russia by sea or by rail.

Second, this view minimizes the extent to which Russian preparatory actions were successful in sowing confusion and uncertainty within the Georgian government and preventing any real deterrence of Russian escalation from Georgia's western partners. In short, it was Russia's skilful use and abuse of its mandate and prerogatives as a peacekeeping force in both Abkhazia and South Ossetia that allowed it to set the strategic conditions for success, while preventing its adversary from doing so.

Timing of the Hostilities Outbreak

While in hindsight it seems obvious that Russia was determined to fight if war came, that fact was not obvious to Georgian decision-makers.

Despite the increase in tensions with Russia, the Georgian leadership expected a repeat of previous skirmishes in South Ossetia, in which the Georgian army would confront South Ossetian militias backed by volunteer forces from the Russian North Caucasus and only limited artillery and aviation support from the Russian armed forces. The reasons for this failure are several—Georgia's poor intelligence set-up, the degradation in Georgian decision-making capabilities brought on by sustained Russian pressure, and probably plain wishful thinking—but the consequences for the Georgian armed forces were dire. Poor Georgian planning and an early breakdown of Georgian command and control once the operation began compounded these effects.

If the Georgian leadership misread the Russian determination to fight, Russian decision makers—having set the strategic conditions for success in the upcoming war—seemed to have been caught off-guard by the timing of its outbreak. When war came during the night of August 7-8, Russian Prime Minister Vladimir Putin, largely seen as the architect of the Russian political strategy, was at the opening ceremonies of the Beijing Olympics. On the military side, Chief of the General Staff General Nikolai Makarov was newly appointed, while the Chief of the Main Operations Directorate had been dismissed and no replacement had been named. Finally, the Russian General Staff was in the process of moving into a new building on 7 August, thus its ability to coordinate operations and communicate securely were temporarily degraded.

There is also a Georgian narrative that the Russian plan was for the war to begin later in August, and that the Georgian move on Tskhinvali pre-empted it. Whatever the case, the outbreak of the war was precipitated by a months-long series of Russian strategic moves that deftly set the conditions for political and military success in the campaign.

Operations

Having set the conditions for success on the strategic level, Russia now had to undertake offensive operations to translate this to success on the battlefield. The introduction of volunteer forces from the North Caucasus Republics and the lead elements of the 135th and 693rd Motorized Rifle Regiments into South Ossetia prior to the outbreak of the war allowed Russia and its South Ossetian allies to prevent Georgia from fully achieving its objectives of securing the critical road junctions north of Tskhinvali and blocking the exit of the Roki Tunnel to prevent the deployment of additional Russian forces. Georgian forces did move through Tskhinvali and engaged Russian forces, probably the advance elements of the 135th and 693rd Regiments, north of the town.

Although the tactical outcome of this first engagement between Georgian and Russian forces was inconclusive, the presence of Russian forces that far south in significant strength caused the Georgian Land Forces Command to adjust its plan which originally called for the main body of its forces to move quickly through Tskhinvali and seize the key road junctions and villages to the north of the city. The engagement with Russian forces, in significant numbers, forced the Georgians to commit first one, then two, and finally all three infantry battalions of the 4th Brigade in support of the effort in and north of Tskhinvali. This left a gap in the west of the Georgian zone of operations, which was eventually filled by the deployment of the 2nd Brigade, initially held in reserve at its base in Senaki in western Georgia. The need for Georgia to commit the 4th Brigade to the effort and reinforce it with the 2nd Brigade had two adverse effects for the Georgian effort. First, the change in mission for the 4th Brigade temporarily left a critical road unguarded. This road leads northwest out of Tskhinvali through the towns of Dzari and Didi Gupta to the town of Java, where Russia had upgraded its refuelling facility a year earlier. Leaving it unguarded meant that Russian forces moving south from Java could reach the northern outskirts of Tskhinvali unmolested, and Russia took advantage of this Georgian error. By the afternoon of 8 August, the 135th, 693rd, and 503rd Motorized Rifle Regiments of the 19th Motorized Rifle Division had moved south from Java along this road all the way to the north-western edge of Tskhinvali, where they engaged in battles with Georgian forces. The second consequence of the commitment of the Georgian 4th Brigade to the main effort and its reinforcement by the 2nd Brigade would not be felt until later. The commitment of the 2nd Brigade to South Ossetia left western Georgia essentially undefended, and Russia would exploit this situation when the forces it committed in Abkhazia rolled into western Georgia on 11 August and destroyed critical military infrastructure there, most notably the 2nd Brigade base in the town of Senaki and the Georgian Naval base in Poti.

The first significant Georgian defeat came in the opening stages of the war. Georgia was unable to secure or block the exit of the Roki Tunnel—the only route into South Ossetia from Russia—primarily due to the fact that Georgian artillery lacked the range and accuracy to hit the tunnel's exit, and the fact that Russian forces had secured the tunnel's exit and deployed advance forces through it before the outbreak of the war. Georgia was therefore reduced to attempting to interdict the movement of Russian forces south by air attacks (the Georgian air force did not fly after 8 August) and cluster munitions fired from BM-21 rocket launchers. This did slow the movement of Russian forces south temporarily by damaging the bridge at the town of Gupta, but once the road and bridge had been cleared and repaired, the movement of Russian forces through the tunnel and down the road to Tskhinvali resumed. By 10 August, in addition to the three regiments from the 19th Motorized Rifle Division committed earlier, Russia had deployed the following forces to South Ossetia: the 70th and 71st Motorized Rifle Regiments of the 42nd Motorized Rifle Division; elements of the 104th and 234th Airborne Regiments from the 76th Air Assault Division; elements of the 45th Intelligence Regiment; and elements of the 10th and 22nd Special Forces Brigades, as well as significant armour, artillery and air defence formations. By this time, Russia had opened a second front in Abkhazia by deploying units from the 7th Airborne and 76th Air Assault Divisions, the 20th Motorized Rifle Division, and two battalions of Naval Infantry from the Black Sea Fleet.

Thus, the strategic preparation for war allowed Russia to begin it on advantageous terms—even though the timing of the war's outbreak seems to have come as a surprise to the Russian political and military leadership—and the rapid introduction of significant forces into the theatre of operations allowed Russia to translate strategic preparation into operational advantage. In summary, successful preparation for war on the strategic level translated into a significant advantage for Russian forces on the operational level. Russia exploited this advantage by committing a significantly greater number of forces to the fight than Georgia was able to; by using its better-trained units in key roles; by adequate coordination between units, including artillery; by relying on typical Soviet doctrinal tenets of operational speed and overwhelming concentration of force at key points; and by making good use of irregular forces to complement the efforts of its conventional forces.

Tactics

Russian strategic and operational advantages were such that victory in the war against Georgia did not depend to any great degree on Russian tactical skill. Indeed, at the tactical level, in direct fire engagements between Russian and Georgian units of relatively equal size, Georgian forces seem to have inflicted more damage than they suffered. In part, this was due to superior Georgian equipment—many Georgian tanks and infantry fighting vehicles were equipped with reactive armour, night vision equipment, advanced radios, and superior fire control systems installed under contract by an Israeli defence firm, while most Russian vehicles lacked these improvements. Georgian forces also benefited from training administered by US and other Western countries designed to prepare them for their deployments to Kosovo and Iraq. While generally focused on stability operations or counterinsurgency, this training taught skills relevant to conventional engagements at the tactical level such as reacting to contact and using firepower to support manoeuvre against the enemy.

Russian forces, in contrast, generally used Soviet tactics, moving in column formation, fighting from the lead elements and continuing to press forward after making contact. They generally made no attempt to stop, establish support by fire positions, and manoeuvre to the flanks of the Georgian units they encountered. These tactics, employed as they were against a Western-trained force, nearly had disastrous consequences for the Russian effort when the command group of the 58th Army, including the commander, General Anatoly Khruliev, was almost completely destroyed by Georgian forces. Of the 30 vehicles in the command group, 25 were destroyed, killing a significant number of officers and soldiers, and wounding the Army Commander. In another engagement, Georgian reconnaissance units identified a convoy of Russian armour and mechanized forces descending a mountain road northwest of Tskhinvali on the evening of 9 August. When Georgian tanks engaged this column, the Russian vehicles appeared confused, failing to return fire and acting as if they were coming under artillery fire.

Despite the high risk entailed by the use of Soviet tactics in the war against Georgia, they did provide a number of advantages to Russian units. The first of these was speed. Declining to deploy upon contact, using support by fire positions, and manoeuvring to the flank of enemy units allowed Russian forces—at the cost of higher casualties—to continue to press their advance southward through South Ossetia and into Georgia proper. This kept up the pressure on Georgian forces and certainly had an advantageous psychological effect, since the Georgian military did not believe Russia would fight for South Ossetia on such a significant scale.

The second advantage to the use of Soviet tactics lies in their simplicity. For units in which vehicles are not equipped with navigation systems, night vision systems, advanced radios, and advanced fire control systems, the use of tight column formations with the lead elements fighting and the rest of the formation pushing through contact might be the best way to maintain unit integrity and sustain the advance. Finally, Russian manoeuvre tactics—especially combined as they were with massive air and artillery attacks against Georgian forces—seem to have had a significant shock effect on Georgian forces, as testified to by the significant number of Georgian vehicles left abandoned on the battlefield.

In general, then, the higher the level of analysis, the more effective the Russian effort appears to have been. At the strategic level Russia was able to execute a combined political-military strategy that isolated Georgia from its Western partners while setting the conditions for military success. At the operational level, these advantages were parlayed into success by the early commitment of a decisive amount of forces to the theatre of operations and sufficient, if not especially elegant, operational coordination. At the tactical level, despite disadvantages in capabilities at the small-unit level and use of tactics that exposed its forces to the risk of higher casualties, the offensive-mindedness, superior numbers, and speed of Russian forces committed to the fight overwhelmed their enemy and translated into battlefield victory.

Personnel

Assessments of the effectiveness of the Russian personnel system in the war have highlighted two key deficiencies. The first of these is the lack of adequate numbers of professional soldiers (*kontraktniky*), a deficiency that forced Russian commanders to deploy conscripts despite an official policy banning their use in wars. Only 70 percent of the soldiers who fought in the war against Georgia were *kontraktniky*, the rest were conscripts. The problem with the deployment of conscripts is their generally low level of training for war. In a war against a more substantial foe this deficiency might have extremely negative effects on Russian performance.

A second problem with the personnel system exposed by the war was the failure of the system of cadre units within the Russian military. While the existence of these cadre units has long been a fact within the Russian armed forces—their purpose being to allow Russia to rapidly expand its armed forces in case of major war—their existence and their role in the war against Georgia point to a structural problem for the Russian military. First, the fact that personnel from cadre units had to be deployed in the war highlights the fact that even Russia's first-line units are not prepared to go to war "as is," without outside augmentation. Second, when the Russian military leadership called on the staffs of these cadre units to serve in Georgia, they were apparently shocked by how incompetent many of them were. The Russian Military High Command was forced to handpick colonels and generals from all over Russia to replace the ineffective commanders of cadre units. Both of these problems—the role of conscripts and the status of cadre units—are significant areas of emphasis in Russia's current military reform effort.

Equipment and Weapons Systems

Georgian forces were better equipped than their Russian counterparts. Some 80 percent of Russian weaponry had not been refurbished since the collapse of the Soviet Union in 1991. The effects of this were felt in reduced capability as well as maintenance problems. There were reports of scores of broken Russian vehicles lining the road to South Ossetia, impeding the movement of follow-on forces. This fact, combined with the flow of civilians fleeing the fighting, jammed the single road into South Ossetia and hampered the movement of Russian equipment into the area of operations.

Georgian tanks and infantry fighting vehicles were generally better equipped than were their Russian counterparts, but this comparison held for other equipment as well. Most Georgian Su-25s had been upgraded by the same Israeli firm that upgraded Georgia's tanks; the result was that Georgian aircraft tended to have superior communication, avionics, and weapon-control systems than did Russian aircraft.

Even on the individual soldier level, the comparison held, as Georgian soldiers were equipped with advanced helmets and body armour that Russian soldiers lacked. There are a number of reports of Russian soldiers stripping the helmets and body armour from dead Georgians in order to improve their personal protection. Russian forces apparently failed to use even the protective equipment they had. Russian tanks and infantry carriers were subject to destruction by Georgian rocket-propelled grenades (RPGs) because they failed to fill their reactive armour canisters before they deployed.

Russian equipment deficiencies were not limited to the manoeuvre forces. There was a lack of counter battery radars, lack of access to satellite imagery for intelligence planning, lack of electronic warfare capability, and a shortage of unmanned aerial vehicles as well as the poor quality of those available as factors that significantly degraded the Russian effort. The lack of reliable UAVs and satellite imagery is what apparently led the Russian air force to send a Tu-22 bomber deep into Georgia on a reconnaissance and targeting mission, where it was shot down by Georgian air defences.

Within the air force, two related deficiencies stand out. The first is the fact that GLONASS, the Russian answer to the US Global Positioning System (GPS), had not been completed in time for the war. This, combined with the fact that GPS data for Georgia were interrupted during the war, made the use of GPS or GLONASS guided precision munitions impossible. The second problem was the overall lack of precision-guided munitions (PGMs), meaning that even munitions with other guidance systems (laser, for example) were not available in sufficient numbers. These deficiencies led to a significant degradation of the Russian air force's ability to identify and engage important targets.

Joint Operations: An Assessment of Operational Coordination

The war against Georgia represents possibly the first case in which Russian ground, air, and naval components fought together in significant numbers since the end of World War II. Most analyses of the performance of these components give the ground component passing marks but note several deficiencies, give the naval component high marks but admit that it faced no serious opposition, and reserve their harshest criticism for the air component. As far as the coordination among them is concerned, most analysts describe it as coordination in timing of operations only; in other words, Russian operations were coincident in time but can be characterized as joint on only the most superficial level. There did not appear to be unity of command in the joint sense, either. For instance, the commander of the North Caucasus Military District, the nominal overall commander, is said to have had no control over the air force aircraft operating in his theatre. Instead, air force operations were personally directed by Commander of the Air Force Colonel-General Aleksander Zelin, who controlled his forces via mobile phone from his office in Moscow.

The war exposed significant weaknesses in several key capabilities of the Russian air element. Russian aircraft lacked the ability to operate at night, had very little electronic-warfare capability, and made sparing use of precision-guided missiles (PGMs). Russian tactical aviation assets in their close air support (CAS) role were also criticized for providing little to no support to Russian ground forces in contact with the enemy. Poor coordination between Russian ground and air forces certainly played a role in this. The lack of interoperable radios between army and air force units and the lack of forward air controllers severely limited the extent to which the air force could support ground units in contact. It is also likely that the Georgian air defence threat, which proved much more robust than expected, contributed to this deficiency.

The Russian strategic attack plan executed by long-range aircraft suffered from a lack of good intelligence on potential targets, a higher than expected Georgian air defence threat, and a lack of PGMs. The result was a poorly planned and executed strategic attack effort that bombed military infrastructure of no importance while neglecting important military infrastructure and resulted in high levels of collateral damage. Russian aircraft bombed the airfields at Vaziani near Tbilisi and Kopitnari, west of Kutaisi, neither of which has been used for military flights since the collapse of the Soviet Union. While bombing these unimportant targets, Russian aircraft completely neglected to attack the new Georgian military bases at Gori and Khoni, both of which were of considerable importance. The base at Gori was eventually damaged, but only after Russian ground forces rolled into it and began to dismantle and destroy military infrastructure and capture idle military vehicles.

Given the poor intelligence picture, what appears to have happened is that instead of constructing a coherent and comprehensive targeting plan for the war against Georgia, the leadership of the Russian air force relied on old Soviet maps and data to determine which military targets to attack. There are even indications that the pilot of the Tu-22 shot down by Georgian air defences was transferred from an academic assignment to a combat flying assignment upon the outbreak of the war because he had been stationed in Georgia during the Soviet period and knew where Georgian airfields were located.

There were also several instances in which Russian aircraft attacked civilian targets, such as apartment buildings, schools, and hospitals. Since these have no military value as targets and since attacking them resulted in significant public relations problems for the Russian military, it is highly unlikely that they were deliberately attacked. A more likely scenario is that the lack of PGMs, the high air defence threat, and the poor intelligence picture caused pilots either to accidentally attack civilian infrastructure that had been misidentified as military, or to release their bombs at the wrong time or place due to an understandable reluctance to fly low and slow enough to attack the proper target with the dumb bombs available to them.

The Russian air force was unaware that Georgia had purchased the BUK M1 (SA11) anti-aircraft missile system from Ukraine prior to the outbreak of the war, even though Georgia had publicly reported this purchase. This system accounted for a significant portion of the Russian aircraft losses during the war. Russia also appeared to have been unaware that Georgia had purchased the Rafael *Spyder* anti-aircraft system from Israel, although this was also public knowledge.

The only air force assets that avoided significant criticism of their performance in the war were transport aviation, both fixed-wing and rotary-wing. Units from as far away as Moscow and St. Petersburg were airlifted to the theatre on short notice, although all of them, including airborne units, were landed at friendly airfields instead of making combat jumps. Once in theatre, airborne and air assault units fought in a standard infantry role. Their use in an airmobile or air assault role was restricted by the air defence threat and the fact that the Russian air force controlled the transport helicopter fleet and was unwilling to use it in support of ground operations. This has led some of the Russian army leadership to argue that some or all of the transport helicopter fleet should be transferred to the army.

Naval Forces

Little has been written on the role and performance of the Russian navy in the war with Georgia. As mentioned, the Russian naval force was built around the cruiser, *Moskva*, and the destroyer, *Smetlivy*, and included two battalions of naval infantry, which landed on the coast of Abkhazia and from there moved into Georgia proper. Three landing ships appear to have been used in the amphibious operation: the *Caesar Kunikov, Jamal*, and *Saratov*. The landing was successful as it was unopposed.

Russian forces did eventually destroy several Georgian navy ships at anchor in Poti where they were based, after the two sides declared a ceasefire. The Georgian coast guard, which had received significant US training and equipment and was thus in many ways more capable than the navy, relocated from Poti south to the port of Batumi in order to preserve its vessels.

Special Forces and Irregular Forces

Georgian reports mention several instances in which Russian helicopters inserted troops in black uniforms behind Georgian lines, where they may have engaged in subversion and espionage. There are a number of reports in the Russian media that Russian special forces (GRU) units operated in Georgian territory. The veracity of these reports is unknown. What is known is that North Caucasus volunteer forces—especially the Chechen "East" and "West" Battalions—as well as South Ossetian and Abkhazian militia forces, played significant roles in the war. All of the irregular forces, both those from Russia and those from the separatist provinces, were deployed prior to the outbreak of the war and likely conducted reconnaissance and advance-guard operations for their Russian allies.

In South Ossetia, militia forces deployed in Tskhinvali continually harassed Georgian forces as they moved through the town.These forces appear to have engaged in standard partisan operations—using small hit-and-run engagements where their chances of survival were higher and using civilian clothing to blend in with the local population. South Ossetian militia forces and the Chechen battalions also conducted some of the most egregious ethnic cleansing in the wake of the war, burning ethnic Georgian villages in South Ossetia and ejecting their inhabitants. The EU, the UN and several human rights organizations documented this ethnic cleansing and criticized the Russian military for its inability or unwillingness to control forces it had trained and which were fighting alongside it.

Logistical Support and Strategic Mobility

Despite the short duration of the war and the relatively small area over which it was fought, there are indications that the Russian ground logistics system was severely taxed. The Georgian side was aware of serious Russian problems keeping up with the demand for food, fuel, and ammunition. Perhaps, one of the reasons the Russian army halted its advance at the town of Igoeti, some 30 kilometres from the capital of Tbilisi, was its logistical incapability of advancing further. Russian accounts support this picture of a logistics system unable to cope with the demands placed on it.

Cyber Warfare and Information Operations

The area of cyber warfare and information operations is one of the most illuminating areas of study in this conflict. The war against Georgia marks the first time in its history that Russia has used cyber war and information operations in support of its conventional operations. The Russian cyber campaign attacked a total of 38 Georgian and Western websites upon the outbreak of the war, including those of the Georgian President, the Ministry of Foreign Affairs, the National Bank, the Parliament, the Supreme Court, and the US and UK embassies in Georgia. These attacks appear to have been centrally directed and coordinated, judging from the fact that they started and ended within 30 minutes of one another—beginning at about 1715 hours on 8 August and ending at about 1245 hours on 11 August, at the time when Russia announced its ceasefire.

Despite this fact, it is unlikely that the attacks were conducted directly by the Russian government. Although Russia has been a source of many of the most sophisticated cyber attacks in recent years, most of these are thought to originate from a shadowy group called the Russian Business Network (RBN), which has not been definitively shown to have links to the Russian government. Indeed, the fact that the RBN is not a registered company and that its internet domains are registered to anonymous addresses makes pinning down the origins and ownership of the RBN a challenge for the intelligence community. In any case, the RBN is notorious for cybercrimes such as identity theft, phishing, spam, and malware distribution, but it has also specialized in the type of distributed denial of service (DDOS) attacks that were aimed at Georgian websites during the war. In an earlier spat between Russia and Estonia over the removal of a Soviet war memorial from the Estonian capital, the Estonian government was subjected to a similar series of attacks also thought to have been conducted by the RBN. The most likely scenario in both cases is that RBN conducted the attacks on behalf of the Russian government, providing the government with plausible deniability.

Interestingly, the cyber attacks on Georgia were less effective than they might have been against a more wired government. Although the Georgian internet infrastructure proved relatively simple for Russian cyber warriors to overwhelm, the Georgian government proved adept at getting itself back up online. The Georgian President's website was re-established as a page on the website of the President of Poland, which Russia proved unable or unwilling to attack; other Georgian government websites quickly re-established themselves as blogs behind the protection of *google.com*, and again Russia was unwilling or unable to bring them down. The result was an explosion in the size and importance of the Georgian blogosphere, which has continued to be a thorn in Russia's side since the end of the war. A final reason that Russian cyber attacks were limited in their effectiveness is that in August 2008 Georgia had only recently set up official email accounts for its government and military. At the start of the war, many, if not most, Georgian officials still used their personal accounts (gmail, yahoo, etc.) for official communication, meaning that attacks on Georgian government email servers had little effect on their ability to communicate.

Concurrent with the cyber war against Georgia was a Russian attempt to seize the initiative in the information war by ensuring that its narrative dominated the discussion of the causes and results of the conflict. The Russian narrative consistently emphasized three major themes: first, Georgia in general and President Saakashvili in particular were the aggressors; second, Russia was forced to intervene in defence of its citizens and to prevent a humanitarian catastrophe; and finally, the United States and the West had no basis on which to criticize Russia because of Western actions in Kosovo and elsewhere.

Key elements of this narrative took hold, especially the idea that Russian actions were defensive in nature and that Georgia was the aggressor. Even after extensive evidence came to light from multiple sources that Russian forces had entered South Ossetia prior to the outbreak of war, the idea that Georgia moved first and Russia responded persisted. Perhaps the clearest evidence of this mindset appears in the official EU report on the conflict. While acknowledging that there is ample evidence that Russian forces entered South Ossetia prior to the Georgian intervention, the report surprisingly argues that there was not enough information about the number and activities of Russian forces to conclude definitively that an invasion was underway.

In addition to having a narrative prepared and effectively propagating it in the early days of the war, Russia seems to have been significantly savvier in dealing with the media than it had been in previous conflicts, especially those in Chechnya. Russian General Staff briefers appeared to have studied US briefings from the wars in Iraq and Afghanistan and attempted to model their performances on these. The Russian government also demonstrated an increased willingness to work with the Russian media, as evidenced by the fact that it flew some 50 reporters to Tskhinvali several days prior to the outbreak of the war—another indication that the Russian attack was imminent. It also effectively used Russian television to portray Georgia as a Western surrogate by showing US equipment from the recently concluded exercise Immediate Response '08 as "proof" that American forces had assisted the Georgians in planning and executing their intervention in South Ossetia. Russian interactions with Western media were less frequent, and Russian officials repeatedly complained that Georgian officials—especially President Saakashvili— were given too much air time on Western networks.

What are some of the operational and intelligence lessons that can be drawn from these conclusions?

(a) First, a country has to employ their people's patriotic 'hacker militia' to conduct a network attack against a target nation-state, they must engage them first—to motivate and 'sell' them on the concept; steer them toward appropriate targets; synchronize those cyberspace operations with combat activity in the physical realm; and discuss the most effective cyberspace tactics, techniques and procedures to be used. These hackers and cyber militias need to understand the opponent's centre of gravity in order to develop cyberspace domain approaches and techniques to effectively attack it. These preliminary cyberspace activities often create an identifiable signature that can be tracked and monitored in advance of combat operations. Nations need to monitor hacker chat rooms and communications of potential aggressor nations in order to intercept and understand this activity.

(b) Targets in cyberspace need to be identified and accesses developed prior to any actual military operation. The actual planned attacks and activities need to be practiced at a low level to assess their effectiveness. In future cyber combat, nations will need to conduct these preparatory operations, reconnaissance activities, and probing attacks well in advance of any network attack conducted in support of traditional military operation. There will be an attempt to disguise these activities but it is possible that they can be detected by the target nation networks.

(c) Russian-oriented hackers/militia took out news and local government web sites specifically in the areas that the Russian military intended to attack in the ground and air domains. The Federal and local Georgian governments, military, and local news agencies were unable to communicate with Georgian citizens that were directly affected by the fighting. This provided an intelligence indicator of the ground and air attack locations. It created panic and confusion in the local populace, further hindering Georgian military response. This effect also provides a future aggressor nation with an opportunity to conduct military deception operations via feints and ruses to mislead the target nation population, government, and military. A sudden "blackout' of cyberspace activities in a specific region may provide an indicator of a tactical or operational level conventional attack. Or it could be used as a sophisticated cyberspace operation as part of a larger deception plan, creating a feint in the cyberspace domain to lure opposing forces into believing an attack is imminent in another warfighting domain. Use of patriotic hackers and cyberspace militia themselves might be a deception effort to attract the target nation's attention away from the aggressor nation's top-quality military and intelligence community cyberspace operators that quietly conduct the main effort in the overall cyberspace domain operation.

(d) A target nation's patriot hackers/cyber militia will probably be targeted first (or at least early in combat) by an aggressor nation in order to pre-emptively remove retaliatory capability. There have been a whole series of cyber-militia hacker wars with various levels of government support over the past 20 years. These individual hackers and cyber-militias target each other and often know each other (at least by reputation). It can be reasonably assumed that government and government-sponsored cyberspace domain operations will follow a similar strategy of pre-emptive strike. It is clearly in the interests of any government to watch the status of the internal hacker community—an attack upon this community may very well be an intelligence indicator of potential foreign nation-state hostilities in other domains.

(e) Nations that intend to successfully operate in the cyberspace domain to develop air-gapped cyberspace ranges where various scenarios of attack/defend combinations can be practiced and played out in free-play force-on-force combat within a variety of network topology and technology terrain environments. This exercise environment must be integrated with physical domain exercise scenarios in order to better understand the interplay between cyberspace and the physical domains. It also needs to provide a training ground for cyberspace operators to understand and practice the nuances of both offensive and defensive operations (often two separate communities) and how to synchronize cyberspace operations with full spectrum Information Operations (IO) and political/military objectives in the other domains.

Geopolitical Lessons

Lessons from the Russia-Georgia war abound, and apply both to grand strategy, military operations, cyber warfare, and strategic information operations. The most important of these are:

- *Russian continental power is on the rise.* In 2008 Russia was willing, and may be willing again in the future, to change the borders of Europe by force, making the 1975 Helsinki Accords obsolete. Moscow justifies this policy by citing Kosovo and other Yugoslav examples. The war is intricately linked with Russia's demands to revise European security architecture, do away with NATO, and weaken the US security presence in, and ties with, Europe. The 20-year-long post-Cold War era of joint attempts between NATO and Russia to build a joint European security architecture has come to an end.
- *The war undermined the close relationships the US had developed with post-Soviet states since the collapse of the Soviet Union.* Provoking a militarily strong great power is clearly dangerous.
- *Expressions of US support are an insufficient deterrent short of NATO membership or a separate mutual defence pact.* US expressions of support provided to Georgia (clearly, short of an explicit mutual defence pact) may or may not result in military assistance if/when a post-Soviet state is under attack, especially when the attacker has an effective deterrent, such as nuclear arms deliverable against US targets.
- *US intelligence and military assistance shortcomings are obvious.* U.S. intelligence-gathering and analysis regarding the Russian threat to Georgia failed. The US military assistance to Georgia, worth

around $2 billion over the last 15 years and focussed on the development of counterinsurgency capabilities instead of conventional warfare, did not prevent the August 2008 debacle. No scenarios of a Russian invasion were envisaged, wargamed, or seriously exercised. No force structure to resist a Russian invasion was built by the Georgian authorities with US support. US intelligence managers justified the failure by stating that the satellite capabilities were redeployed for Iraq. Additionally, the war demonstrates that there is no substitute for high-quality human intelligence and raises questions with regards to the reporting chain to the National Security Command Authority.

- *Air power is not sufficient*. Russia used air, armour, the Black Sea Fleet, Special Forces, and allied militias in the attack. Clausewitzian lessons still apply to the August 2008 war: the use of overwhelming force against the enemy's centre of gravity by implementing a combined air-land-sea operation may be 20th-century style, but it does work.
- *Surprise and speed of operations matter, as they have for the 4,000 years of recorded history of warfare*. To be successful, wars must have limited and achievable goals. Russia achieved most of its goals, while the world was watching the Olympics and parliaments were on vacation.
- *Russia is prepared to take military casualties—within reason—and inflict overwhelming military and civilian casualties at a level unacceptable to the enemy*. Georgia lost some 100-200 soldiers and effectively capitulated. A tougher enemy could well suffer a proportionally higher rate of casualties and keep on fighting.
- *Information and psychological warfare is important*. So is cyber security. The Russians conducted repeated denial-of-service attacks against Georgia, shutting down key websites. Russia was ready with accusations and footage of alleged Georgian atrocities in South Ossetia, shifting the information operation playing field to describing Georgia as an aggressor; portraying itself and its Ossetian allies as victims; saving Ossetian civilians from barbaric Georgians. These operations matter domestically, to shore up support and boost morale at home and to isolate the adversary and undermine his reputation internationally.
- *International organizations failed to prevent the war and force Russia to observe the ceasefire conditions*. This was because (1) Russia was classified as a "peacekeeper"—through a CIS-based mechanism before the war, in addition to effectively being a side in the conflict;

and (2) Moscow enjoyed a veto power in two organizations that could play a peacekeeping role in Georgia: OSCE and the UN. Russia would not agree to a NATO peacekeeping force, while the EU expressed no sufficient interest in deploying a credible contingent in the Caucasus.

The Russia-Georgia war indicates that the balance of power in western Eurasia has shifted, and that US power may be deteriorating in the face of its lengthy and open-ended commitments in Iraq, Afghanistan, Libya, and the Global War on Terror, which are leading to global overstretch. While the Middle East, and especially the Persian Gulf, will remain a top priority in US foreign policy, Russia is playing an increasingly active role in the strategic environment along its southern tier, from the Black Sea to Afghanistan and western China.

Conclusion

The Russian leadership focused on Georgia as the key element in its strategy to reassert its power in Eurasia. For years before the 2008 invasion, Moscow sought a pretext for a war that would provide a payback for the NATO operation solidifying Kosovo independence, re-establish Russian domination in Abkhazia and South Ossetia, and demonstrate the consequences of NATO aspirations for a post-Soviet state.

In Eurasia, Moscow is using its entire toolbox to shift the balance of power in the region. Its tools include diplomacy (e.g., recognition of the self-proclaimed republics), strategic information operations, arms sales, status-of-forces agreements, and base construction— even regime change— to secure its control over the "sphere of privileged interests." The 2008 Georgia war was an important step toward the realization of this goal.

13

CONCLUSION

The conflict in Georgia continues to be a threat to peace in the Caucasus, causing destabilising effects in the region and beyond. There are three separate but interconnected levels within this conflict:

(a) The unresolved relationship between Georgian authorities and the minorities living within its borders;
(b) The strained and ambiguous relationship between Georgia and its powerful northern neighbour, the Russian Federation;
(c) The geo-strategic interests of major international players, both regional and non-regional, competing for political influence, access to energy supplies and other strategic assets.

None of these layers of conflict has lost any of its impact or importance since the armed conflict of August 2008.

The Geo-political Scenario

The Caucasus is a broken region. Its constituent countries have chosen different paths for political and economic development, and Russia, the EU and the US have very different ties with them. In addition, the Caucasus is divided between its southern part of three independent republics and a northern Caucasus, which is part of Russia. Caucasian borders have (to various degrees) emerged as obstacles to cooperation, movement of people, and trade.

This fragmented landscape is challenging for regional cooperation leading to integration as Russia aggressively seeks to maintain its influence. Over the years, Georgian attitudes towards the EU have shifted as a result of both regional and domestic developments. During the early years of the Saakashvili presidency, despite a rhetorical emphasis on the country's European identity, integration with the EU was not a key priority; instead, membership in NATO was. The 2008 conflict with Russia – which resulted in the de facto loss of Abkhazia and South Ossetia while also putting an end to the hopes of NATO accession in the short run—marked a turning point.

The ongoing fragility and fragmentation of the South Caucasus will not be fixed anytime soon as the region is prone to domestic instability, inflammable protracted conflicts, and Russia's heavy influence. The South Caucasus region suffers from a security deficit and has entered a new period of change with a significant risk of increased instability and even conflict. The situation in Georgia over Abkhazia and South Ossetia appears stable but there is little progress toward a political settlement between Georgia and the Abkhazian and South Ossetian leaderships. At the same time Georgia-Russia relations remain cool at best. Meanwhile, international organisations have been unable to play a positive security role in the region, mediate in solving the conflicts in the region, or develop confidence-building measures to bring opposing parties together and avoid new conflict. The weakness of multilateral security frameworks was made clear at the December 2010 OSCE Summit, when participating states were unable to agree on the return of a mission to Georgia.

The Russia dominated status quo established in the region during the mid-1990s following a series of conflicts—Abkhazia, South Ossetia and Nagorno-Karabakh—is changing. Previously frozen conflicts have thawed —even leading to 'hot' conflicts such as in the summer of 2008 between Russia and Georgia. Little or no progress was made after 15 rounds at the EU, OSCE and UN hosted Geneva based negotiations between Georgia, Abkhazia, South Ossetia and Russia. The parties remain divided over key issues such as refugee return and possible security mechanisms in South Ossetia with Georgia and Russia blaming each other for failure after each round.

Russia remains the leading actor in the region. Moscow has extended its security sphere into the South Caucasus as a result of the war with Georgia and the subsequent unilateral declarations of independence by

South Ossetia and Abkhazia in 2008. This shift has brought with it new responsibilities for developments in these regions which are proving difficult for Moscow to manage. Russia's recognition of South Ossetian and Abkhazian independence has helped to spur local nationalisms in western parts of the North Caucasus (notably the Circassian movement).

Migration from South Ossetia into North Ossetia following the war has renewed tensions with Ingushetia over the Prigorodnyi district where many South Ossetians are settling, contributing to growing violence in Dagestan and Ingushetia. Georgia introduced visa free travel for Russian citizens from the North Caucasus, with Moscow responding that the initiative was a 'provocation' and an 'attempt to divide Russia's population into different categories.'

Increased links between violence in the north Caucasus and the unstable South Caucasus is a headache for Russia as well as other external powers and organisations. Whereas Europe, the US and Turkey are active in the South Caucasus and have some influence on policy this is not the case in southern Russia. After the second Chechen war in 1999-2000 Russia reasserted itself as a military power and pre-empted external engagement. International leverage on Russian anti-terrorist and 'stabilisation' policies is weak. Russia thus faces a paradox in that its influence remains substantial in the wider Caucasus but it cannot control the North Caucasus nor ensure stable and pro-Russian neighbours on its southern flank.

Russia hoped that Georgian President Saakashvili's position would be untenable after the 2008 conflict and he would be ousted from power due to external pressure or internal discontent. Actually, Saakashvili's internal position strengthened as opposition forces have fragmented and Georgia's economy survived the severe impact of the economic crisis. The EU and US have continued to support Saakashvili.

Security and Conflict

Russia also plays an essential role in the protracted conflicts of the region. The conflicts over Abkhazia and South Ossetia will not be resolved as long as they remain centrepieces of Russia's influence in the South Caucasus and Georgia more specifically. Their integration with Russia seem to only differ on paper and in name with Russia's annexation of Crimea: In November 2014 Russia signed a 'Treaty of Alliance and Strategic Partnership' with Abkhazia, and in March 2015 (on the one year anniversary of the Crimea annexation) Moscow sealed the 'Treaty on Alliance and Integration' with South Ossetia, in effect incorporating the strip of Georgian territory into Russia.

The Geneva talks—the format that brings together Russia and Georgia as well as representatives from Abkhazia and South Ossetia and chairs from the EU, OSCE and the UN—have not had substantial results after 32 rounds of talks. In the last session of 1 June 2015, Russia complained that Georgia's integration into NATO would be a security threat to the South Caucasus, objecting to the planned NATO-Georgia Joint Training and Evaluation Centre and NATO exercises in Georgia. While these talks were previously described as frank, open and even constructive, Russia increased its involvement in drawing borders. A week later on 10 July Russia continued its earlier demarcation of the 'state-border' between South Ossetia and Georgia one and a half kilometres on Georgia-proper territory, swallowing up farmland and houses of Georgian residents, coming dangerously close to Georgia's East-West Highway, and taking control of one kilometre of the BP-operated Baku-Supsa oil pipeline. Other external actors had no response besides expressing disapproval and concern. Georgia is the main partner of the EU and the US in the Caucasus; a situation that is constantly threatened by Russia.

Georgia's Vulnerability

The renewed Russian border demarcation of South Ossetia showed Georgia's vulnerability to Russian influence. Besides creating tensions over Abkhazia and South Ossetia, Russia is probably capable of stirring up tensions in other regions of the country with large minorities. Although Russia currently has almost no grip on mainstream Georgian politics and pro-Russian civil society is weak, the Russian Orthodox Church has some influence on its Georgian counterpart.

Russia's economic influence is substantial and it can exploit it to coerce or punish the Georgian authorities as necessary. Many Georgians work in Russia and families rely on their remittances (although less than before as a result of Russia's economic downturn). The threat that Russia might send migrants home is therefore a powerful one. In addition, Russia is a significant player in Georgia's energy sector through ownership and involvement in electricity production and distribution. It invests in Georgia's oil and chemical industries and agricultural products, and is an important export market for Georgian products. To Tbilisi's surprise Georgian products did not feature on Russia's list of banned imports – although Georgia aligned with Western sanctions against Russia. This could indicate that Georgia is growing in economic importance to Russia since it needs access to EEU member Armenia.

Energy and Trade

The South Caucasus countries depend on each other and on external actors in the energy and trade fields, which makes them vulnerable in some respects. Armenia does not have trade dealings with Azerbaijan and Turkey, and largely depends on Russian energy supplies and to a large extent on transit through Georgia. Georgia receives most of its gas supplies from Azerbaijan; it also receives, as a transit fee, 10% of gas shipped by Russia to Armenia through a pipeline running via Georgia.

Azerbaijan will become increasingly dependent on new markets for gas and current markets for oil, since the government has neglected to diversify its economy. Deliveries to Turkey—again through Georgia—are essential: From 2019 onwards Azerbaijani gas going west could reach EU countries in modest quantities when the TANAP pipeline through Turkey to South East Europe becomes operational. So far Azerbaijan has been wary of potential competition from other gas-producing Caspian littoral states – Turkmenistan or Iran. Meanwhile Georgia is dependent on transit revenues and delivery of Azerbaijani gas for its own consumption although it has a substantial hydroelectric sector.

In the energy sphere external actors are fairly (inter)dependent on their small South Caucasus neighbours (both as a source of energy and as important transit routes). For the EU, gas imports from Azerbaijan and beyond would constitute a welcome addition to the mix of imports, but would not substantially lessen dependence on Russian gas, especially for Central and Eastern European countries. Turkey relies on Russian gas deliveries (mostly via the Blue Steam pipeline through the Black Sea) for over half its needs, but also has other sources (Azerbaijani gas for instance); a Southern Corridor as foreseen by the EU would be the basis of Turkey's envisioned geopolitical role as an energy transit hub. For Russia the main dependency is on the South Caucasus not becoming a viable and substantial alternative for the EU to Russian gas.

Russia is the dominant power in the Caucasus and is itself a Caucasus country. One of its main concerns is controlling the borders between the Russian northern Caucasus republics (most of which remain unstable and violent) and the South Caucasus. In the South Caucasus Russia's main interest is not to lose ground to EU and possibly US interests—Turkey has presented itself as less of a threat since it does not seek to influence South Caucasus countries directly, and is regarded as a partner by Moscow despite its NATO membership. In the wake of Russia's declining trade position in the region and its feeling of being besieged by NATO and the EU, Moscow seeks to avoid developments rather than encourage new initiatives in the region. This also applies to energy diplomacy where Russia seeks to avoid the establishment of a Southern Corridor that would link Azerbaijan, Turkey and Europe at the expense of Russian exports and control of infrastructure.

Russia's primary interest is to help shape regimes in neighbouring countries that are friendly to Moscow's interests; do business in a similar 'way' and want to integrate into joint structures (the EEU and CSTO). To this end Moscow also uses soft power mechanisms, foremost through Russian media active in Armenia, Azerbaijan and to a lesser extent Georgia. It tends also to use coercive instruments such as military action and trade embargos. However, South Caucasus countries prefer to keep integration with Russia at bay while seeking a constructive relationship with their northern neighbour. This has led to a situation in which Georgia sees Moscow as a direct threat but pursues practical ties in trade and at the Geneva talks; Armenia feels forced to accept Russia's patronage but explores modest alternatives through cooperation with the EU; and Azerbaijan develops relations with Russia as part of its policy to play third parties off each other.

Since Russia cannot rely on healthy relations with its three southern neighbours it tries to apply a divide and rule policy through protracted conflicts. In recent years Moscow has beefed up and modernised its military presence in Armenia, Abkhazia and South Ossetia. In Georgia the conflicts of Abkhazia and South Ossetia are controlled by Russia, in part because these regions border Russian territory and have been largely incorporated into the Federation.

Washington's democracy promotion agenda in the South Caucasus has long focused on Georgia (as a 'beacon of democracy' in President George W. Bush's narrative). The US has been active in the South Caucasus since the fall of the Soviet Union and is the only country with a truly global reach. American priorities in the South Caucasus are difficult to define. Over the last decade, US interest in the region has been rather low and it has tended to rely on its close partners' more active involvement—the EU and Turkey (as well as confidence in Russia as part of the then US-Russia 'reset'). Currently US energy and trade dealings are small and its main interests are stability and democracy promotion. With this stability the US hopes that the region can be a bulwark against Russian revisionism and an unstable Middle East.

From the 1990s to the mid-2000s the US was an active player in South Caucasus energy politics, and took initiative in the Minsk Group on Nagorno-Karabakh. After the December 2003 Rose revolution, Georgia became central to almost all US priorities in the region. The US has been inclined to extend NATO membership to Georgia but its European allies have been hesitant owing to concerns about Russian reactions. Armenia is also relevant to Washington, in part because of the politically vocal Armenian diaspora in the US. Meanwhile Azerbaijan played an important transit role for the US and NATO in Afghanistan, although current relations have been severely damaged (as with the EU) over human rights and the notion in Baku that the US might be developing plans for a democratic revolution in Azerbaijan.

The Russia-Georgia conflict has caused several analysts to state that Moscow's main goal was to ensure its energy dominance in the region. Though this may not be entirely correct—other Russian security interests were equally at play—energy issues did have a large role. Ever since Vladimir Putin took over the reins, he had time and again reiterated the importance of energy in Russia's regional, and indeed its global, policy. It is well known that Moscow will not allow its supremacy to be compromised.

Though Russia appears to have emerged as the winner in the Georgian conflict, with its status as the main energy supplier for Europe remaining unscathed, in the long term it cannot afford to be sanguine. For one, given the growing concerns expressed by its European customers and their determination to seek alternative sources of supply, Russia may have to act on its "threat" and actually look eastwards to lessen its dependence on the European market.

The Russian invasion of Georgia was the most significant event of

2008 in the area of European security. Although some of the factors that led Russia and Georgia to war grew out of the unique history of Georgia and its separatist conflicts, many more were the result of deliberate Russian attempts to set the conditions for crisis in the Caucasus and thereby undercut NATO's enlargement efforts, threaten energy corridors that bypass Russia and demonstrate its power in its self-described "Near Abroad", all of which amount to threats to US interests.

The IIFFMCG Report

The IIFFMCG, which has provided the most comprehensive documented analysis of the conflict, has stated that the war was started by a Georgian attack that was an infraction under international law. It declares that the shelling of Tskhinvali during the night of August 7-8, 2008, was unjustifiable under global law. It states that although the South Ossetian defensive actions conformed to international laws, any operations of South Ossetian forces outside of the purpose of repelling the Georgian armed attack, in particular acts perpetrated against ethnic Georgians inside and outside South Ossetia, must be considered as having violated International Humanitarian Law and in many cases also Human Rights Law. In addition, all external military actions specifically directed against the Georgian armed forces after the signing of the ceasefire agreement on 12 August 2008 were deemed illegal. Georgian action or use of force against Russian peacekeeping members on Georgian territory also ran contrary to international law.

The IIFFMCG has conducted extensive research on the legality of Russian armed forces attacking the Georgians. The report divides the examination into two phases: the first concerns the immediate response from the Kremlin to defend Russian peacekeepers, and second, the full invasion of Georgia by the Russian military stretching far past the South Ossetian boundaries to the Georgian capital. The first phase was defended by appeal to international law because Russian peacekeepers were attacked and Russia had "the right to defend them using military means proportionate to the attack. Thus according to the tribunal, the Russian use of military force proportionate to protect innocent peacekeepers during the conflict was legal. The second issue analyzed by the IIFFMCG concerned whether the deep penetration of the Russian military campaign was necessary and proportionate in regard to defensive measures undertaken against the initial Georgian attack. Evidence of extended military action includes bombing the Kodori Valley, setting up military positions in major Georgian metropolitan areas, controlling principal highways, and releasing large deployments of navy units to the Black Sea. All these actions indicate that Russian military action went far beyond the reasonable limits of defence. Another example of disproportionate use of force was the continuing presence of advancing Russian military forces in Georgian territory after the signing of the ceasefire peace agreement. This use of excessive force was in clear violation of international statutes. The IIFFMCG declared that Russian military action outside the boundaries of South Ossetia and Abkhazia was conducted in violation of international law.

In summary, the IIFFMCG has confirmed that both nations violated international law and human rights; that despite being warned and advised against shelling Tskhinvali, Georgia went ahead and lit the match that started the conflict; and that the Russian and South Ossetian persistent military advances deep into Georgian territory, and their excessive use of disproportionate force, was in violation of international law. In conclusion, according to the IIFFMCG, Georgia triggered an unnecessary war by shelling Tskhinvali and shooting at Russian peacekeepers, and Russia responded with a disproportionate, unjustified measure of military force in clear violation of international law.

GEORGIA-RUSSIA CONFLICT TIMELINE

(includes South Ossetia and Abkhazia)

1989-2007

November 1989	South Ossetia declares 'autonomy' from Georgian Soviet Socialist Republic, resulting in three months of armed conflict.
December 1990	Renewed fighting between Georgia and South Ossetia until 1992.
June 1992	Officials from Georgia, Russia, and South Ossetia meet in Sochi for a peace deal, which includes the formation of a peacekeeping force of 500 troops from each of three parties.
July 1992	Abkhazia declares independence from Georgia, resulting in intense fighting through 1994, mass displacement of people, and eventual Georgian military defeat.
1994	Ceasefire between Abkhazia and Georgia, allowing for the deployment of up to 3,000 Russian peacekeeping troops. UN-led mediation with Russia designated 'special role' as a 'facilitator' of the peace process.
November 1996	Election of Eduard Kokoity as first South Ossetian president.
May 1998	Fighting erupts between Abkhazians and Georgians in Gali in Abkhazia, resulting in displacement of 40,000 Georgians from Abkhazia.

March 2001	Georgia and Abkhazia sign a peace deal not to use armed force against one another.
2002	South Ossetian President Eduard Kokoity requests Moscow's recognition of autonomy of South Ossetia, and its eventual annexation to Russia.
May 2003	Work begins on the BTC pipeline.
November 2003	Georgian President Eduard Shevardnadze ousted in bloodless change of government, dubbed the 'Rose Revolution'.
January 2004	Mikhail Saakashvili elected president of Georgia.
October 2004	Presidential elections in Abkhazia not recognized by Tbilisi. Electoral tension in Abkhazia between presumed winner Sergei Bagapsh and allegedly Moscow-backed Raul Khadzhimba.
January 2005	Georgian President Saakashvili offers a plan for eventual autonomy of South Ossetia, who rejects it in favour of complete independence. Saakshivili presents the same proposal for Abkhazia, on the condition of right of return of Georgian refugees from 1993 conflict.
May 2005	Shooting in South Ossetia results in death of a Georgian policeman and four South Ossetians.
January 2006	Blasts on Russian side of border with Georgia cuts gas and electricity. President Saakashvili implicates Russia in the disruption of supplies.
July 2006	Official opening of the BTC pipeline.
	Georgian parliament insists on the departure of Russian peacekeepers from South Ossetia and Abkhazia, and requests international troops in their place.
September 2006	Tensions flare when Georgian helicopter carrying Defence Minister Okruashvili is shelled in South Ossetia.
November 2006	South Ossetia formalises break from Tbilisi in a referendum. Georgian foreign minister accuses Russia of provoking a potential war in its support of South Ossetia.
April 2007	Tense relations between Georgia and Russia as Georgian parliament elects to create a provisional government in South Ossetia.

June 2007	South Ossetia asserts Tskhinvali shelled by Georgian mortar and sniper fire; claim rejected by Tbilisi.
August 2007	Georgia claims Russia intruded its airspace twice; rebuffed by Moscow.
October 2007	OSCE talks on South Ossetia collapse.

2008

February-March 2008	Kosovo declares independence, triggering South Ossetia's push for recognition of independence by the international community.
March 2008	Georgia's request to join NATO provokes Russian parliament to push for complete independence of Abkhazia and South Ossetia.
April 2008	At NATO Bucharest Summit, members postpone decision on Georgian membership until December.
April 2008	Tbilisi accuses Moscow of mapping out 'de facto annexation' of South Ossetia and Abkhazia after Russia formalizes ties with both territories.
25 April 2008	Russia tells Tbilisi not to rely on NATO to resolve conflicts in Abkhazia and South Ossetia.
25 April 2008	Russian Foreign Ministry claims Georgia is potentially planning a military intervention in Abkhazia.
25 April 2008	Russia vows to use 'all' its resources to protect Russian citizens in Abkhazia and South Ossetia.
30 April 2008	NATO points to Russia's role in 'raising tensions', stating that its troop deployment 'undermines' Georgia's 'territorial integrity'.
2 May 2008	US Secretary of State Condoleezza Rice expresses Washington's concern over rise in troop levels in Abkhazia.
4 May 2008	Separatist forces in Abkhazia declare they have shot down two Georgian UAVs, bringing the total to four since March. Georgia claims the flight of drones is its 'sovereign right', and any aggression against them would be seen as a 'blatant violation of sovereignty'.
5 May 2008	Georgian news agency reports of the construction of a new Russian military base for peacekeepers in Abkhazia.
9 May 2008	Reports that Georgian Deputy Prime Minister Giorgi

	Baramidze maintains that war between Georgia and Russia could break out 'tonight, tomorrow, anytime.'
15 May 2008	Reports of Russian warning of troop increases in South Ossetia.
15 May 2008	Russian defence chief Yuri Baluyevsky urges NATO to help stop the 'military build-up' in Georgia, and names the US, Turkey, the Czech Republic, and Bulgaria as the top providers of military resources to Georgia.
26 May 2008	UN Observer Mission in Georgia (UNOMIG) confirms Georgian UAV shot down by Russian jet in Abkhazia on 20 April; Russian Foreign Minister claims video has 'serious inconsistencies'.
31 May 2008	Russia deploys 300 'unarmed' soldiers to Abkhazia, claiming they are required for railway repair works. Georgia indicts Russia in planning a military intervention.
June 2008	Abkhazia breaks all ties with Georgian government
5 June 2008	EU foreign policy chief Javier Solana declares EU's will to 'try to assist all sides in lowering the temperature' in Abkhazia.
6-7 June 2008	Presidents Saakshivili and Medvedev meet, but agree that they cannot resolve 'all of their problems'; Georgia declares the two sides must meet for a longer discussion.
14-15 June 2008	Reports of an 'intensive' exchange of fire in the outskirts of Tskhinvali between Georgian and South Ossetian troops.
17 June 2008	Four Russian peacekeepers detained in Abkhazia for allegedly transporting illegal ammunition; Russian Defence Ministry demands their return.
30 June-2 July 2008	Blasts in Sukhumi market and Russian peacekeepers' checkpoint on Georgian-Abkhaz border. Russia blames Georgian special forces for the incidents.
3-4 July 2008	Explosions in South Ossetia prompt Russia to accuse Georgia of military intervention and to condemn its 'aggression'.
10 July 2008	In a press conference with President Saakashvili, US Secretary of State Condoleezza Rice calls for an end to violence in Abkhazia and South Ossetia.
22 July 2008	UN Security Council holds a special closed-session

	regarding reports of the flight of Russian jets over South Ossetia; no unanimous decisions are made.
29-30 July 2008	South Ossetia accuses Georgia of shelling villages outside of Tskhinvali. Georgia asserts that South Ossetians directed fire towards its monitoring group.
1 August 2008	Explosion in South Ossetia; Georgia reports injury of two policemen.
7 August 2008	Georgia claims South Ossetia igniting a 'war'; Russia calls the situation 'extremely dangerous.
8 August 2008	Both South Ossetia and Georgia lay claim to the disputed territory during intense shelling of Tskhinvali by both sides. Georgia accuses Russia of provoking 'undeclared war.' Russia warns Georgia that its 'aggression' will not go 'unpunished.' President Saakashvili declares a 'state of war.'
9 August 2008	Georgia claims to shoot down two Russian warplanes. Abkhazian Foreign Minister Sergei Shamba claims Abkhaz forces have embarked upon an operation to drive Georgian forces out of the hotly-disputed Kodori gorge.
10 August 2008	Russian diplomat reports death count of 2,000 in South Ossetia; the numbers have not been verified. Reports of bombs dropped outside of Tbilisi, near a military airport. US President George W. Bush declares Russia's troop build-up to be a 'disproportionate response'; UK Foreign Secretary David Miliband denounces Russia's bombing of targets 'well beyond' South Ossetia. Georgia reports death of 130 Georgian civilians and 1,165 injuries. Russia rejects the claim that it has hit civilians. Georgia reports to have offered Russia a peace deal, saying it would withdraw its troops from South Ossetia. Russia denied any cessation of armed conflict by the Georgians, and demanded an unconditional withdrawal from South Ossetia.
11 August 2008	Russia moves troops and armour into Abkhazia. French Foreign Minister, Bernard Kouchner, arrives in Georgia in the hope of bringing about an armistice between Russia and Georgia, while the two sides continue fighting.

	Russia delivers an ultimatum to Georgia: that it must disarm 1,500 troops in Zugdidi, near Abkhazia, which Georgia rejects.
	European Commission calls on Russia to 'stop immediately all military activity on Georgian territory.'
	Russia stations more than 9,000 paratroopers in Abkhazia, thus exceeding the limit of 3,000 from the 1994 peace agreement. It continues to move more troops and armour across the border; there are reports that the movement also includes T-72 tanks and Hurricane rocket launchers.
	As 2,000 Georgian troops prepare to leave Iraq and return home, Russian Prime Minister Vladimir Putin criticizes the US for facilitating the move of troops 'practically to the conflict zone.'
	Kouchner visits recent bombardments in Gori, approximately 50 kilometres outside of Tbilisi. Kouchner and French President Nicolas Sarkozy expected to travel to Moscow.
16 August 2008	President Medvedev signs six-point EU-brokered ceasefire, which includes a promise to withdraw troops to pre-conflict positions.
17 August 2008	Medvedev tells President Sarkozy in a telephone conversationthat Russian troops will begin to withdraw from Georgia on 18 August.
19 August 2008	Medvedev tells Sarkozy that—contrary to the EU ceasefire—Russian troops will remain in a buffer zone inside Georgia proper on the border with South Ossetia, and the remainder of troops will go back to South Ossetia and to Russia.
	NATO freezes its partnership with Russia, and declares normal relations with Russia to be impossible. Statement issued by NAC (North Atlantic Council) emphasizes concern over Georgia´s territorial integrity and the humanitarian situation.
20 August 2008	US and EU countries reprimand Russia for failing to adhere to the EU-brokered ceasefire agreement.
20-21 August 2008	As Russia pushes its own proposal forward, the UN Security Council remains deadlocked over the

	conflict; Western powers demand Russia to step up its troop withdrawal from Georgia.
21 August 2008	In response to statement by NATO, Russia suspends its military cooperation arrangements until further notice.
	Thousands protest in Abkhazia, pleading Russia to recognise its own independence.
22 August 2008	Russia promises a 'partial' withdrawal of troops by the end of the day, but claims some "peacekeepers" will be left inside Georgia. US General Craddock calls the move 'far too little, far too slow'.
26 August 2008	Russian President Medvedev formally recognizes the independence of South Ossetia and Abkhazia and accuses Georgian President Saakashvili of using 'genocide to solve his political problems.'

CEASEFIRE AGREEMENT
(15-16 August)

Council Conclusions on the situation in Georgia

GENERAL AFFAIRS and EXTERNAL RELATIONS Council meeting

Brussels, 13 August 2008

The Council adopted the following conclusions:

1. The Council recalls that the Union had expressed its grave concern at recent developments in Georgia, and the open conflict that has broken out between Russia and Georgia. Military action of this kind is not a solution. This war has caused the loss of many human lives, inflicted suffering on the population, resulted in substantial material damage and further increased the number of displaced persons and refugees. A peaceful and lasting solution to the conflict in Georgia must be based on full respect for the principles of independence, sovereignty and territorial integrity recognised by international law and UN Security Council resolutions.
2. In this context, the absolute priority is to stop the suffering and bring the fighting to an end. In this respect the Council welcomes the agreement subscribed to by the parties yesterday on the basis of the mediation efforts carried out by the Union.

   The principles to which the parties have subscribed are as follows:

   (1) Not to resort to force;
   (2) To end hostilities definitively;
   (3) To provide free access for humanitarian aid;
   (4) Georgian military forces will have to withdraw to their usual bases;

(5) Russian military forces will have to withdraw to the lines held prior to the outbreak of hostilities. Pending an international mechanism, Russian peace-keeping forces will implement additional security measures;

(6) Opening of international talks on the security and stability arrangements in Abkhazia and South Ossetia. The Council calls on the parties to honour all these commitments, beginning with an effective ceasefire, and to ensure that they are implemented effectively and in good faith both on the ground and in the relevant fora. The international mechanism should be set up rapidly.

3. The Council emphasises the Union's commitment to contribute actively to effective implementation of these principles. They will be embodied in a UN Security Council resolution as soon as possible.

   Rapid reinforcement of the OSCE's observer capabilities on the ground is crucial. The Union will take action along to this effect at the OSCE. The Council urges the parties not to obstruct the observers' activities. The Council also considers that the European Union must be prepared to commit itself, including on the ground, to support every effort, including those of the UN and the OSCE, with a view to a peaceful and lasting solution to the conflict in Georgia. It asks the SG/HR, in liaison with the Commission, to prepare proposals on the matter with a view to the informal meeting in Avignon on 5 and 6 September.

4. The Council stresses the humanitarian emergency and the Union's resolve to provide vital assistance to the population. An outline has been given of initial measures undertaken, both by the Commission and by the Member States. The Council requests the Commission, in liaison with the Presidency, to continue to coordinate European assistance and to encourage pooling arrangements designed to enhance its effectiveness and relevance.

   It is essential that all parties undertake to respect international humanitarian law and to facilitate the unimpeded deliver y of humanitarian assistance to all the population groups affected, without discrimination.

   In addition, in view of the destruction caused by the conflict, the Council emphasises the need to identify reconstruction requirements as of now and to prepare to make a significant contribution to meeting those requirements at Union level. It invites the Commission to report back to it on this matter before its next meeting.

SELECT BIBLIOGRAPHY

Books

Chris Hedges, *War is a Force That Gives Us Meaning (*New York: Anchor Books, 2002).

David M. Glantz, "Soviet Operational Art Since 1936: The Triumph of Maneuver Warfare," in *Historical Perspectives of the Operational Art*, ed. Michael D. Krause and R. Cody Phillips (Washington, DC: Center of Military History, 2005)

Geoffrey Blainey, *The Causes of War* (New York: The Free Press, 1988)

R. Craig Nation and Dmitri Trenin, *Russian Security Strategy Under Putin: U.S. and Russian*

Perspectives, (Carlisle, PA: U.S. ArmyWar College Strategic Studies Institute November, 2007)

Richard W. Harrison, *The Russian Way of War: Operational Art, 1904-1940*, (Lawrence, KS: University Press of Kansas, 2001)

Robert Kagan, *The Return of History and the End of Dreams* (New York: Alfred A. Knopf, 2008)

Roger E. Kanet, (ed), *Russia: Re-emerging Great Power (*Basingstoke: Palgrave Macmillan, 2007)

Ronald D.Asmus, *A Little War That Shook the World: Georgia, Russia and the Future of the West*, (New York: Palgrave/Macmillan, 2010)

Roy Allison, Margot Light and Stephen White, *Putin's Russia and the Enlarged Europe* (Malden, MA: Wiley-Blackwell, 2006)

S.E. Cornell and F. Starr (eds.) *The Guns of August 2008: Russia's War in Georgia* (London: Armonk and M.E. Sharpe, 2009)

Stephen J. Blank, *Afghanistan and Beyond: Reflections on the Future of Warfare*, (Carlisle Barracks, PA: U.S. Army War College, Strategic Studies Institute: June 28, 1993)

Svante E. Cornell, *Small Nations and Great Powers* (London: Curzon Press, 2001)

Thomas Goltz, *Georgia Diary: A Chronicle of War and Political Chaos in the Post-Soviet Caucasus* (London: M.E. Sharpe, 2006)

V. Cheterian, *War and Peace in the Caucasus, Russia's Troubled Frontier* (New York: Hurst/Columbia University Press, 2008)

V. K. Triandafillov, *The Nature of the Operations of Modern Armies*, trans. William A Burhans, ed. Jacob W. Kipp (Portland, Oregon: Frank Cass, 1994)

Zbigniew Brzezinski, *The Grand Chessboard: American Primacy and Its Geostrategic Imperatives*, (New York, Basic Books, 1997),

Mearsheimer, John (2001) *The Tragedy of Great Powers*. New York: W.W. Norton.

Journals

Alexander Cooley and Lincoln A. Mitchell (2009), "No Way to Treat Our Friends: Recasting Recent U.S.-Georgian Relations", *The Washington Quarterly*, Vol. 32 No. 1 (January), pp. 27-41

Ariel Cohen, "The Real World: Georgia War Lessons for the Middle East," *Middle East Times*, August 22, 2008

C. Welt, The Thawing of a Frozen Conflict: The Internal Security Dilemma and the 2004 Prelude to the Russo-Georgian War, *Europe-Asia Studies*, 62 (1), 2010, pp. 63–97.

Charles King, "The Five-Day War", *Foreign Affairs*, Vol. 87, Issue. 6 (Nov-Dec 2008), pp. 2-11.

Edward Mansfield, Jack Snyder, "Democratization and War", *Foreign Affairs*, Vol. 74 No. 3 (May 1995), pp. 79-97

J. Birch, Ossetiya – Land of Uncertain Frontiers and Manipulative Elites, *Central Asian Survey*, 18 (4), 1999, pp. 501–534.

Oksana Antonenko, (2008), "A War with No Winners", *Survival*, Vol. 50, No. 5 (Oct-Nov), pp. 23-26

Pavel Felgenhauer," The Russian-Georgian War Was Pre-planned in Moscow," *Eurasia Daily Monitor* 5, no. 156 (August 14, 2008)

Roy Allison, "Russia Resurgent? Moscow's Campaign to Coerce Georgia to Peace", *International Affairs*, Vol. 86 No. 6, (November 2008), pp. 1145-1171

Stephen Sestanovich, (2008), "What has Moscow done?" *Foreign Affairs*, Vol 87, Issue 6 (Nov-Dec), pp. 12-28.

Svante E. Cornell, "War in Georgia, Jitters All Around", *Current History*, Vol. 107, Issue 711 (Oct 2008), pp. 307-317.

Thom Shanker, "Russian Blitz Melded Old-School Onslaught with Modern Military Tactics," *The New York Times*, August 16, 2008

V. Papava, Georgia's Economy: Post-War Development And Post-War Difficulties, *Central Asian Survey*, 28 (2), 2009, pp. 199–213.

Internet Resources

Donald Rayfield, "The Georgia-Russia Conflict: Lost Territory, Found Nation", *Open Democracy*, (18 August 2008), [Available at http://www.opendemocracy.net]

George Friedman, "The Russo-Georgian War and the Balance of Power", (12 August 2008) [Available at http://www.stratfor.com/weekly/russo_georgian_war_and_balance_power;]

International Crisis Group report (2008), "Russia vs. Georgia: The Fallout", Europe Report n. 195, (August), pp. 1-35. [Available at http://www.crisisgroup.org]

Ivan Krastev (2008), "Russia and the Georgia war: the great-power trap", *Open Democracy*, (August 31), [Available at http://www.opendemocracy.net]

Jim Nichol, "Russia-Georgia Conflict in South Ossetia: Context and Implications for U.S. interests", *CRS Report for Congress*, RL34618 (24 Oct 2008), pp. 1-35. [Available at http://opencrs.com/document/RL34618]

Stratfor, "Georgia, Russia: The Cyberwarfare Angle," August 12, 2008

Tagliavini Commission, 2009. Report by an Independent International Fact-Finding Mission on the Conflict in Georgia (IIFFMCG) (3 vols) [online]. September, 2009. [Available from: www.ceiigf.ch/]

V. Cheterian, Georgia's arms race, *Open Democracy*, 4 July 2007. Available from: http://www.
opendemocracy.net/conflicts/caucasus_fractures/georgia_military#comments_for_node

Index